SILENT HILL
PAST LIFE

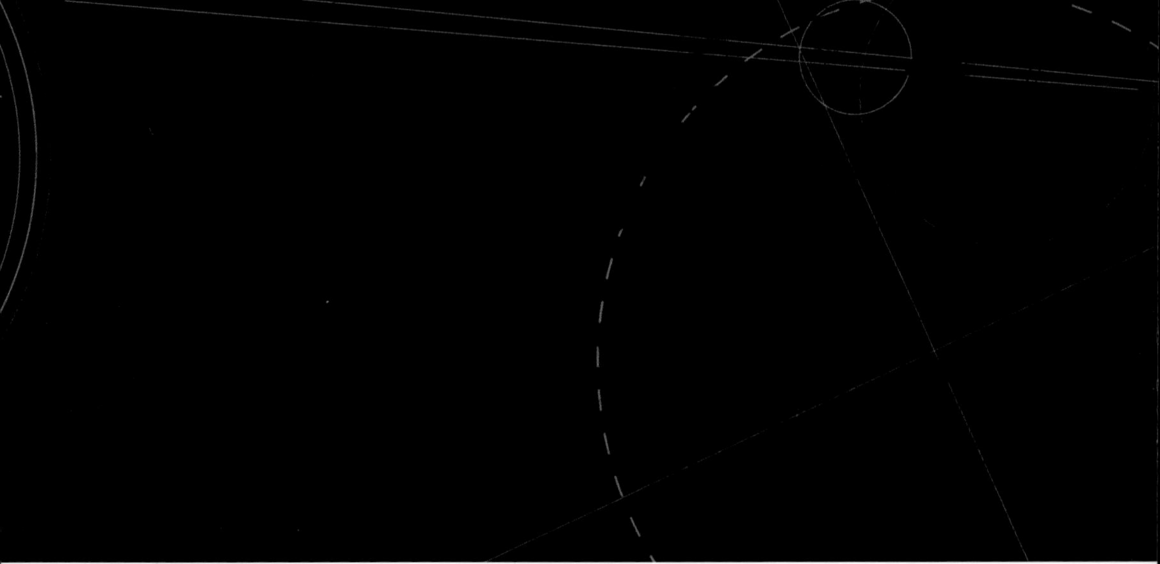

IDW™

Special thanks to Devin Shatsky and Tomm Hulett for their invaluable assistance.

ISBN: 978-1-60010-907-2   14 13 12 11   1 2 3 4

www.IDWPUBLISHING.com

Originally published as SILENT HILL: PAST LIFE Issues #1–4.

"The future is like a wide open plain, you see, filled with endless possibilities.
But the past—that ain't nothin' but a dark pit, just waitin' to swallow you up."

If you're reading this introduction, then you've probably already picked up *Silent Hill: Past Life* and you don't need me to convince you that Silent Hill, the titular town, is special. In fact, you probably already know more about that strange and haunted piece of hard-to-locate real estate than I could presume to reveal. *Silent Hill* is, after all, a long-running franchise now in the world of video games.

But let me tell you: this comic is special and it wouldn't even matter if you didn't know a video game from a velociraptor. *Silent Hill: Past Life* is a story of American gothic horror in line with the best the country has to offer, the kind of horror we usually get from old short stories that make you wonder if the shadows are empty—stories from your Shirley Jacksons and H.P. Lovecrafts.

What do we mean when we say "gothic horror"? Just to define our terms, there are a lot of kinds of horror out there, from roller-coaster horror like *The Mist*, to creepy, psychological horror like *The Orphanage*. *Silent Hill: Past Life* belongs to that second kind, the kind of horror that worries us as we drive home because it makes us question the safety of our souls. And the "gothic" in gothic horror? That refers to a love of the past that has curdled into something unhealthy; it refers to a feeling of spiritual magic given off by old curling paint and old sagging structures. Not every story that loves the past is gothic, in other words—a new Sherlock Holmes story is not gothic, but *From Hell* certainly is.

In *Silent Hill: Past Life*, a man named Jeb Foster travels with his very pregnant wife Esther to the town of Silent Hill, where the couple hope to fix up Esther's empty family home. The time is the late 1800s, with the Civil War still in recent memory. Esther is a picture of Protestant piety, gentle and kind and quick to calm Jeb's anger and chastise his profane tongue.

But Jeb is a man who lives on the edge of disaster. As written by Tom Waltz and drawn by artist Menton3, Jeb is a big, muscular man who hides his face behind a beard and struggles to stay sober and calm. But just below the surface we get the impression that there is not a dark deed that Jeb has committed that he doesn't think about constantly, and we are to learn that there are many, many dark deeds for him to think about. Silent Hill is going to remind him.

Jeb has turned over a new leaf—we've all felt this, haven't we?—the notion that *just for today I'll make the right choices, just for today I'll do the next right thing, just for today I won't kill anyone for pay or commit any of the cardinal sins.* But what about yesterday, and what makes you so sure about today, Jeb? Does Esther make you sure?

We watch Jeb as though even *he* doesn't completely believe he can run for long. The house that he and Esther move into is a reflection of Jeb's world: a hulking, dark and decaying place that all the prayers in the world may not be able to save.

And why not? Because this is Silent Hill.

American horror often has a palpable sense of place, and Waltz's Silent Hill is a near *Twilight Zone* of a town; once Jeb and Esther roll in, they seem to pass through an invisible skein and into a more vivid dimension, where matters of spirit can erupt into the real world.

As Jeb and Esther enter it, Silent Hill as presented here is a withering boomtown, now sparsely populated, dusty and quiet. Every part of the town seems to have a past and a darker past before that—of peacetime and wartime prisons and slaughtered Indians. And the town has a bead on Jeb—no sooner does Jeb arrive than he keeps running into people who hint at knowing about him, from a creepy, elderly Indian woman with a big knife, to a sheriff who isn't very interested in protecting Jeb and Esther when they feel threatened, to folks in the saloon who seem to be acting out a drama all their own and expecting Jeb to join in.

As you read these scenes, you wonder: is Silent Hill like a dream? Does it make you unable to recognize the path you're walking down even if you've walked down it before?

With a few exceptions, the comic stays riveted to Foster's own intense, fevered point of view. What must it be like for him to walk into a town and be surrounded by people from his own past, some of whom should have a definite attitude problem about him? But more than this—when Jeb and Esther go to church, we have to wonder: do Esther and Jeb see the same people in the pews? How much of this town is actually there, and how much of it is being sculpted for each new visitor, a show of horrors along rotting acres presented for one lucky patron?

And in the middle of it all is a baby on the way—Esther will soon give birth, and what kind of town is Silent Hill to choose as a place to start a family? Pregnancy is a terrifying thing to encounter in a gothic horror story, because pregnancy is wonderful and dangerous and involves so many lives. It's a physical manifestation of something spiritual: the creation of life—itself the piercing of the veil between the spiritual and the physical. We're terrified for the baby throughout the story because we know that the spiritual justice of Silent Hill might not spare a child. Evil deeds have a way of coursing through the evildoer's life and poisoning everyone near.

I don't want to give too much away about what happens in *Silent Hill: Past Life* because you'll enjoy it more if you read it yourself. But know this: this is fine American gothic horror, and there is no better kind.

–Jason Henderson

Jason Henderson is the author of Alex Van Helsing: Vampire Rising *(Summer 2010) from HarperTeen, which has been named by the Texas Library Association to the 2011 Lone Star Reading List, a list of the top 20 books published in the previous year for middle grade readers. His next book,* Alex Van Helsing: Voice of the Undead, *comes out in Summer 2011. You can find him online at http://alexvanhelsing.com.*

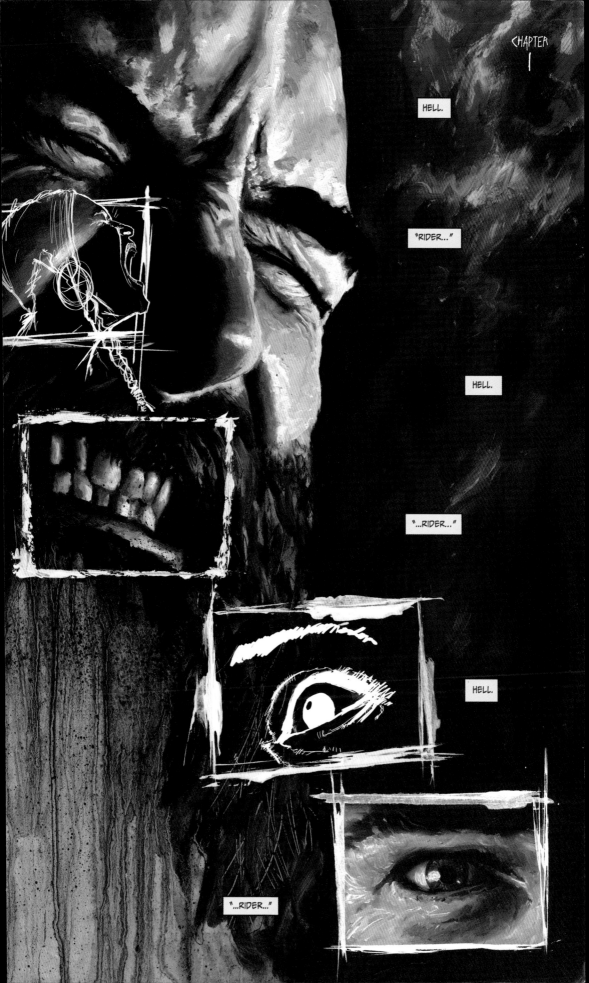

HELL.

"RIDER..."

HELL.

"...RIDER..."

HELL.

"...RIDER..."

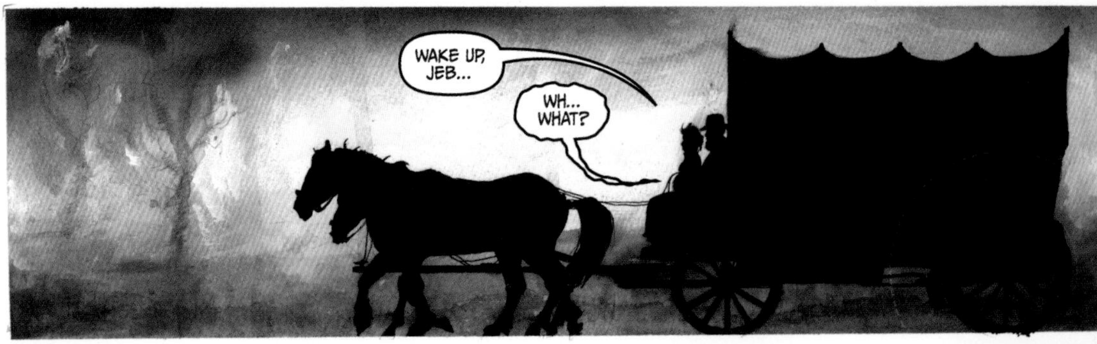
WAKE UP, JEB...
WH... WHAT?
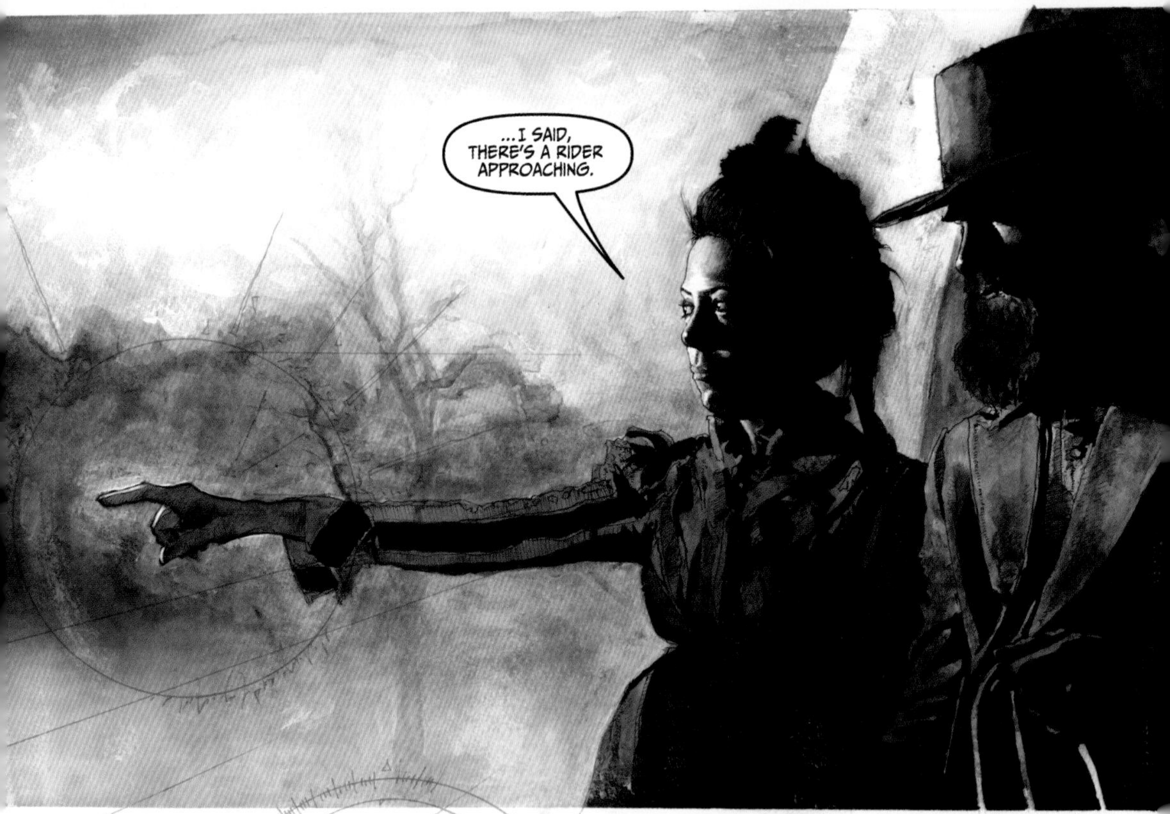
...I SAID, THERE'S A RIDER APPROACHING.
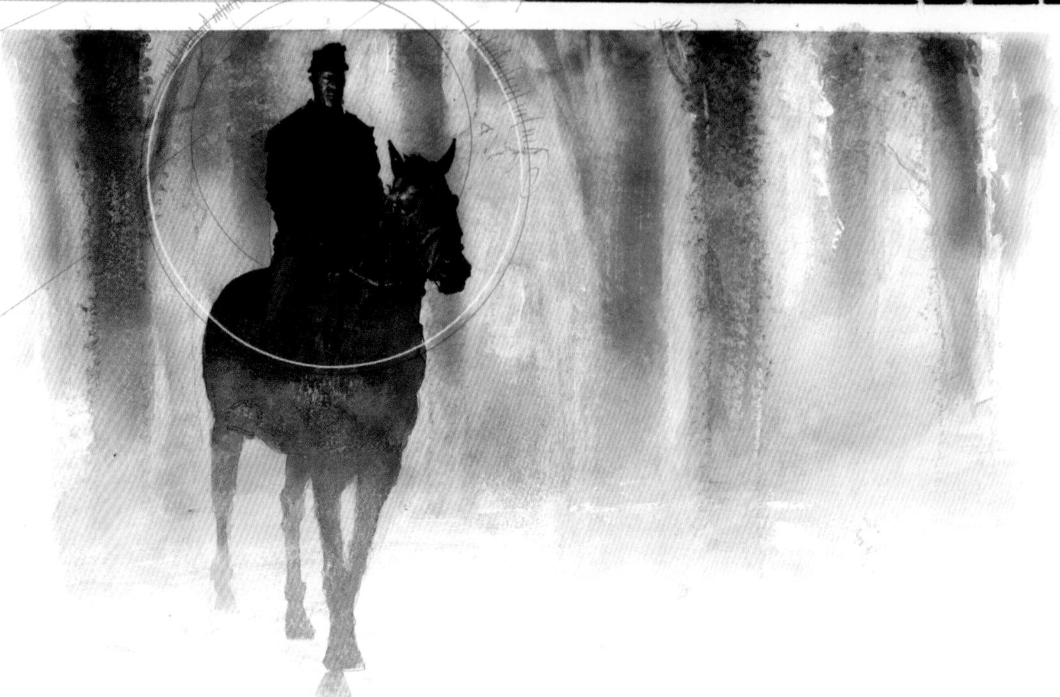

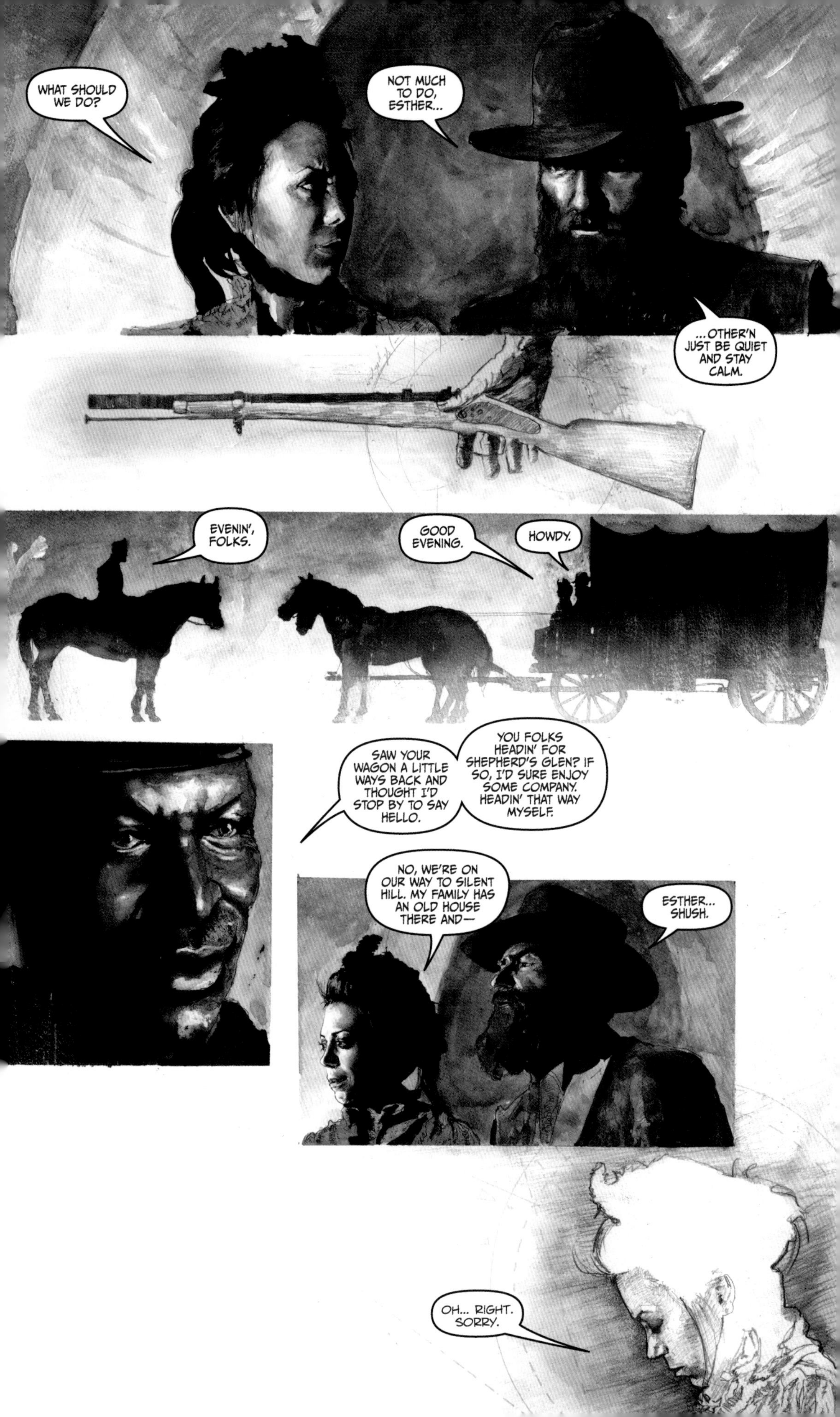
WHAT SHOULD WE DO?
NOT MUCH TO DO, ESTHER...
...OTHER'N JUST BE QUIET AND STAY CALM.
EVENIN', FOLKS.
GOOD EVENING.
HOWDY.
SAW YOUR WAGON A LITTLE WAYS BACK AND THOUGHT I'D STOP BY TO SAY HELLO.
YOU FOLKS HEADIN' FOR SHEPHERD'S GLEN? IF SO, I'D SURE ENJOY SOME COMPANY. HEADIN' THAT WAY MYSELF.
NO, WE'RE ON OUR WAY TO SILENT HILL. MY FAMILY HAS AN OLD HOUSE THERE AND—
ESTHER... SHUSH.
OH... RIGHT. SORRY.

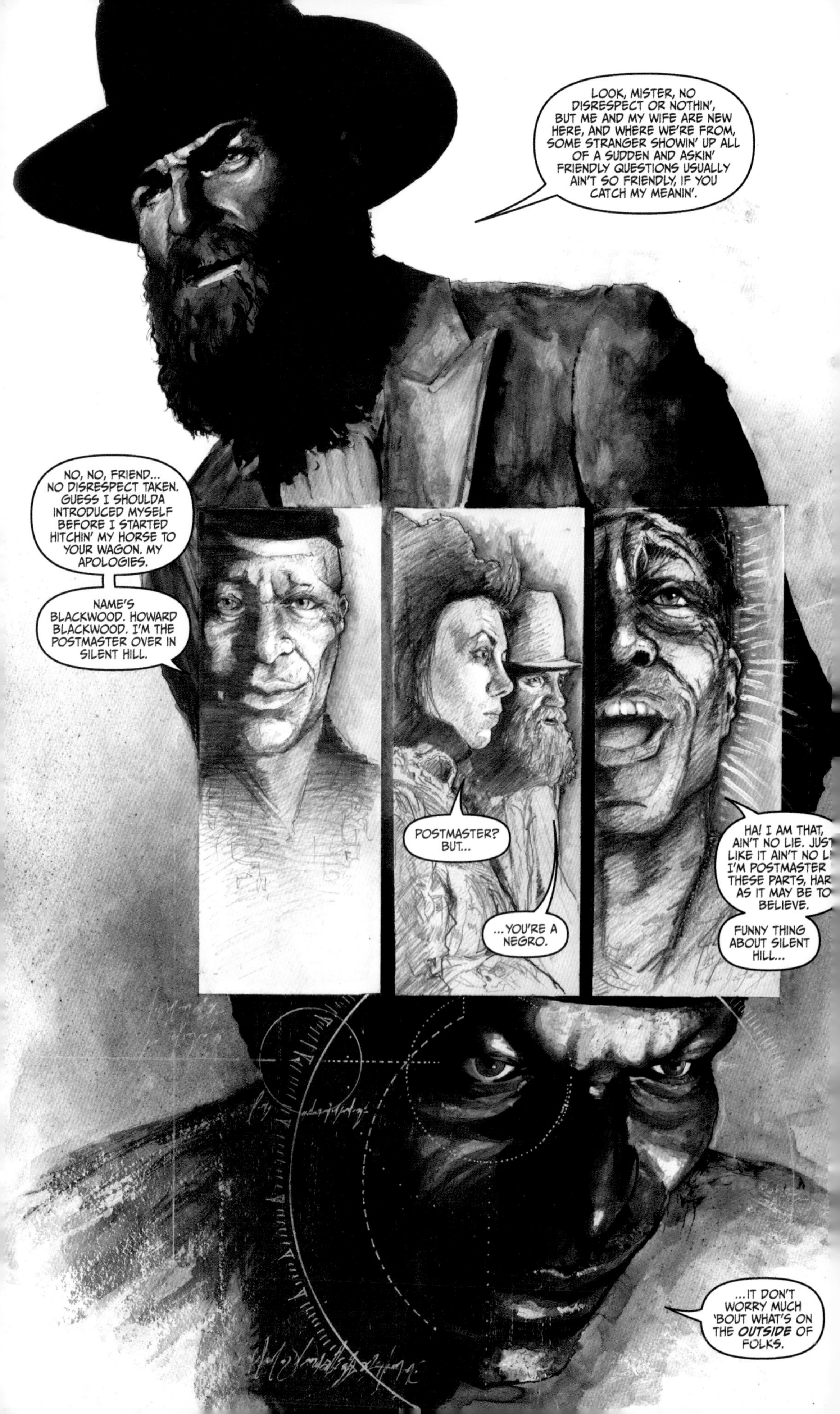
LOOK, MISTER, NO DISRESPECT OR NOTHIN', BUT ME AND MY WIFE ARE NEW HERE, AND WHERE WE'RE FROM, SOME STRANGER SHOWIN' UP ALL OF A SUDDEN AND ASKIN' FRIENDLY QUESTIONS USUALLY AIN'T SO FRIENDLY, IF YOU CATCH MY MEANIN'.
NO, NO, FRIEND... NO DISRESPECT TAKEN. GUESS I SHOULDA INTRODUCED MYSELF BEFORE I STARTED HITCHIN' MY HORSE TO YOUR WAGON. MY APOLOGIES.
NAME'S BLACKWOOD. HOWARD BLACKWOOD. I'M THE POSTMASTER OVER IN SILENT HILL.
POSTMASTER? BUT...
...YOU'RE A NEGRO.
HA! I AM THAT, AIN'T NO LIE. JUS LIKE IT AIN'T NO LI I'M POSTMASTER THESE PARTS, HAR AS IT MAY BE TO BELIEVE.
FUNNY THING ABOUT SILENT HILL...
...IT DON'T WORRY MUCH 'BOUT WHAT'S ON THE *OUTSIDE* OF FOLKS.

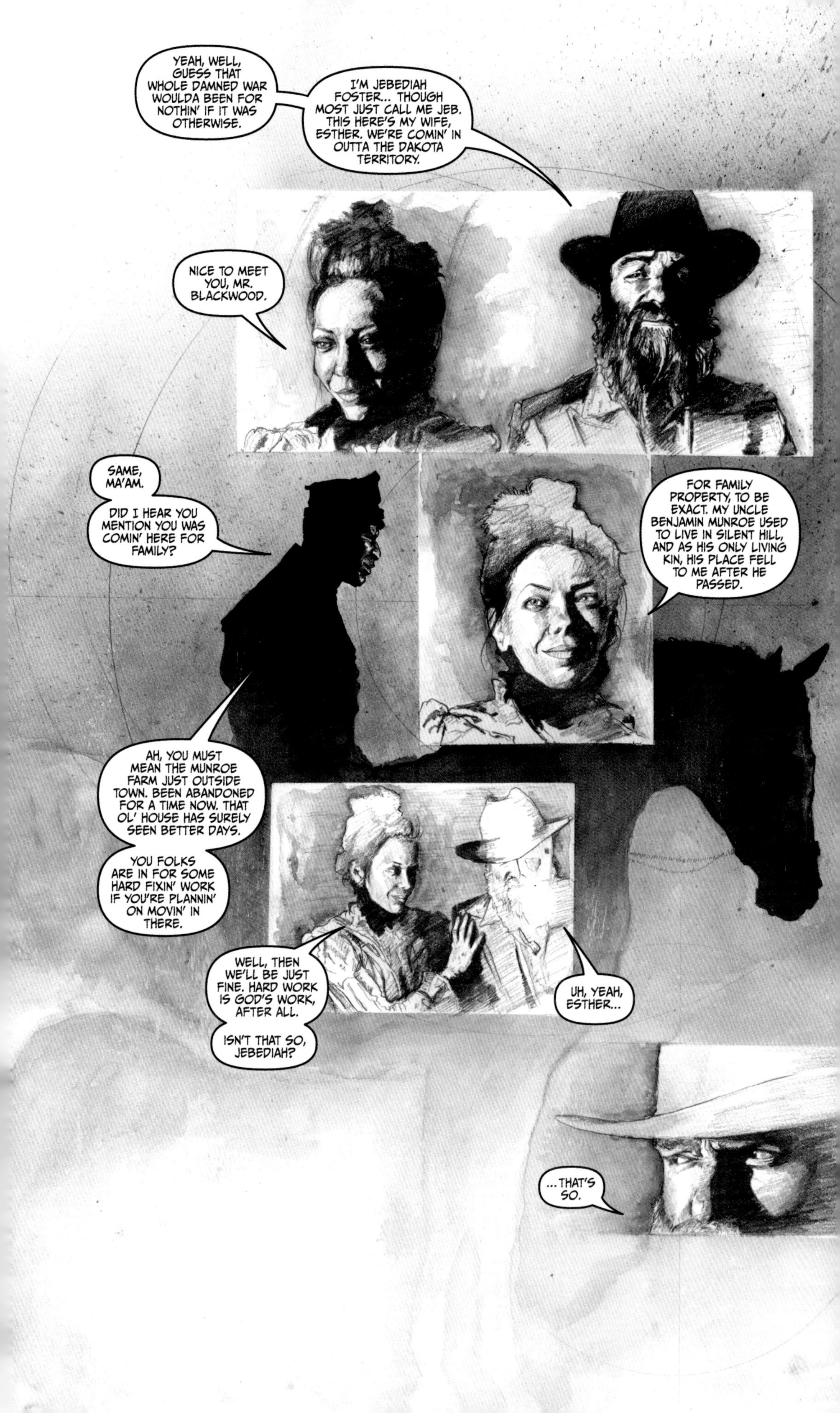
YEAH, WELL, GUESS THAT WHOLE DAMNED WAR WOULDA BEEN FOR NOTHIN' IF IT WAS OTHERWISE.
I'M JEBEDIAH FOSTER... THOUGH MOST JUST CALL ME JEB. THIS HERE'S MY WIFE, ESTHER. WE'RE COMIN' IN OUTTA THE DAKOTA TERRITORY.
NICE TO MEET YOU, MR. BLACKWOOD.
SAME, MA'AM.
DID I HEAR YOU MENTION YOU WAS COMIN' HERE FOR FAMILY?
FOR FAMILY PROPERTY, TO BE EXACT. MY UNCLE BENJAMIN MUNROE USED TO LIVE IN SILENT HILL, AND AS HIS ONLY LIVING KIN, HIS PLACE FELL TO ME AFTER HE PASSED.
AH, YOU MUST MEAN THE MUNROE FARM JUST OUTSIDE TOWN. BEEN ABANDONED FOR A TIME NOW. THAT OL' HOUSE HAS SURELY SEEN BETTER DAYS.
YOU FOLKS ARE IN FOR SOME HARD FIXIN' WORK IF YOU'RE PLANNIN' ON MOVIN' IN THERE.
WELL, THEN WE'LL BE JUST FINE. HARD WORK IS GOD'S WORK, AFTER ALL.
ISN'T THAT SO, JEBEDIAH?
UH, YEAH, ESTHER...
...THAT'S SO.

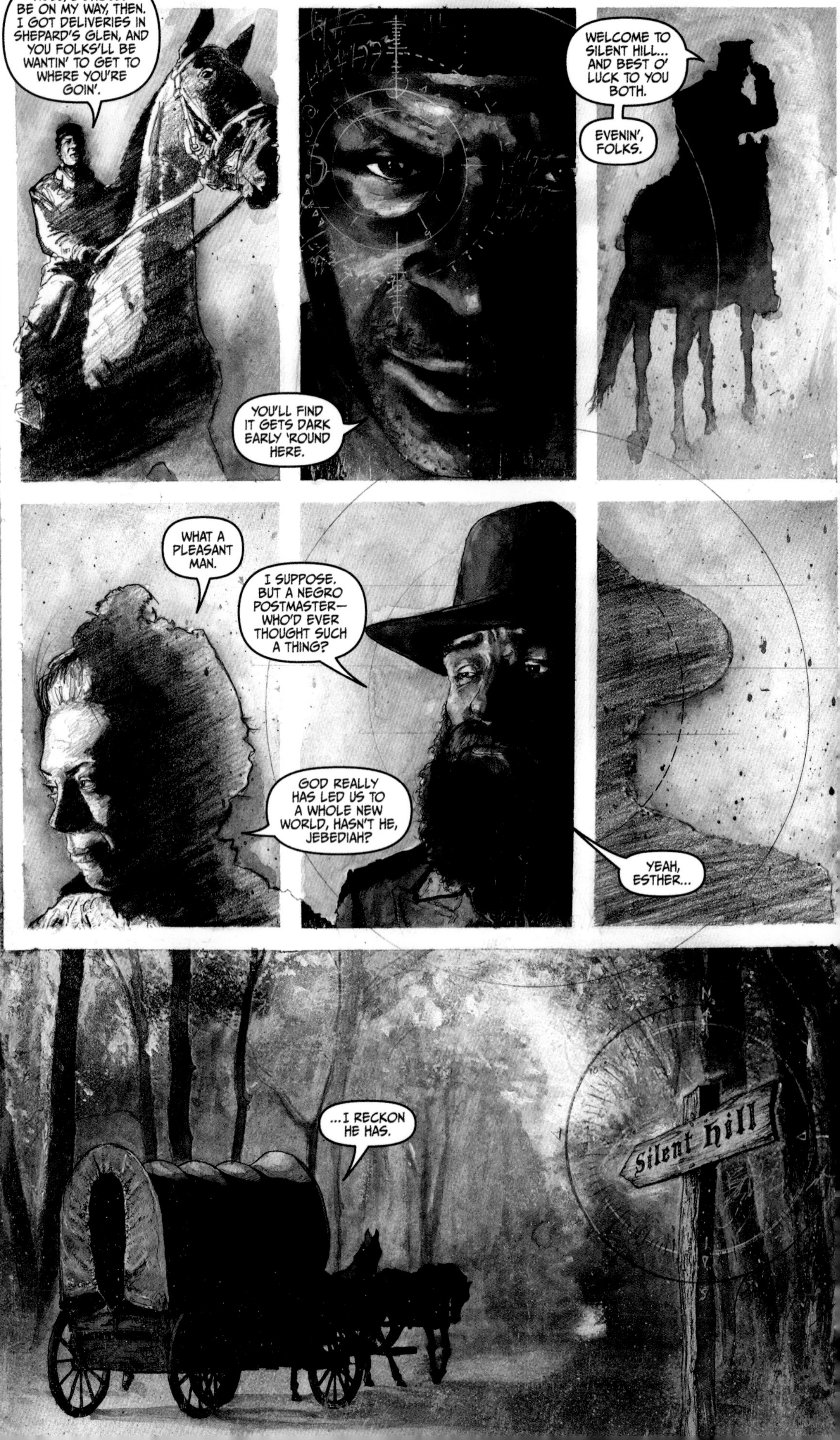
WELL, I SHOULD BE ON MY WAY, THEN. I GOT DELIVERIES IN SHEPARD'S GLEN, AND YOU FOLKS'LL BE WANTIN' TO GET TO WHERE YOU'RE GOIN'.
YOU'LL FIND IT GETS DARK EARLY 'ROUND HERE.
WELCOME TO SILENT HILL... AND BEST O' LUCK TO YOU BOTH.
EVENIN', FOLKS.
WHAT A PLEASANT MAN.
I SUPPOSE. BUT A NEGRO POSTMASTER— WHO'D EVER THOUGHT SUCH A THING?
GOD REALLY HAS LED US TO A WHOLE NEW WORLD, HASN'T HE, JEBEDIAH?
YEAH, ESTHER...
...I RECKON HE HAS.
Silent hill

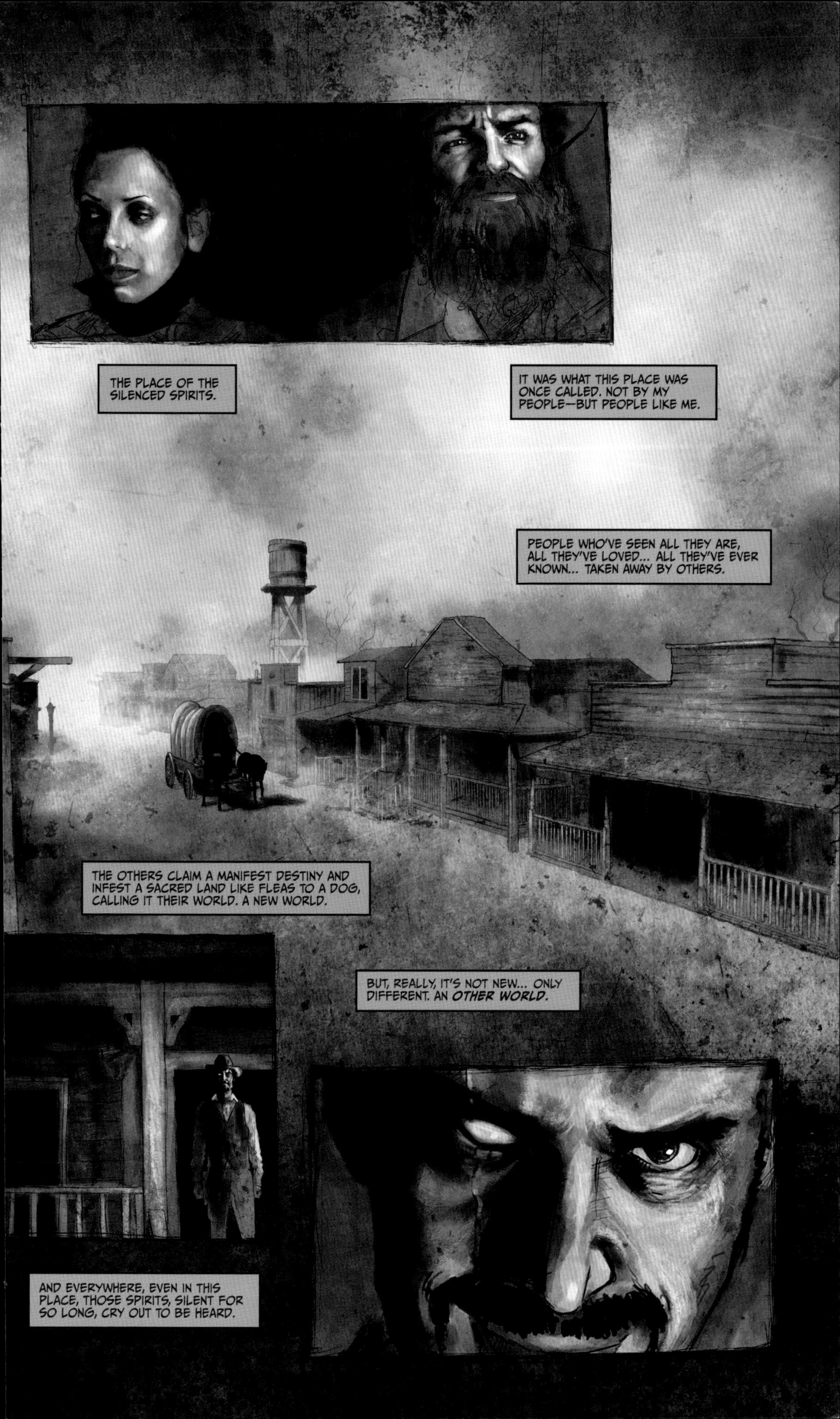
THE PLACE OF THE SILENCED SPIRITS.
IT WAS WHAT THIS PLACE WAS ONCE CALLED. NOT BY MY PEOPLE—BUT PEOPLE LIKE ME.
PEOPLE WHO'VE SEEN ALL THEY ARE, ALL THEY'VE LOVED... ALL THEY'VE EVER KNOWN... TAKEN AWAY BY OTHERS.
THE OTHERS CLAIM A MANIFEST DESTINY AND INFEST A SACRED LAND LIKE FLEAS TO A DOG, CALLING IT THEIR WORLD. A NEW WORLD.
BUT, REALLY, IT'S NOT NEW... ONLY DIFFERENT. AN *OTHER WORLD.*
AND EVERYWHERE, EVEN IN THIS PLACE, THOSE SPIRITS, SILENT FOR SO LONG, CRY OUT TO BE HEARD.

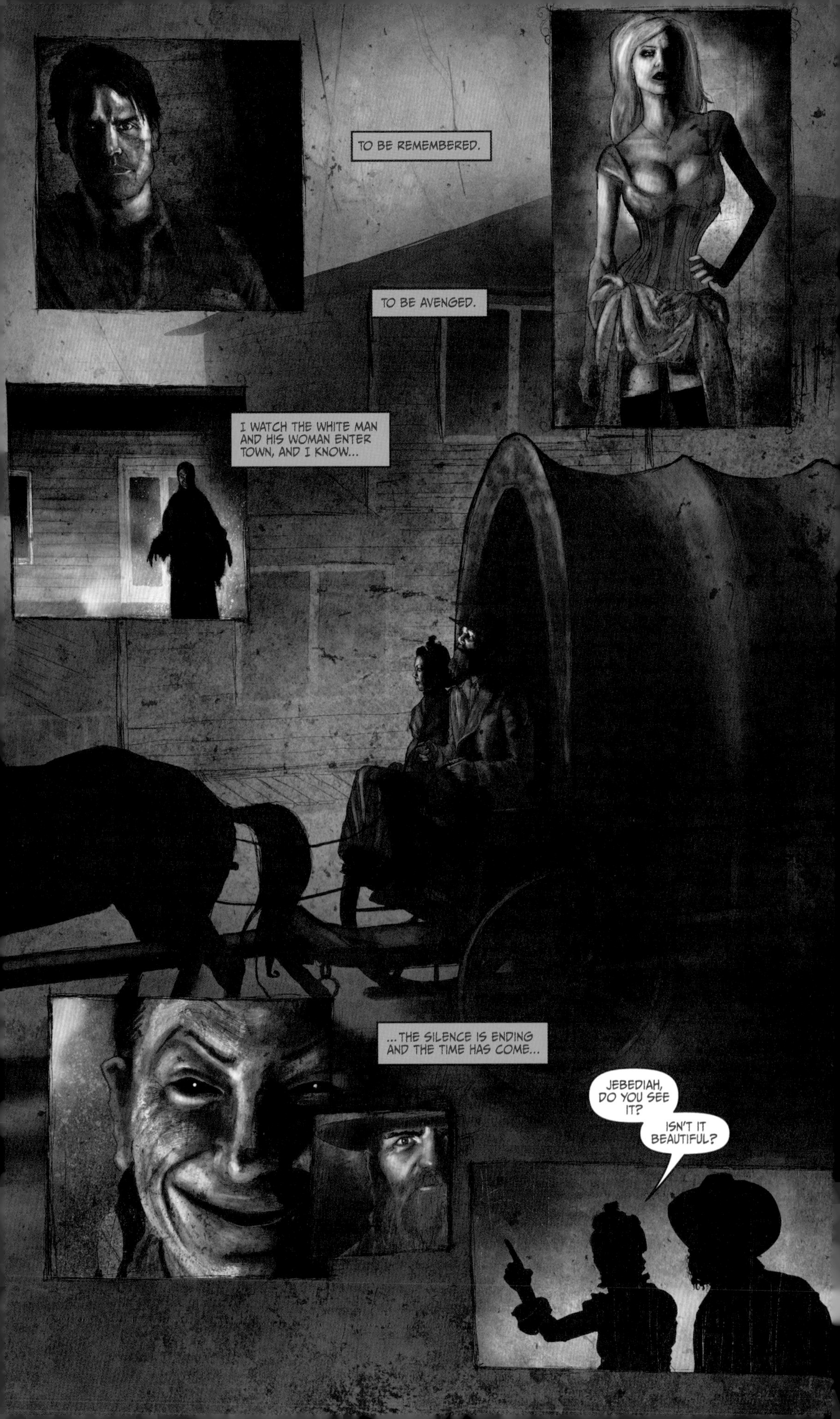
TO BE REMEMBERED.
TO BE AVENGED.
I WATCH THE WHITE MAN AND HIS WOMAN ENTER TOWN, AND I KNOW...
...THE SILENCE IS ENDING AND THE TIME HAS COME...
JEBEDIAH, DO YOU SEE IT?
ISN'T IT BEAUTIFUL?

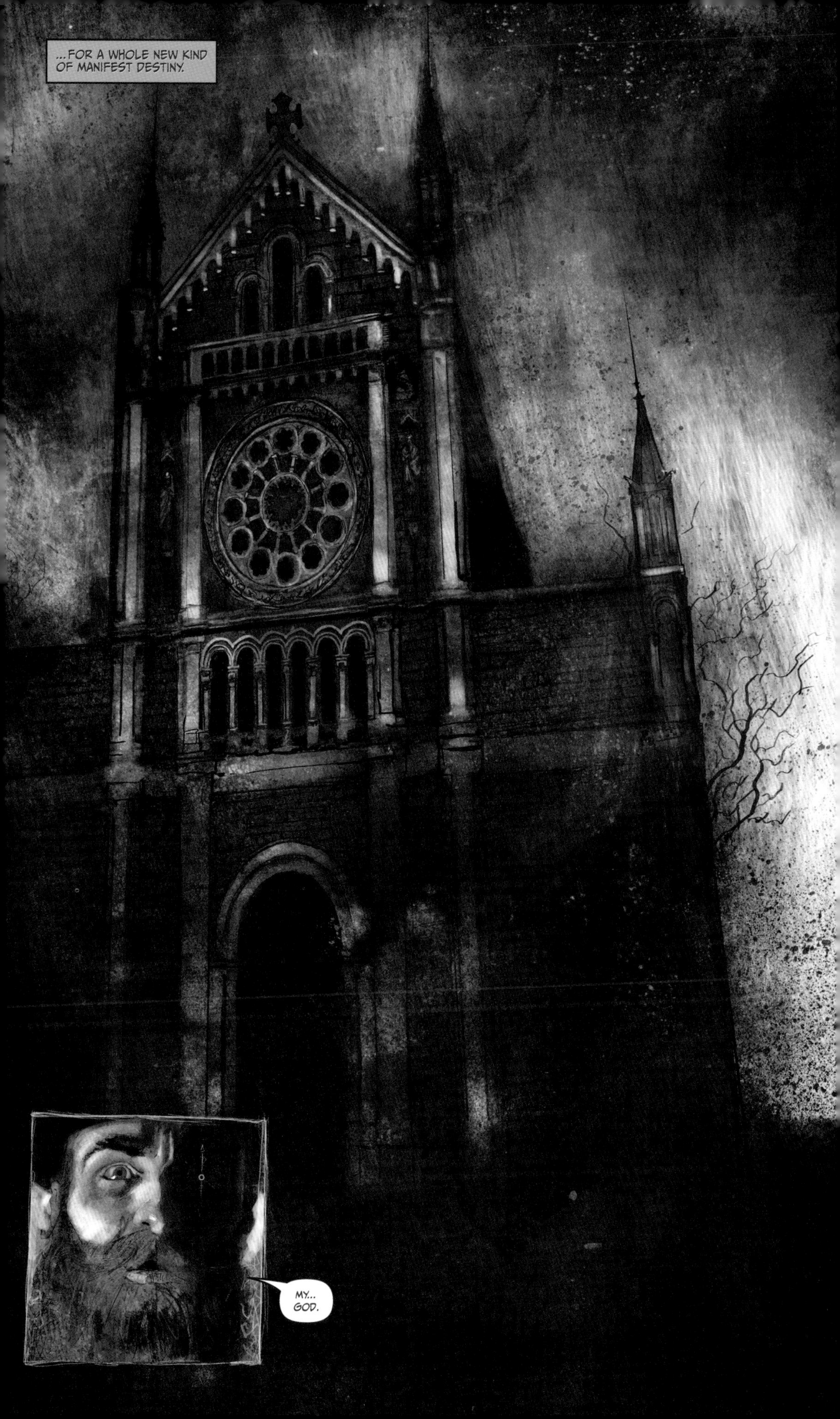
...FOR A WHOLE NEW KIND OF MANIFEST DESTINY.
MY... GOD.

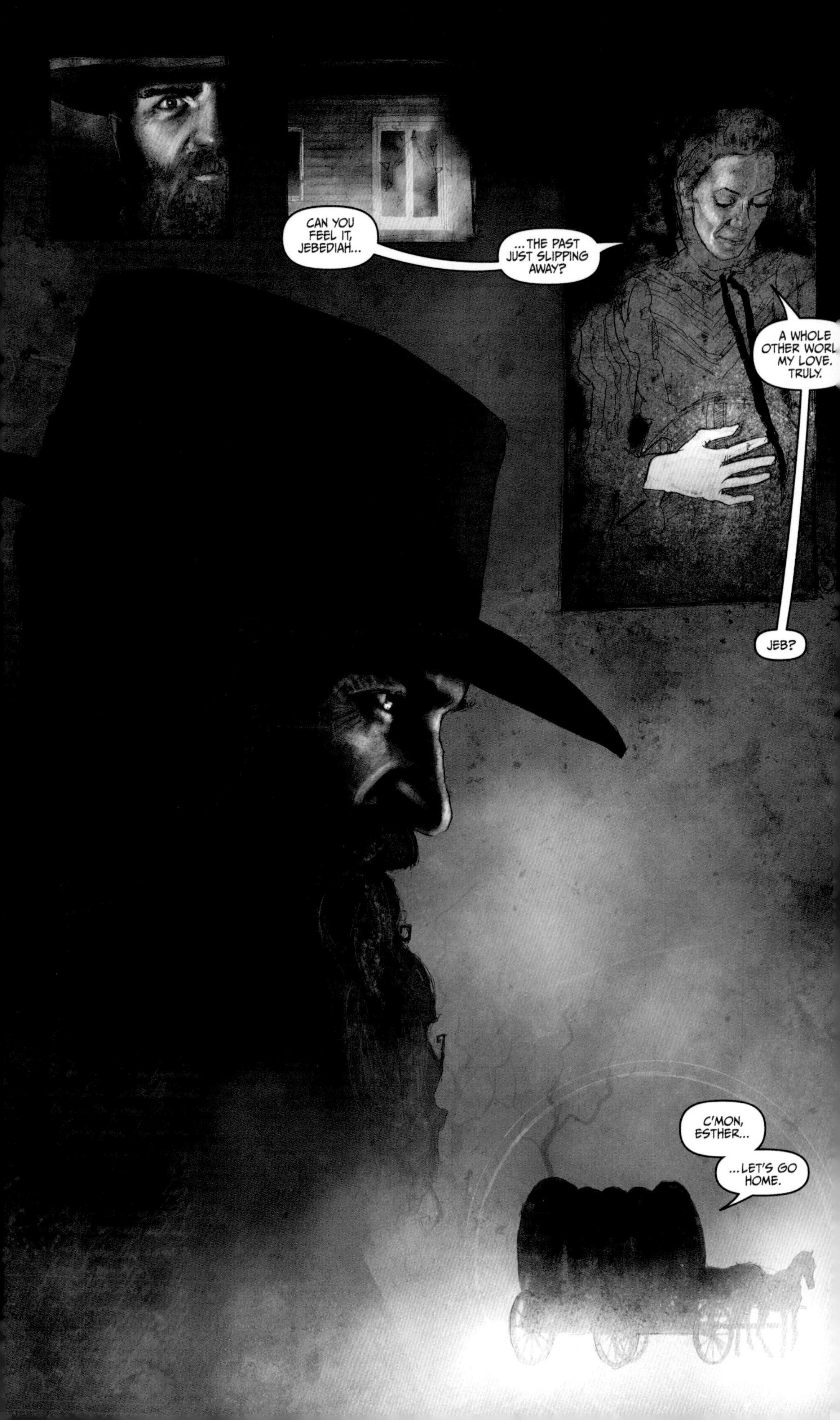
CAN YOU FEEL IT, JEBEDIAH...
...THE PAST JUST SLIPPING AWAY?
A WHOLE OTHER WORL MY LOVE. TRULY.
JEB?
C'MON, ESTHER...
...LET'S GO HOME.

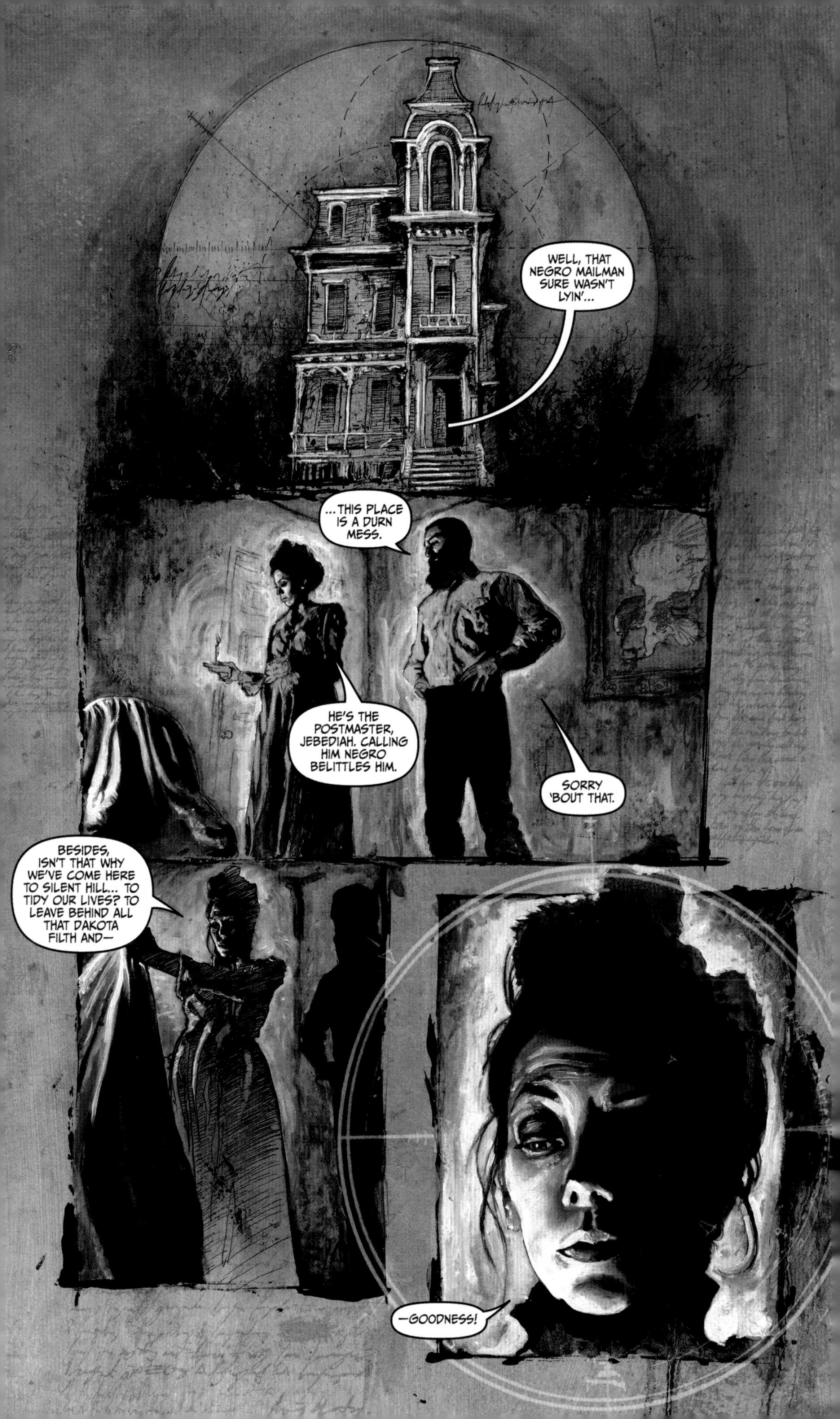
WELL, THAT NEGRO MAILMAN SURE WASN'T LYIN'...
...THIS PLACE IS A DURN MESS.
HE'S THE POSTMASTER, JEBEDIAH. CALLING HIM NEGRO BELITTLES HIM.
SORRY 'BOUT THAT.
BESIDES, ISN'T THAT WHY WE'VE COME HERE TO SILENT HILL... TO TIDY OUR LIVES? TO LEAVE BEHIND ALL THAT DAKOTA FILTH AND—
—GOODNESS!

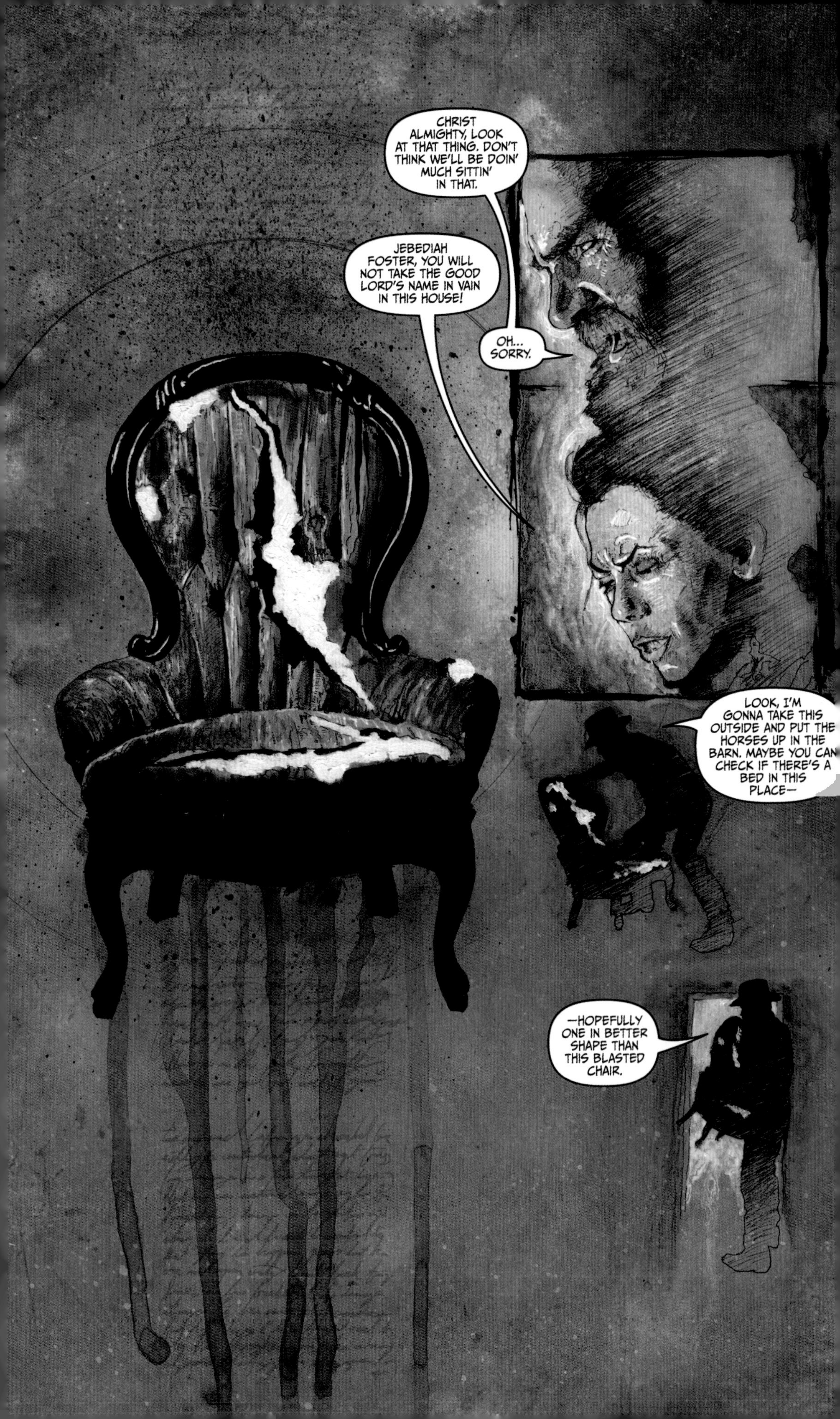
CHRIST ALMIGHTY, LOOK AT THAT THING. DON'T THINK WE'LL BE DOIN' MUCH SITTIN' IN THAT.
JEBEDIAH FOSTER, YOU WILL NOT TAKE THE GOOD LORD'S NAME IN VAIN IN THIS HOUSE!
OH... SORRY.
LOOK, I'M GONNA TAKE THIS OUTSIDE AND PUT THE HORSES UP IN THE BARN. MAYBE YOU CAN CHECK IF THERE'S A BED IN THIS PLACE—
—HOPEFULLY ONE IN BETTER SHAPE THAN THIS BLASTED CHAIR.

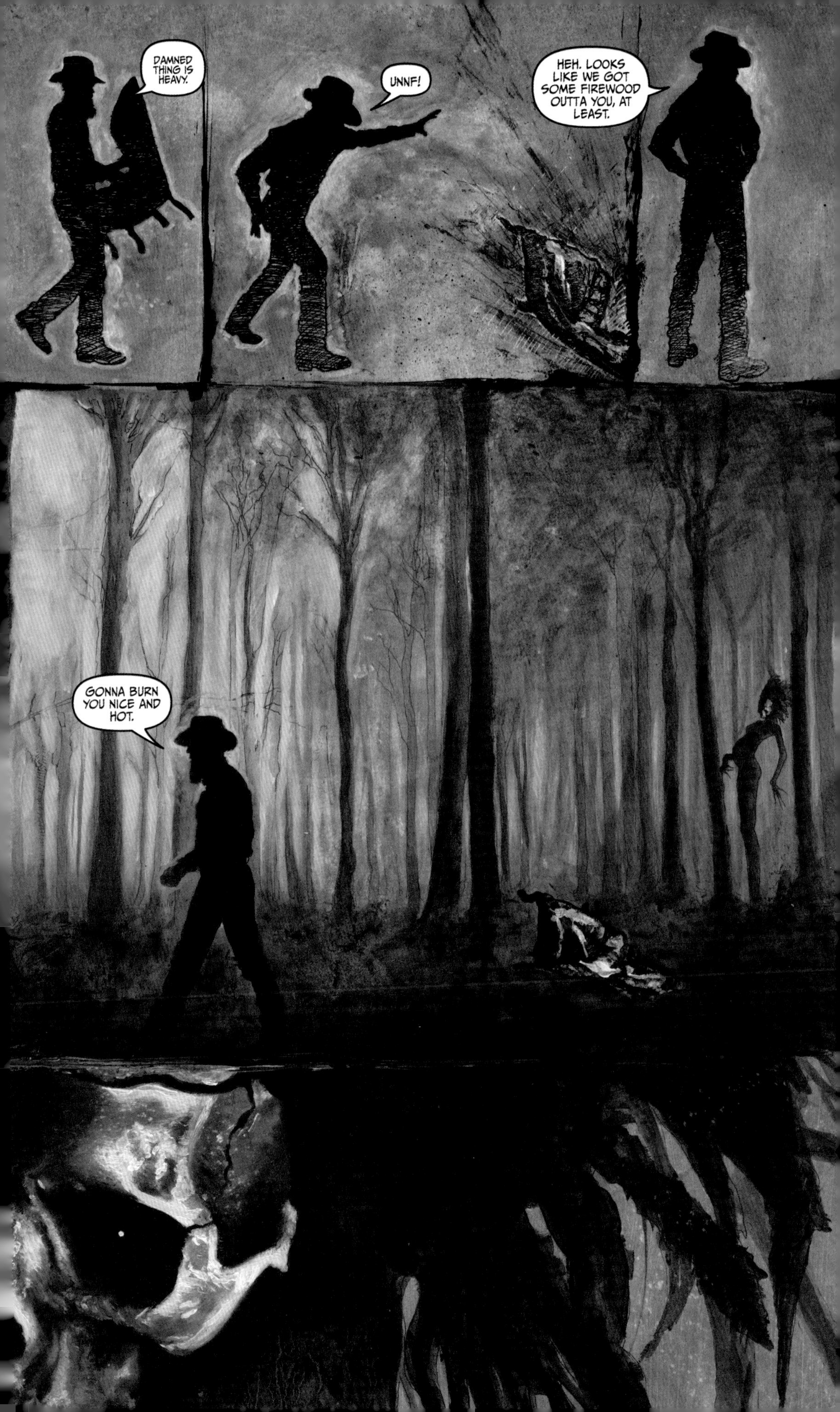
DAMNED THING IS HEAVY.
UNNF!
HEH. LOOKS LIKE WE GOT SOME FIREWOOD OUTTA YOU, AT LEAST.
GONNA BURN YOU NICE AND HOT.

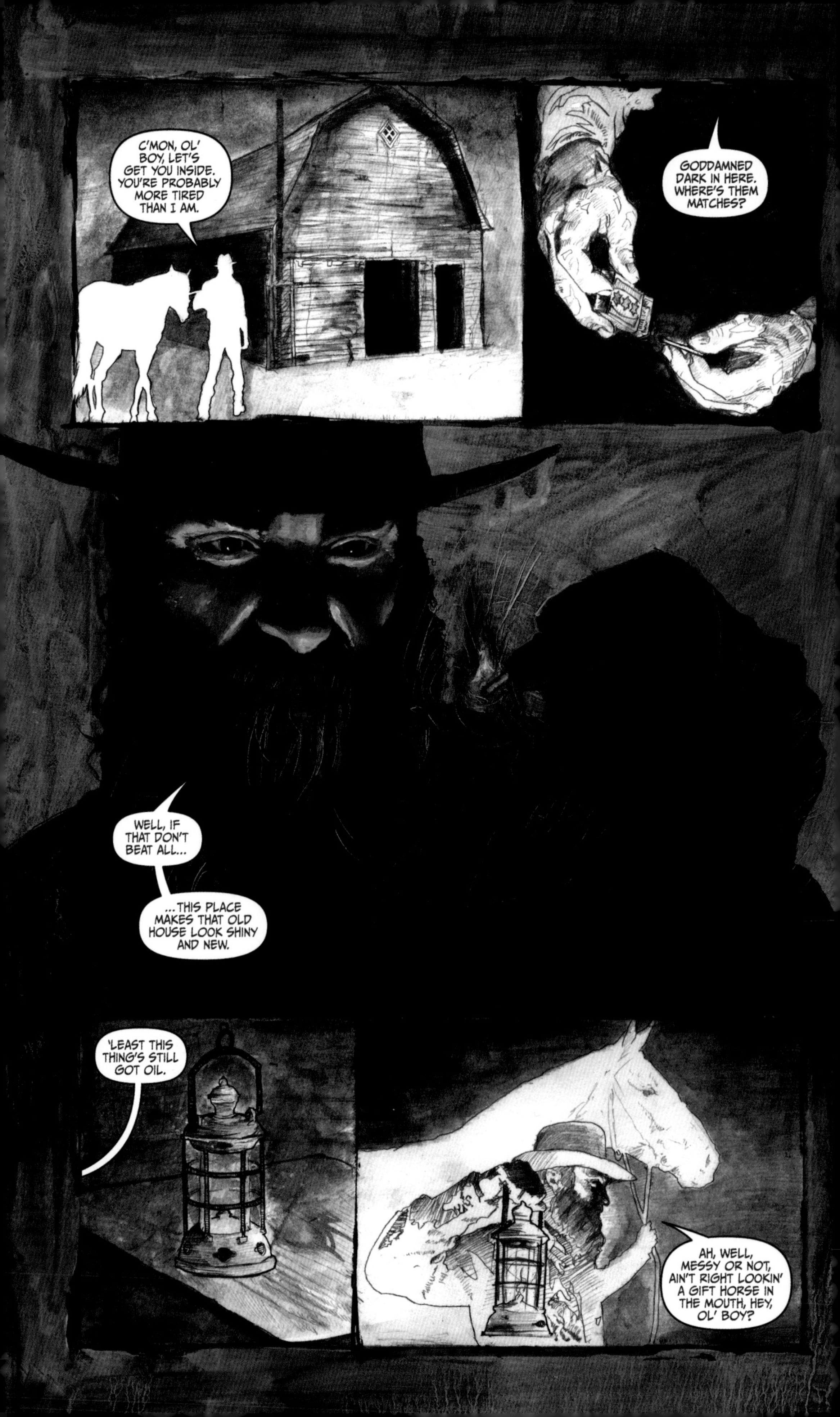
C'MON, OL' BOY, LET'S GET YOU INSIDE. YOU'RE PROBABLY MORE TIRED THAN I AM.
GODDAMNED DARK IN HERE. WHERE'S THEM MATCHES?
WELL, IF THAT DON'T BEAT ALL...
...THIS PLACE MAKES THAT OLD HOUSE LOOK SHINY AND NEW.
'LEAST THIS THING'S STILL GOT OIL.
AH, WELL, MESSY OR NOT, AIN'T RIGHT LOOKIN' A GIFT HORSE IN THE MOUTH, HEY, OL' BOY?

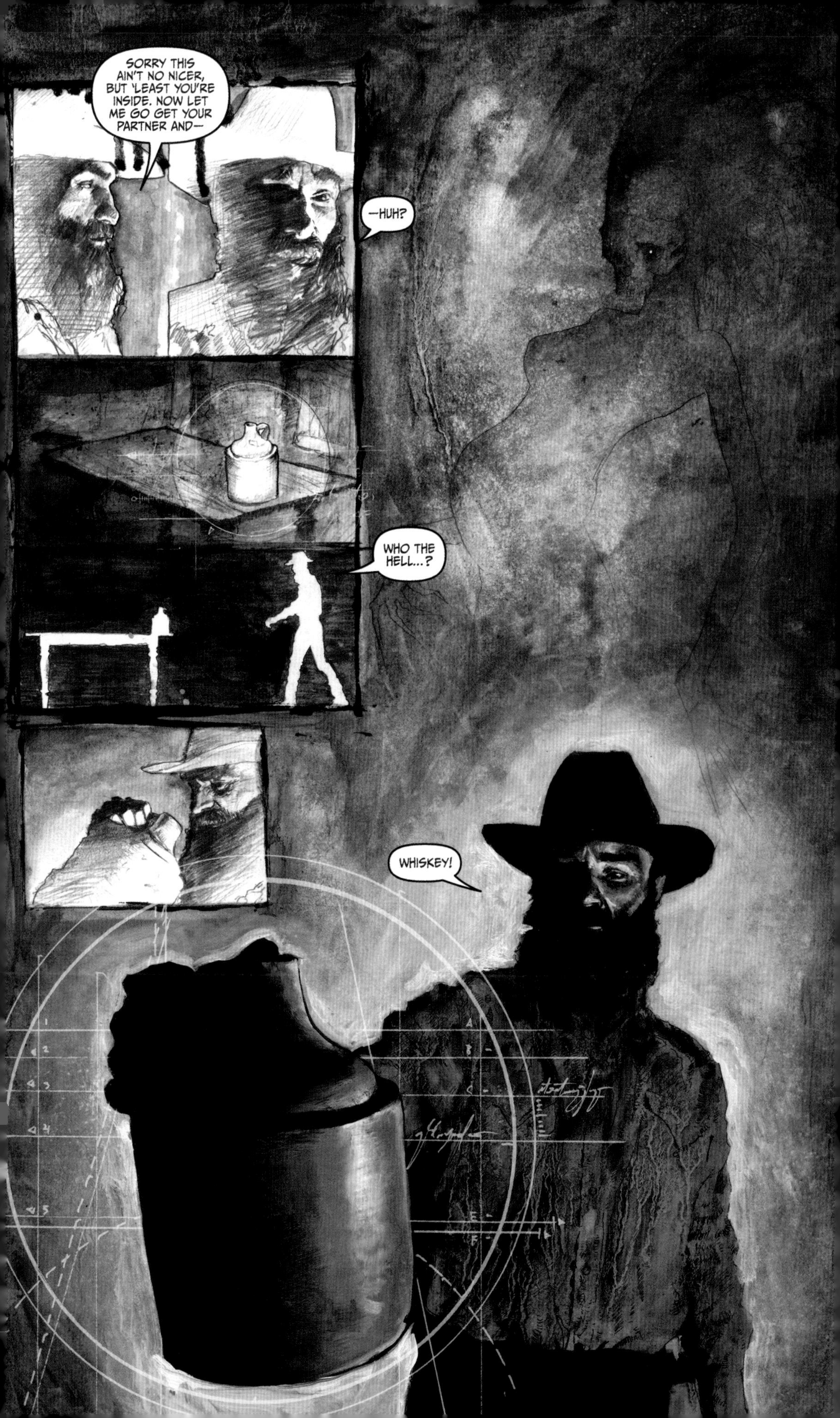
SORRY THIS AIN'T NO NICER, BUT 'LEAST YOU'RE INSIDE. NOW LET ME GO GET YOUR PARTNER AND—
—HUH?
WHO THE HELL...?
WHISKEY!

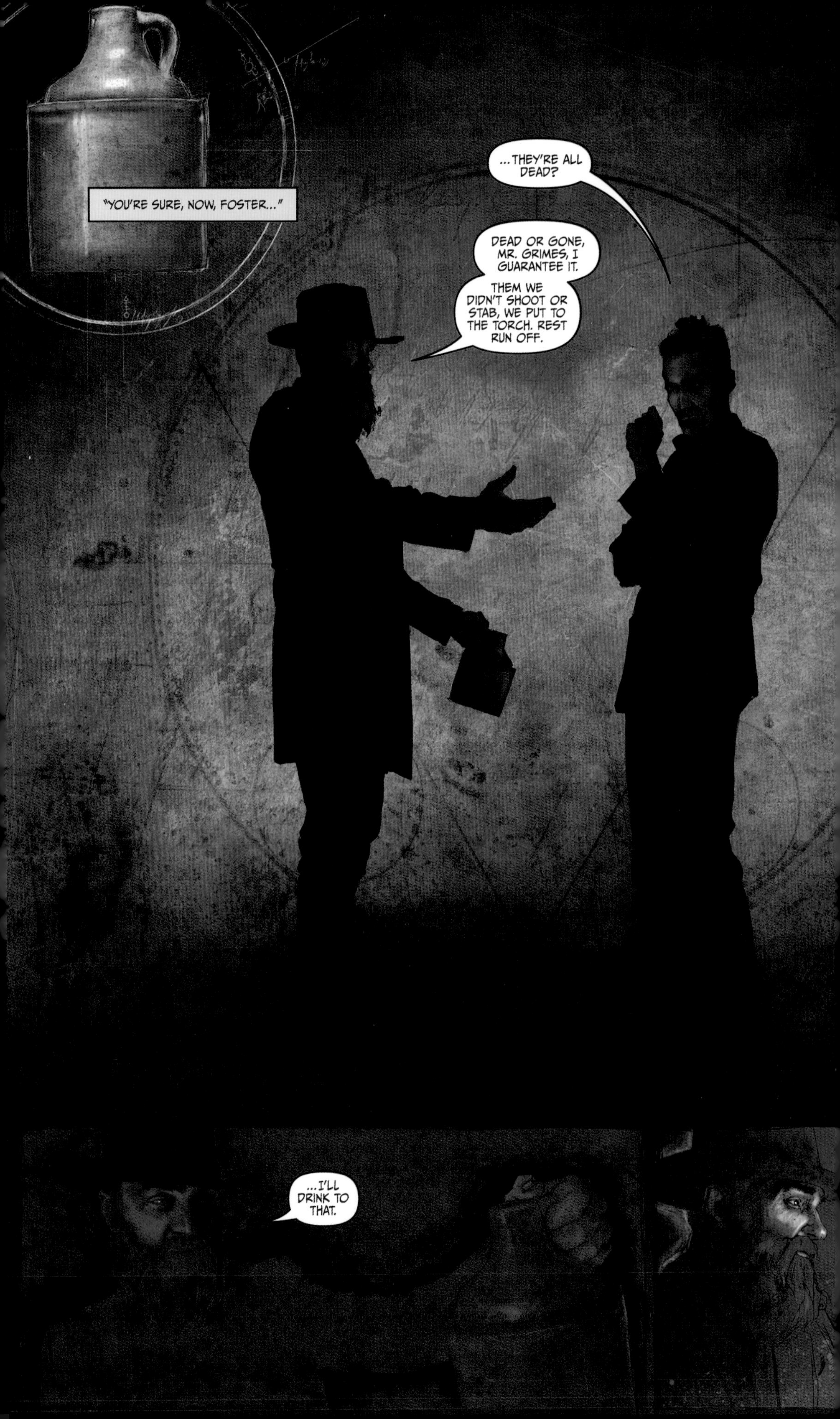
"YOU'RE SURE, NOW, FOSTER..."
...THEY'RE ALL DEAD?
DEAD OR GONE, MR. GRIMES, I GUARANTEE IT.
THEM WE DIDN'T SHOOT OR STAB, WE PUT TO THE TORCH. REST RUN OFF.
...I'LL DRINK TO THAT.

WELL, THAT'S GOOD, FOSTER... REAL GOOD. MONEY WELL SPENT, IF I DO SAY SO MYSELF.
YESSIR, MR. GRIMES...
AAAHHH!
ESTHER?

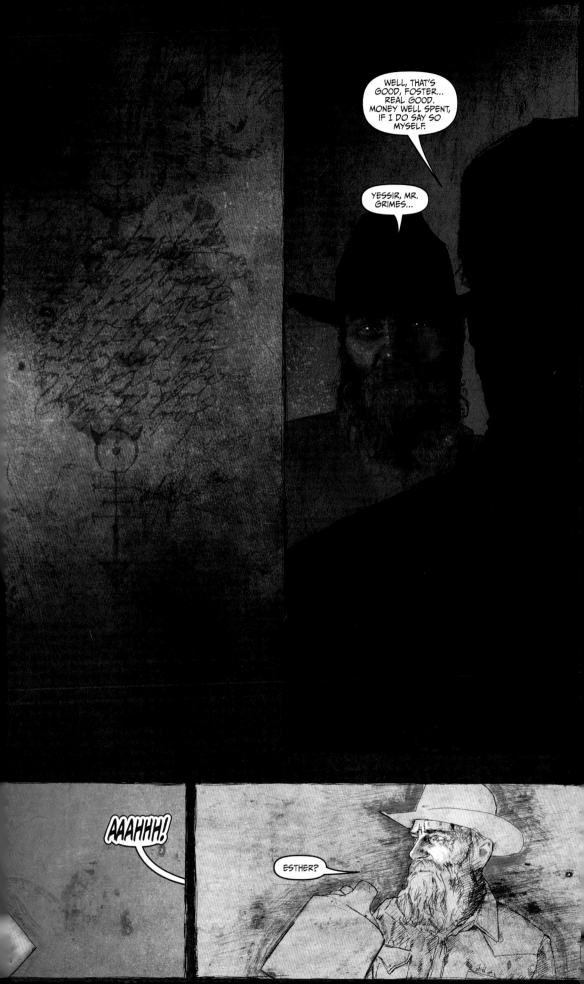

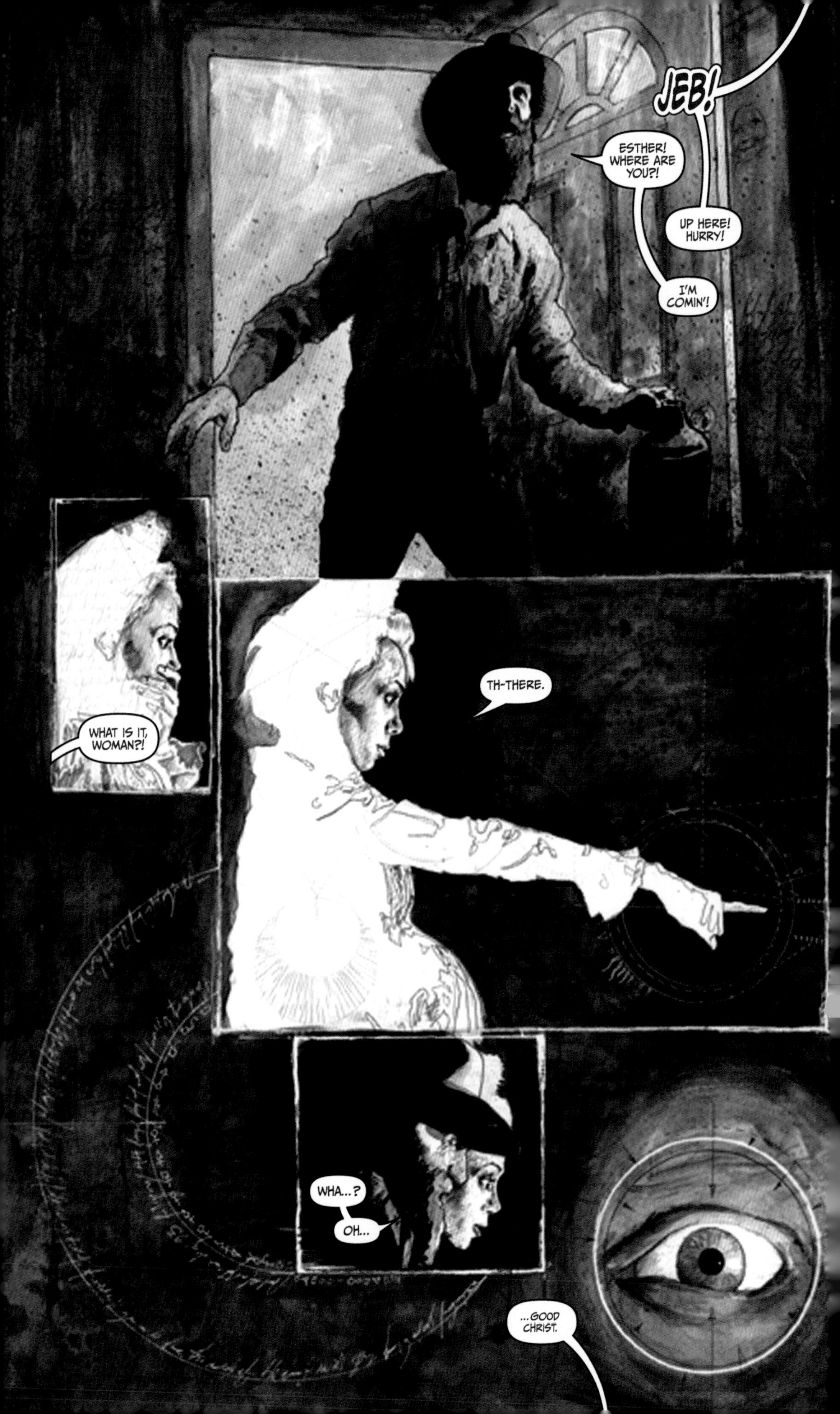
JEB!
ESTHER! WHERE ARE YOU?!
UP HERE! HURRY!
I'M COMIN'!
WHAT IS IT, WOMAN?!
TH-THERE.
WHA...?
OH...
...GOOD CHRIST.

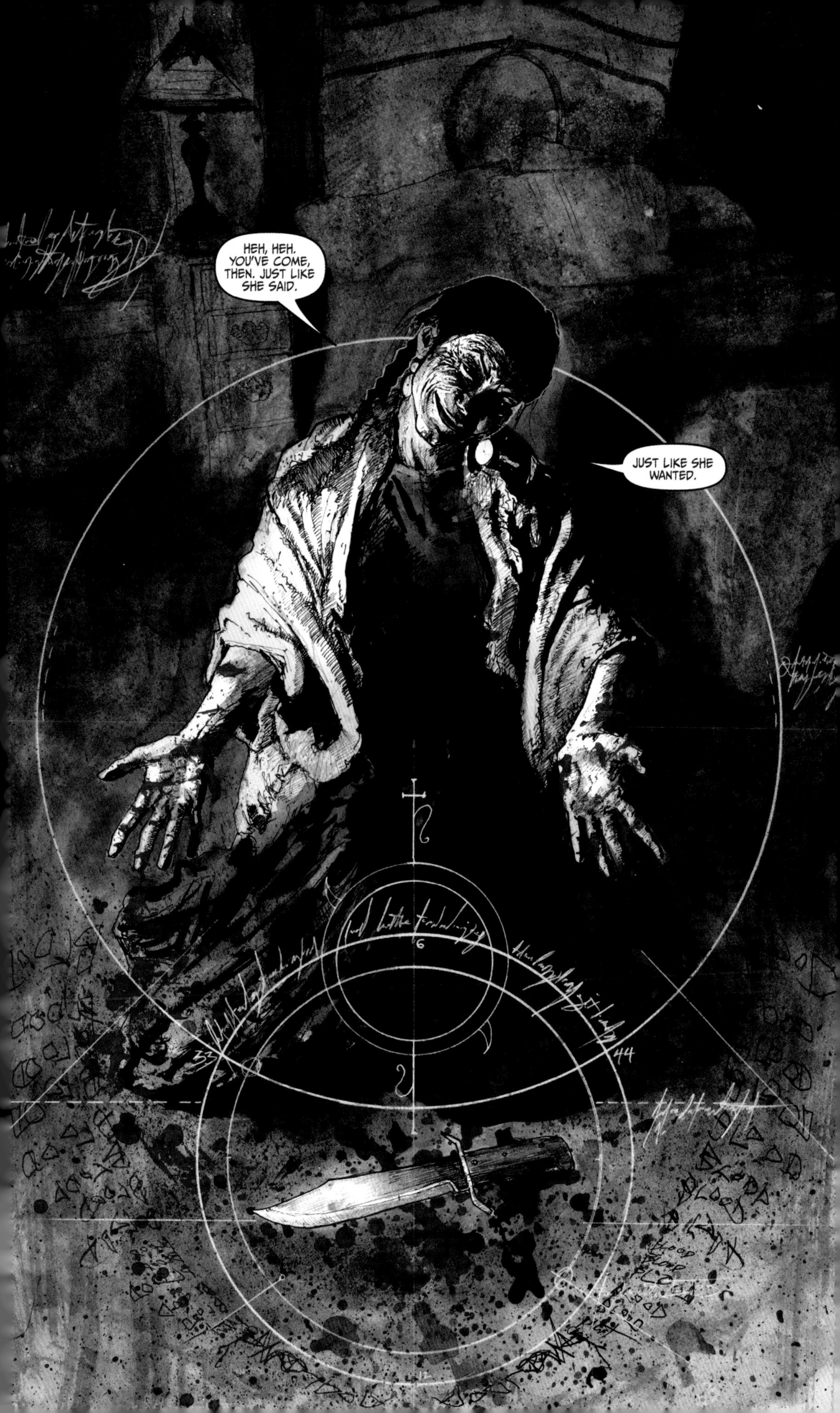
HEH, HEH. YOU'VE COME, THEN. JUST LIKE SHE SAID.
JUST LIKE SHE WANTED.

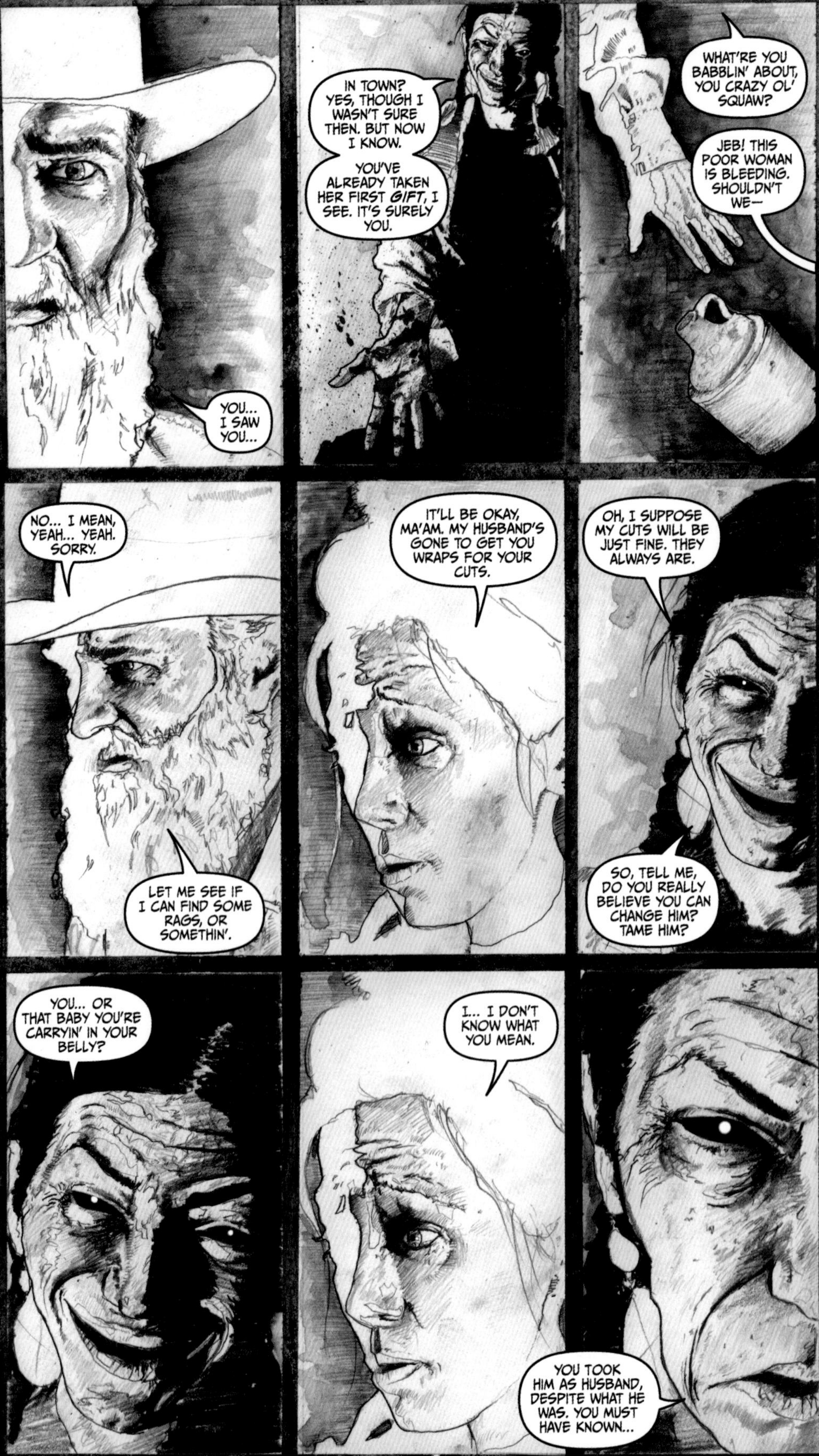
YOU... I SAW YOU...
IN TOWN? YES, THOUGH I WASN'T SURE THEN. BUT NOW I KNOW.
YOU'VE ALREADY TAKEN HER FIRST GIFT, I SEE. IT'S SURELY YOU.
WHAT'RE YOU BABBLIN' ABOUT, YOU CRAZY OL' SQUAW?
JEB! THIS POOR WOMAN IS BLEEDING. SHOULDN'T WE—
NO... I MEAN, YEAH... YEAH. SORRY.
LET ME SEE IF I CAN FIND SOME RAGS, OR SOMETHIN'.
IT'LL BE OKAY, MA'AM. MY HUSBAND'S GONE TO GET YOU WRAPS FOR YOUR CUTS.
OH, I SUPPOSE MY CUTS WILL BE JUST FINE. THEY ALWAYS ARE.
SO, TELL ME, DO YOU REALLY BELIEVE YOU CAN CHANGE HIM? TAME HIM?
YOU... OR THAT BABY YOU'RE CARRYIN' IN YOUR BELLY?
I... I DON'T KNOW WHAT YOU MEAN.
YOU TOOK HIM AS HUSBAND, DESPITE WHAT HE WAS. YOU MUST HAVE KNOWN...

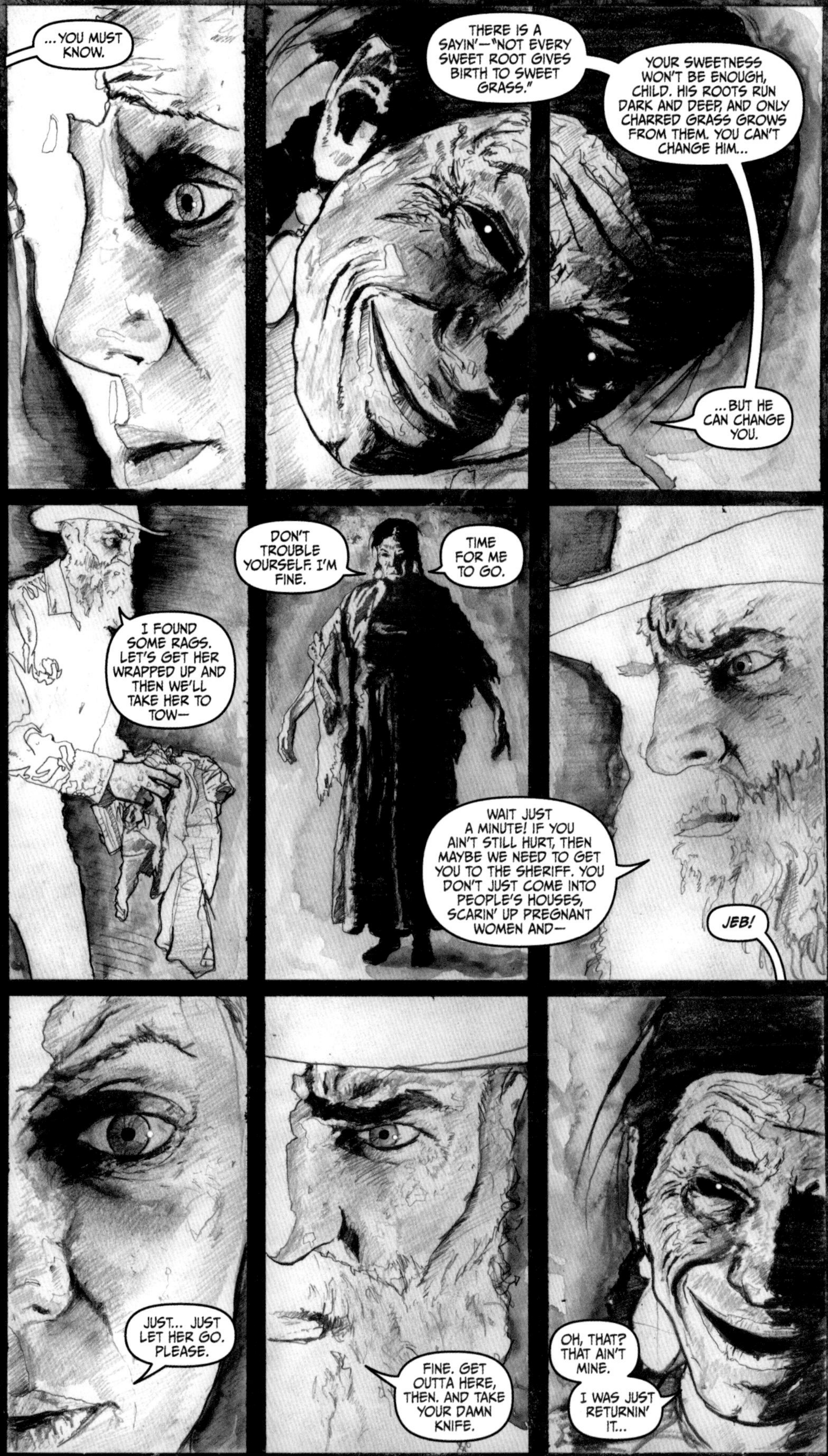
...YOU MUST KNOW.
THERE IS A SAYIN'—"NOT EVERY SWEET ROOT GIVES BIRTH TO SWEET GRASS."
YOUR SWEETNESS WON'T BE ENOUGH, CHILD. HIS ROOTS RUN DARK AND DEEP, AND ONLY CHARRED GRASS GROWS FROM THEM. YOU CAN'T CHANGE HIM...
...BUT HE CAN CHANGE YOU.
I FOUND SOME RAGS. LET'S GET HER WRAPPED UP AND THEN WE'LL TAKE HER TO TOW—
DON'T TROUBLE YOURSELF. I'M FINE.
TIME FOR ME TO GO.
WAIT JUST A MINUTE! IF YOU AIN'T STILL HURT, THEN MAYBE WE NEED TO GET YOU TO THE SHERIFF. YOU DON'T JUST COME INTO PEOPLE'S HOUSES, SCARIN' UP PREGNANT WOMEN AND—
JEB!
JUST... JUST LET HER GO. PLEASE.
FINE. GET OUTTA HERE, THEN. AND TAKE YOUR DAMN KNIFE.
OH, THAT? THAT AIN'T MINE.
I WAS JUST RETURNIN' IT...

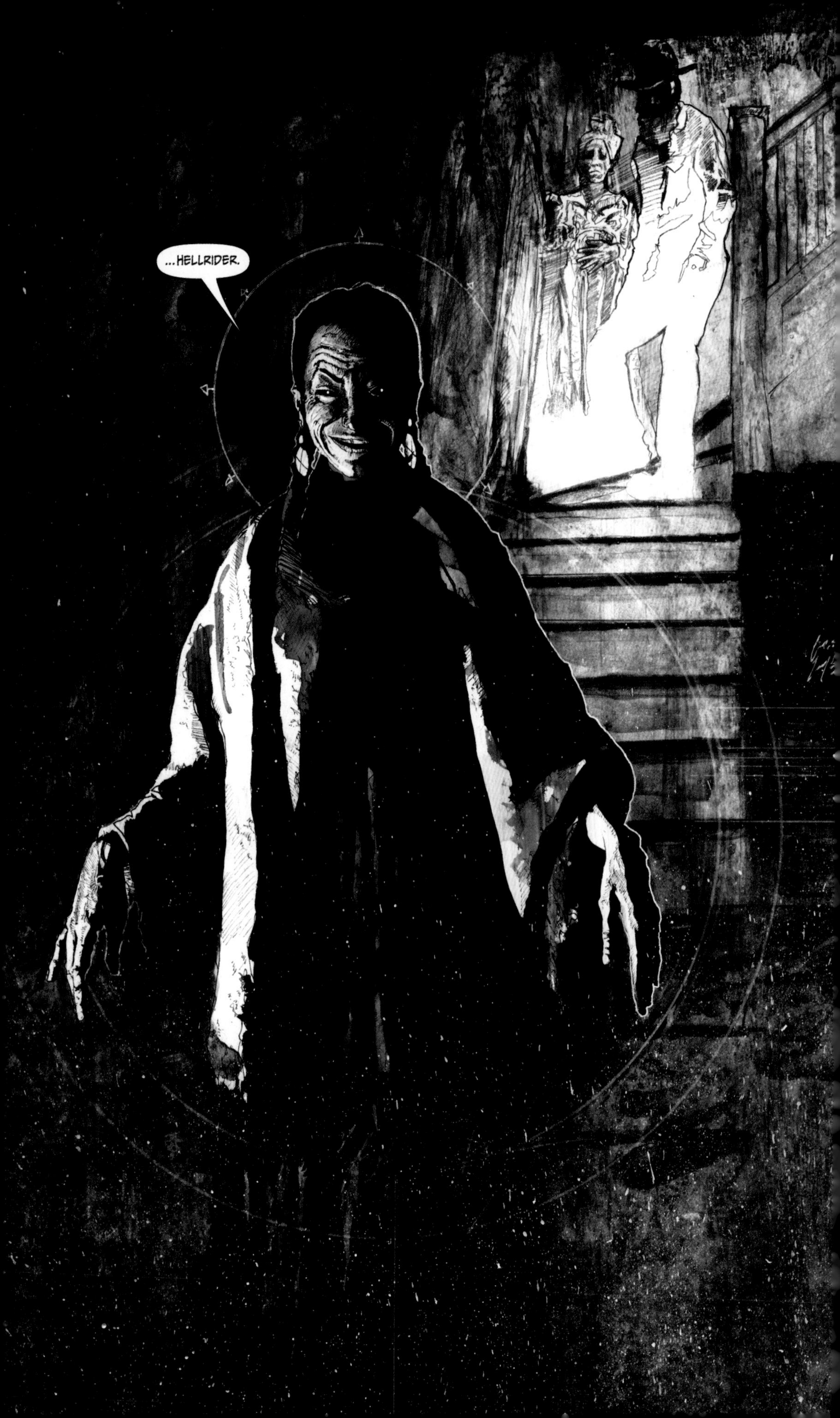
...HELLRIDER.

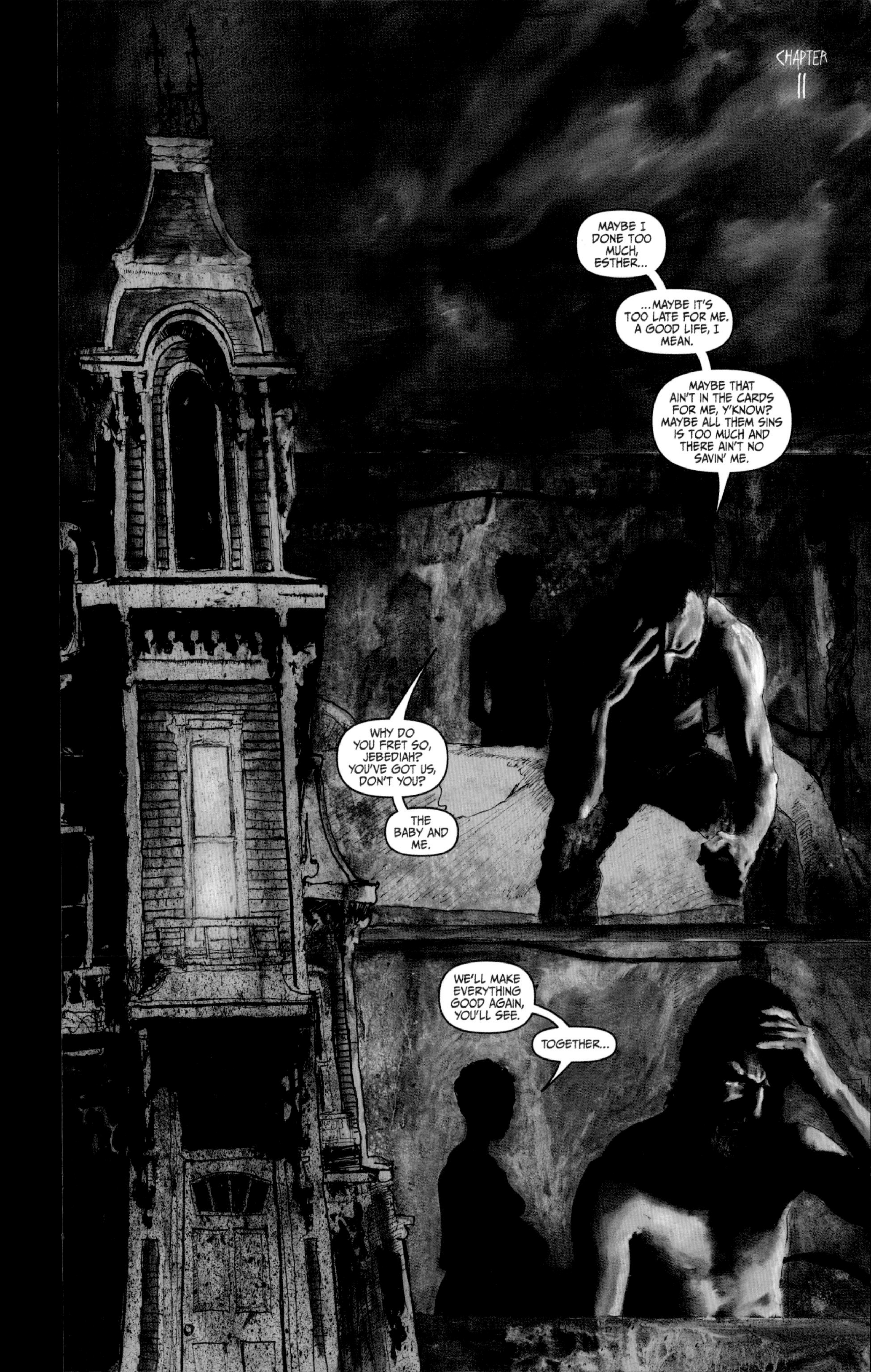
CHAPTER
II
MAYBE I DONE TOO MUCH, ESTHER...
...MAYBE IT'S TOO LATE FOR ME. A GOOD LIFE, I MEAN.
MAYBE THAT AIN'T IN THE CARDS FOR ME, Y'KNOW? MAYBE ALL THEM SINS IS TOO MUCH AND THERE AIN'T NO SAVIN' ME.
WHY DO YOU FRET SO, JEBEDIAH? YOU'VE GOT US, DON'T YOU?
THE BABY AND ME.
WE'LL MAKE EVERYTHING GOOD AGAIN, YOU'LL SEE.
TOGETHER...

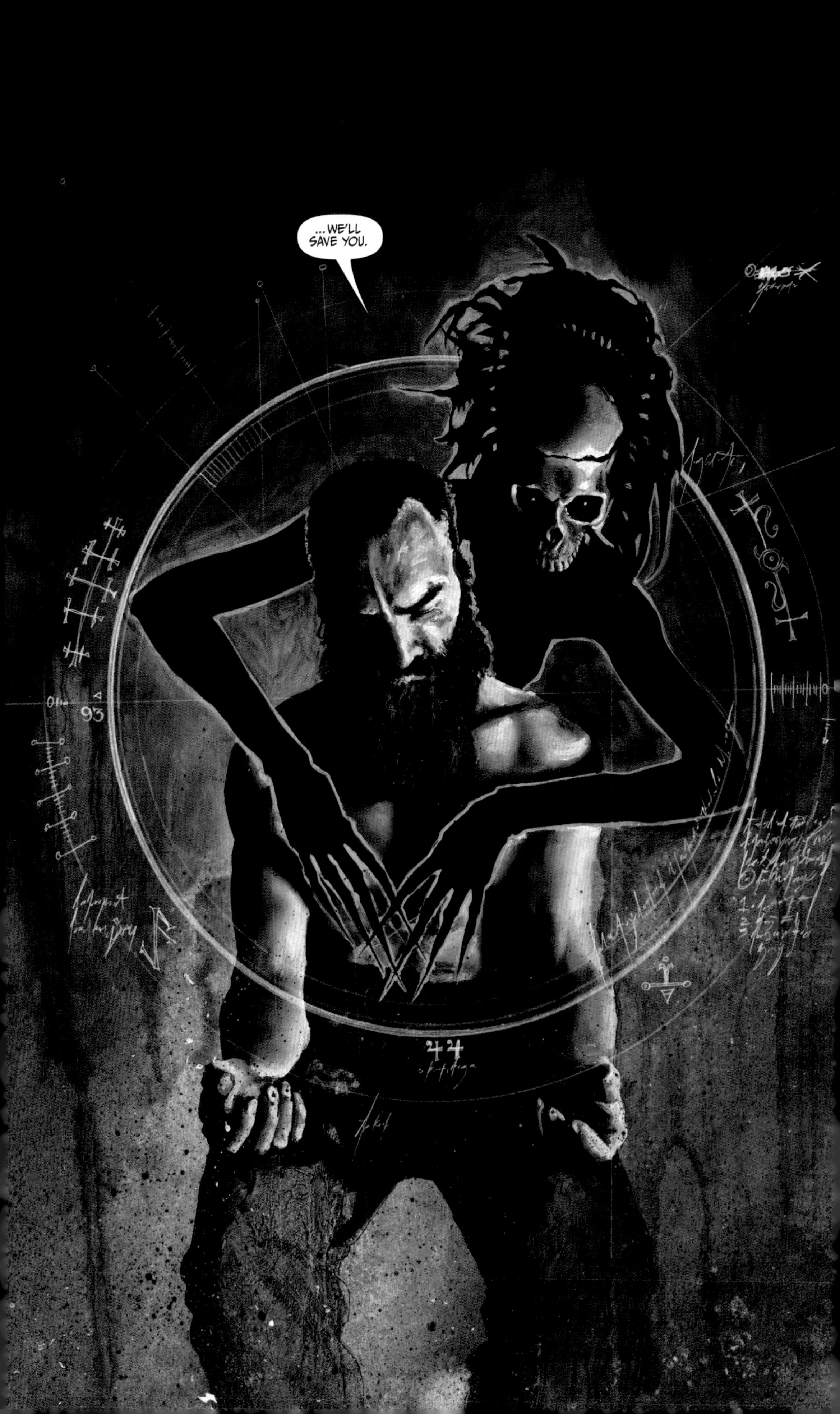
...WE'LL SAVE YOU.

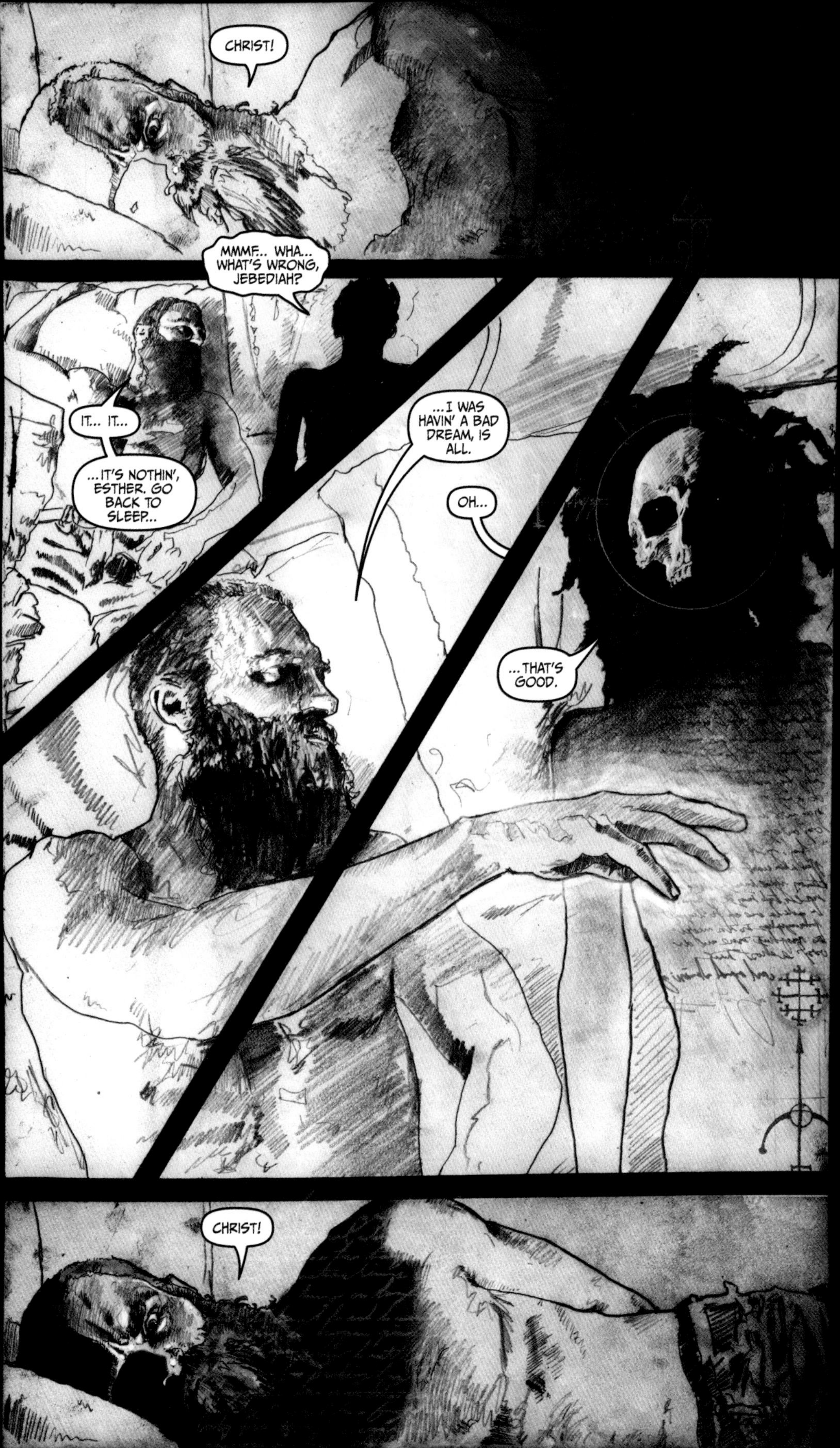
CHRIST!
MMMF... WHA... WHAT'S WRONG, JEBEDIAH?
IT... IT...
...IT'S NOTHIN', ESTHER. GO BACK TO SLEEP...
...I WAS HAVIN' A BAD DREAM, IS ALL.
OH...
...THAT'S GOOD.
CHRIST!

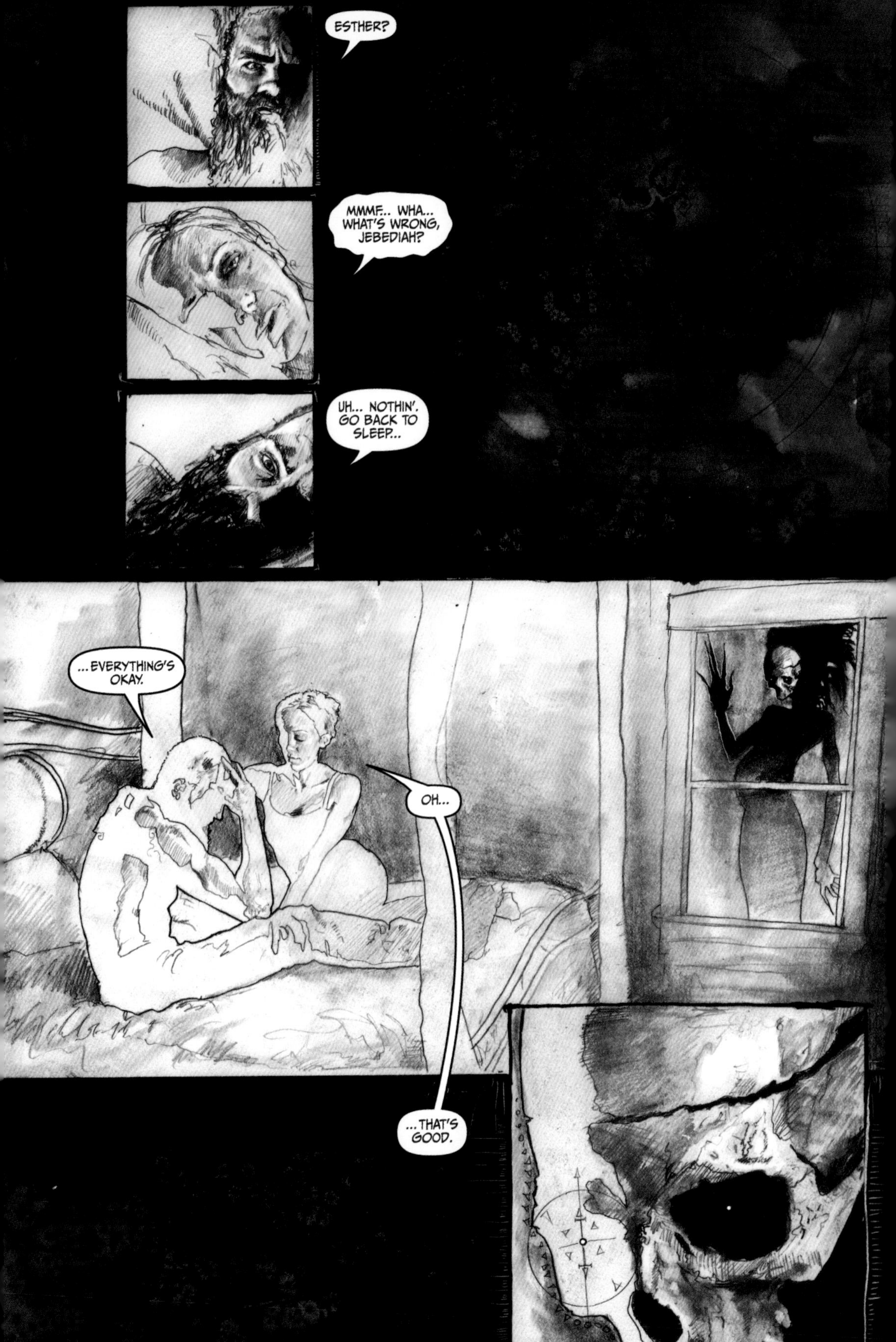
ESTHER?
MMMF... WHA... WHAT'S WRONG, JEBEDIAH?
UH... NOTHIN'. GO BACK TO SLEEP...
...EVERYTHING'S OKAY.
OH...
...THAT'S GOOD.

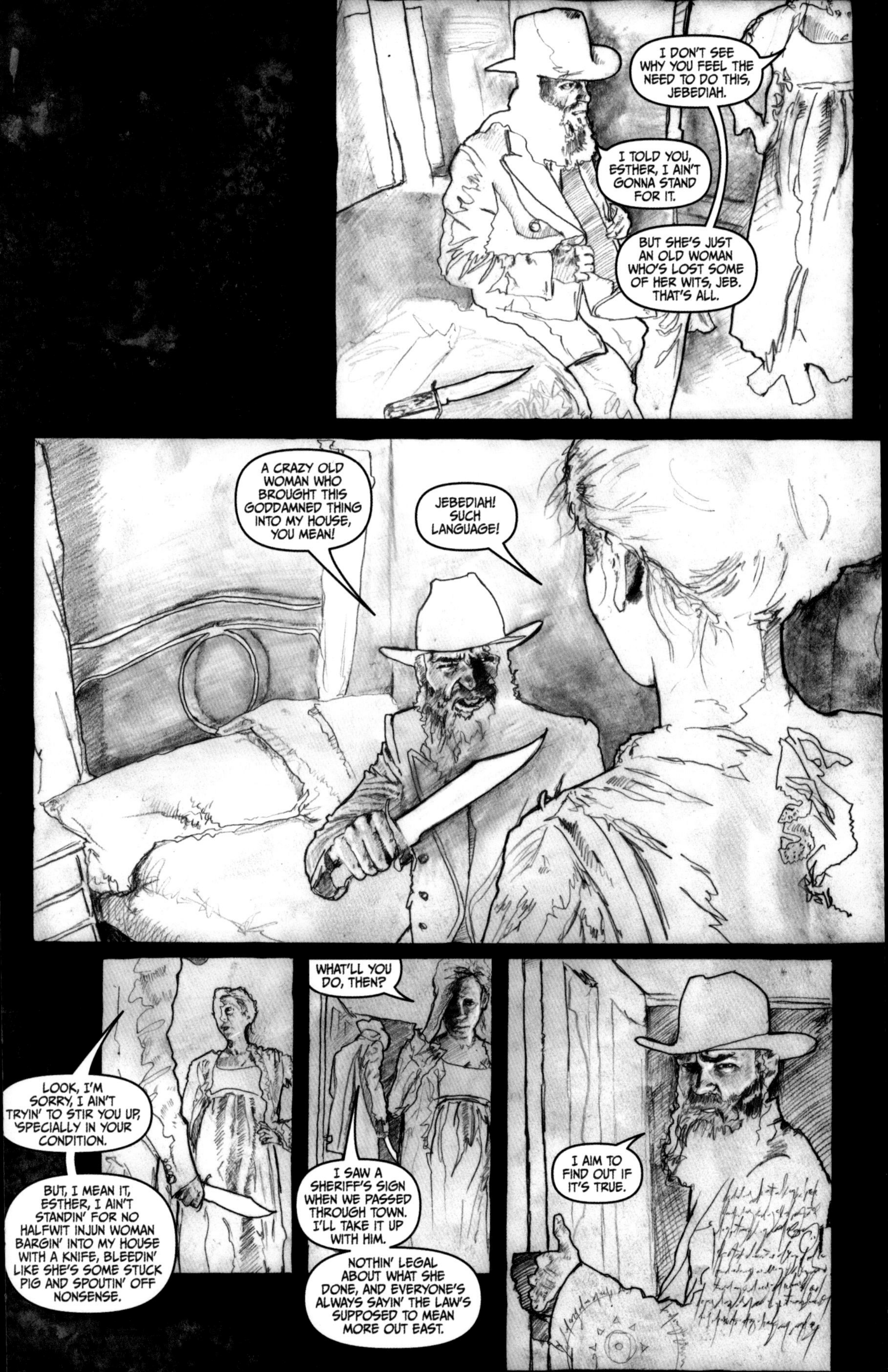
I DON'T SEE WHY YOU FEEL THE NEED TO DO THIS, JEBEDIAH.
I TOLD YOU, ESTHER, I AIN'T GONNA STAND FOR IT.
BUT SHE'S JUST AN OLD WOMAN WHO'S LOST SOME OF HER WITS, JEB. THAT'S ALL.
A CRAZY OLD WOMAN WHO BROUGHT THIS GODDAMNED THING INTO MY HOUSE, YOU MEAN!
JEBEDIAH! SUCH LANGUAGE!
LOOK, I'M SORRY, I AIN'T TRYIN' TO STIR YOU UP, 'SPECIALLY IN YOUR CONDITION.
BUT, I MEAN IT, ESTHER, I AIN'T STANDIN' FOR NO HALFWIT INJUN WOMAN BARGIN' INTO MY HOUSE WITH A KNIFE, BLEEDIN' LIKE SHE'S SOME STUCK PIG AND SPOUTIN' OFF NONSENSE.
WHAT'LL YOU DO, THEN?
I SAW A SHERIFF'S SIGN WHEN WE PASSED THROUGH TOWN. I'LL TAKE IT UP WITH HIM.
NOTHIN' LEGAL ABOUT WHAT SHE DONE, AND EVERYONE'S ALWAYS SAYIN' THE LAW'S SUPPOSED TO MEAN MORE OUT EAST.
I AIM TO FIND OUT IF IT'S TRUE.

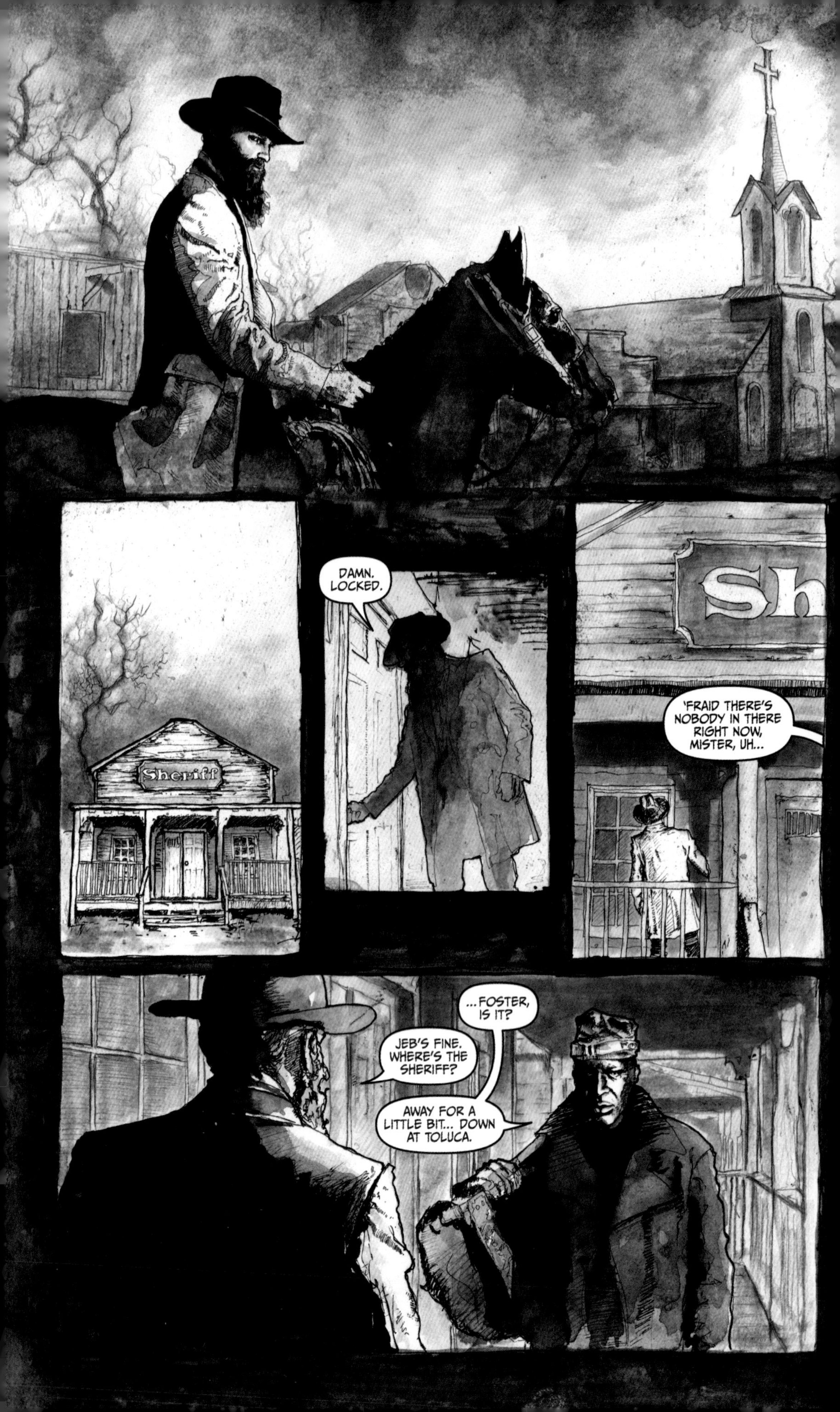
Sheriff
DAMN. LOCKED.
Sh
'FRAID THERE'S NOBODY IN THERE RIGHT NOW, MISTER, UH...
...FOSTER, IS IT?
JEB'S FINE. WHERE'S THE SHERIFF?
AWAY FOR A LITTLE BIT... DOWN AT TOLUCA.

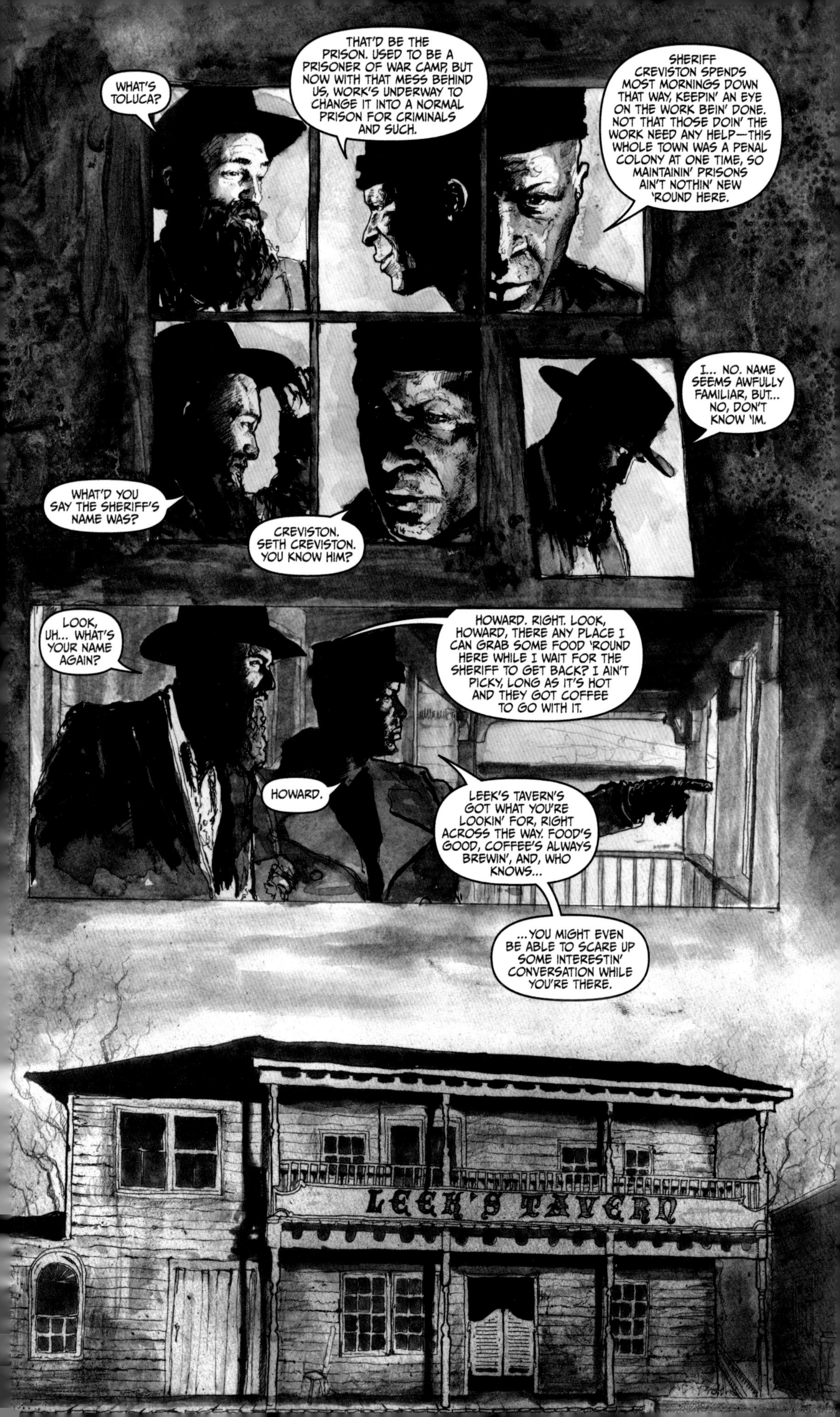
WHAT'S TOLUCA?
THAT'D BE THE PRISON. USED TO BE A PRISONER OF WAR CAMP, BUT NOW WITH THAT MESS BEHIND US, WORK'S UNDERWAY TO CHANGE IT INTO A NORMAL PRISON FOR CRIMINALS AND SUCH.
SHERIFF CREVISTON SPENDS MOST MORNINGS DOWN THAT WAY, KEEPIN' AN EYE ON THE WORK BEIN' DONE. NOT THAT THOSE DOIN' THE WORK NEED ANY HELP—THIS WHOLE TOWN WAS A PENAL COLONY AT ONE TIME, SO MAINTAININ' PRISONS AIN'T NOTHIN' NEW 'ROUND HERE.
WHAT'D YOU SAY THE SHERIFF'S NAME WAS?
CREVISTON. SETH CREVISTON. YOU KNOW HIM?
I... NO. NAME SEEMS AWFULLY FAMILIAR, BUT... NO, DON'T KNOW 'IM.
LOOK, UH... WHAT'S YOUR NAME AGAIN?
HOWARD.
HOWARD. RIGHT. LOOK, HOWARD, THERE ANY PLACE I CAN GRAB SOME FOOD 'ROUND HERE WHILE I WAIT FOR THE SHERIFF TO GET BACK? I AIN'T PICKY, LONG AS IT'S HOT AND THEY GOT COFFEE TO GO WITH IT.
LEEK'S TAVERN'S GOT WHAT YOU'RE LOOKIN' FOR, RIGHT ACROSS THE WAY. FOOD'S GOOD, COFFEE'S ALWAYS BREWIN', AND, WHO KNOWS...
...YOU MIGHT EVEN BE ABLE TO SCARE UP SOME INTERESTIN' CONVERSATION WHILE YOU'RE THERE.
LEEK'S TAVERN

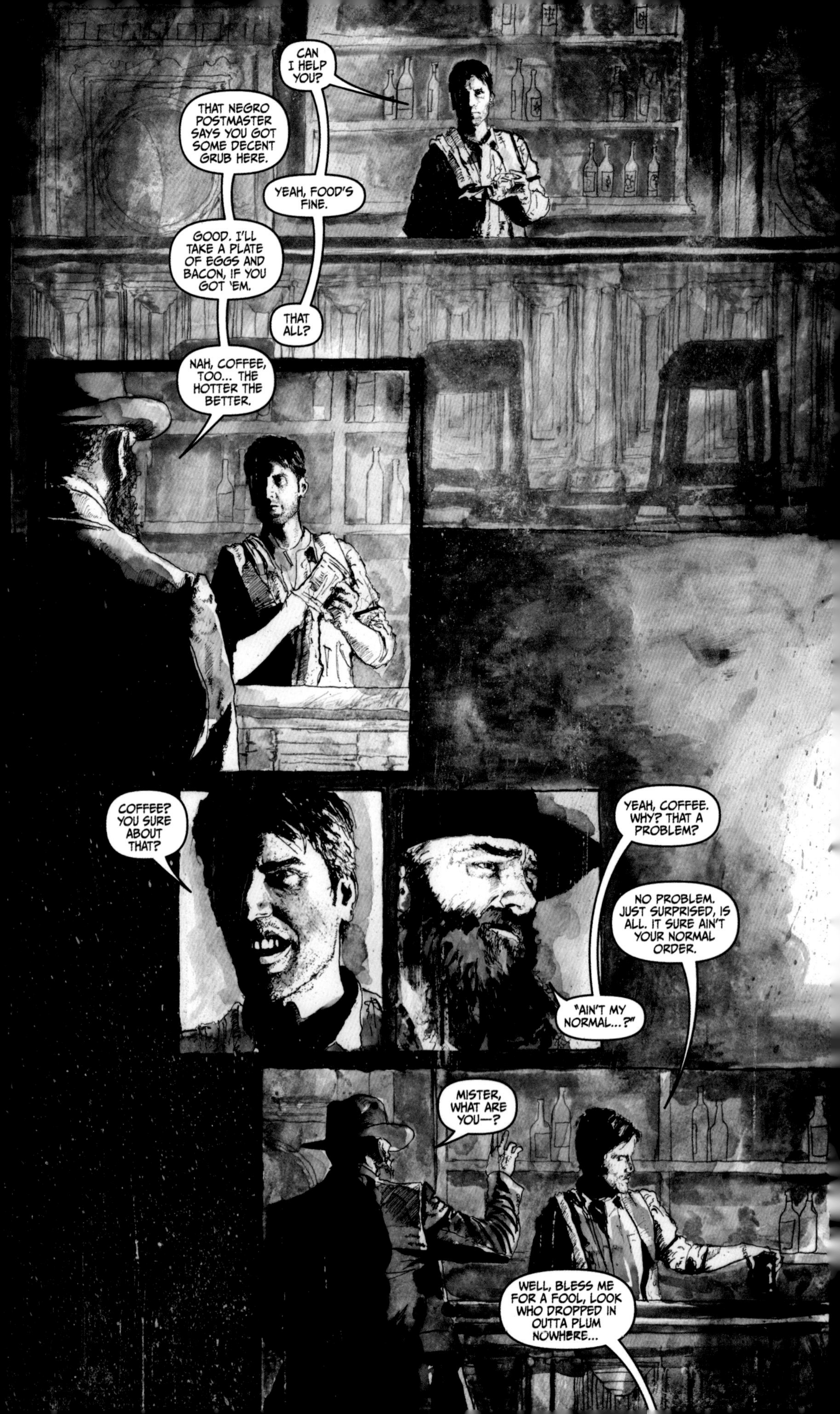
CAN I HELP YOU?
THAT NEGRO POSTMASTER SAYS YOU GOT SOME DECENT GRUB HERE.
YEAH, FOOD'S FINE.
GOOD. I'LL TAKE A PLATE OF EGGS AND BACON, IF YOU GOT 'EM.
THAT ALL?
NAH, COFFEE, TOO... THE HOTTER THE BETTER.
COFFEE? YOU SURE ABOUT THAT?
YEAH, COFFEE. WHY? THAT A PROBLEM?
NO PROBLEM. JUST SURPRISED, IS ALL. IT SURE AIN'T YOUR NORMAL ORDER.
"AIN'T MY NORMAL...?"
MISTER, WHAT ARE YOU—?
WELL, BLESS ME FOR A FOOL, LOOK WHO DROPPED IN OUTTA PLUM NOWHERE...

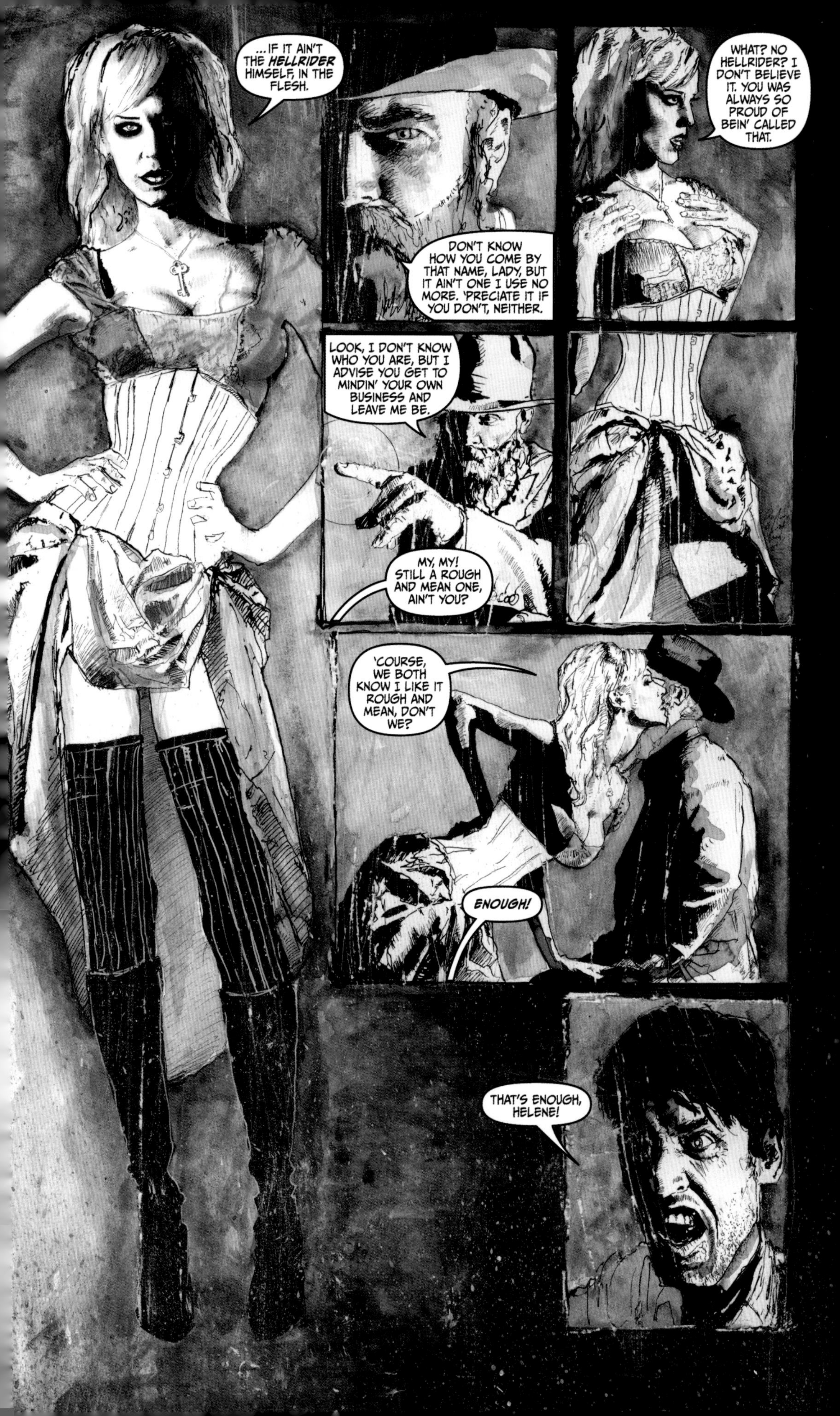
...IF IT AIN'T THE HELLRIDER HIMSELF, IN THE FLESH.
DON'T KNOW HOW YOU COME BY THAT NAME, LADY, BUT IT AIN'T ONE I USE NO MORE. 'PRECIATE IT IF YOU DON'T, NEITHER.
WHAT? NO HELLRIDER? I DON'T BELIEVE IT. YOU WAS ALWAYS SO PROUD OF BEIN' CALLED THAT.
LOOK, I DON'T KNOW WHO YOU ARE, BUT I ADVISE YOU GET TO MINDIN' YOUR OWN BUSINESS AND LEAVE ME BE.
MY, MY! STILL A ROUGH AND MEAN ONE, AIN'T YOU?
'COURSE, WE BOTH KNOW I LIKE IT ROUGH AND MEAN, DON'T WE?
ENOUGH!
THAT'S ENOUGH, HELENE!

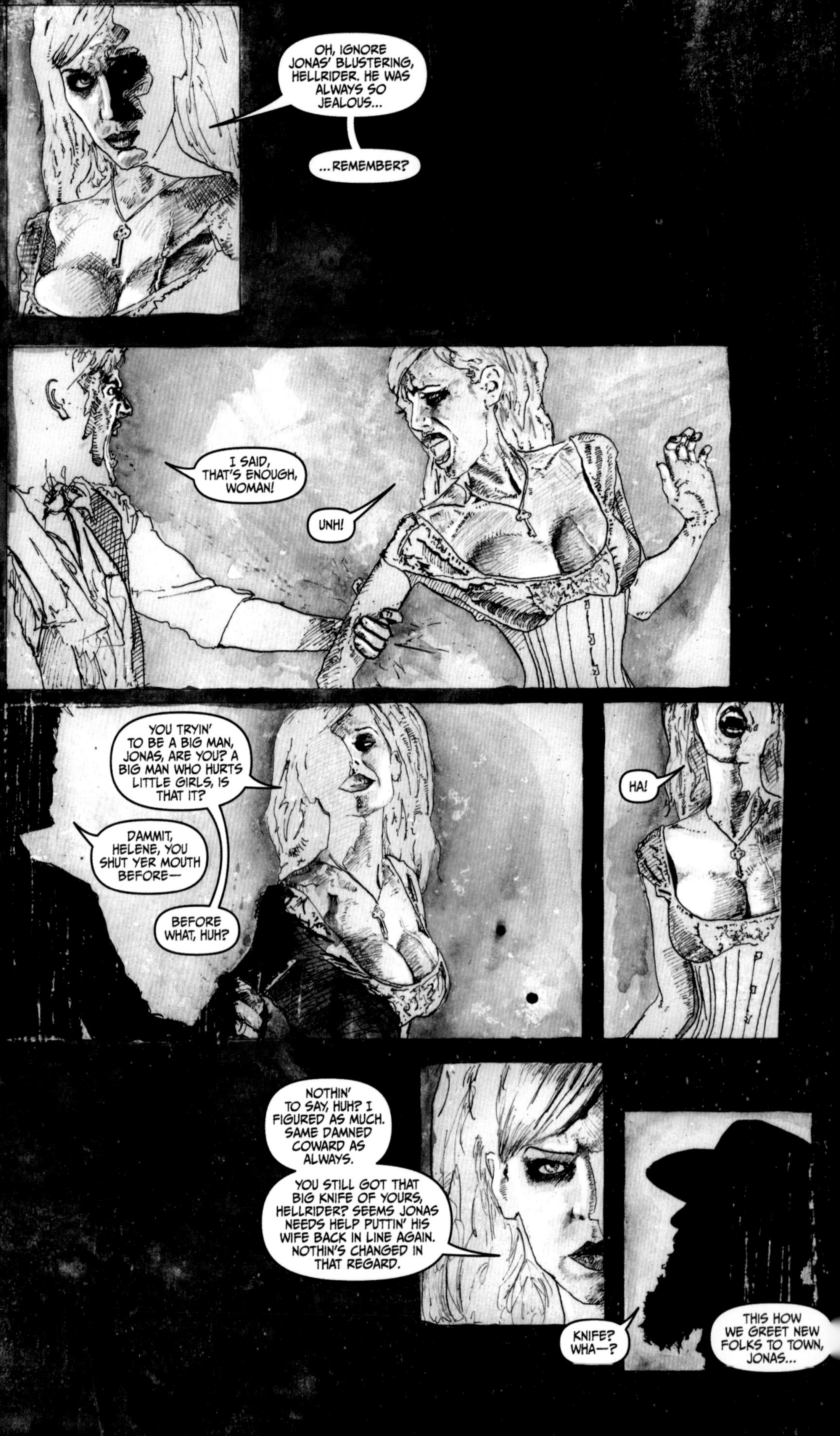

OH, IGNORE JONAS' BLUSTERING, HELLRIDER. HE WAS ALWAYS SO JEALOUS...
...REMEMBER?
I SAID, THAT'S ENOUGH, WOMAN!
UNH!
YOU TRYIN' TO BE A BIG MAN, JONAS, ARE YOU? A BIG MAN WHO HURTS LITTLE GIRLS, IS THAT IT?
DAMMIT, HELENE, YOU SHUT YER MOUTH BEFORE—
BEFORE WHAT, HUH?
HA!
NOTHIN' TO SAY, HUH? I FIGURED AS MUCH. SAME DAMNED COWARD AS ALWAYS.
YOU STILL GOT THAT BIG KNIFE OF YOURS, HELLRIDER? SEEMS JONAS NEEDS HELP PUTTIN' HIS WIFE BACK IN LINE AGAIN. NOTHIN'S CHANGED IN THAT REGARD.
KNIFE? WHA—?
THIS HOW WE GREET NEW FOLKS TO TOWN, JONAS...

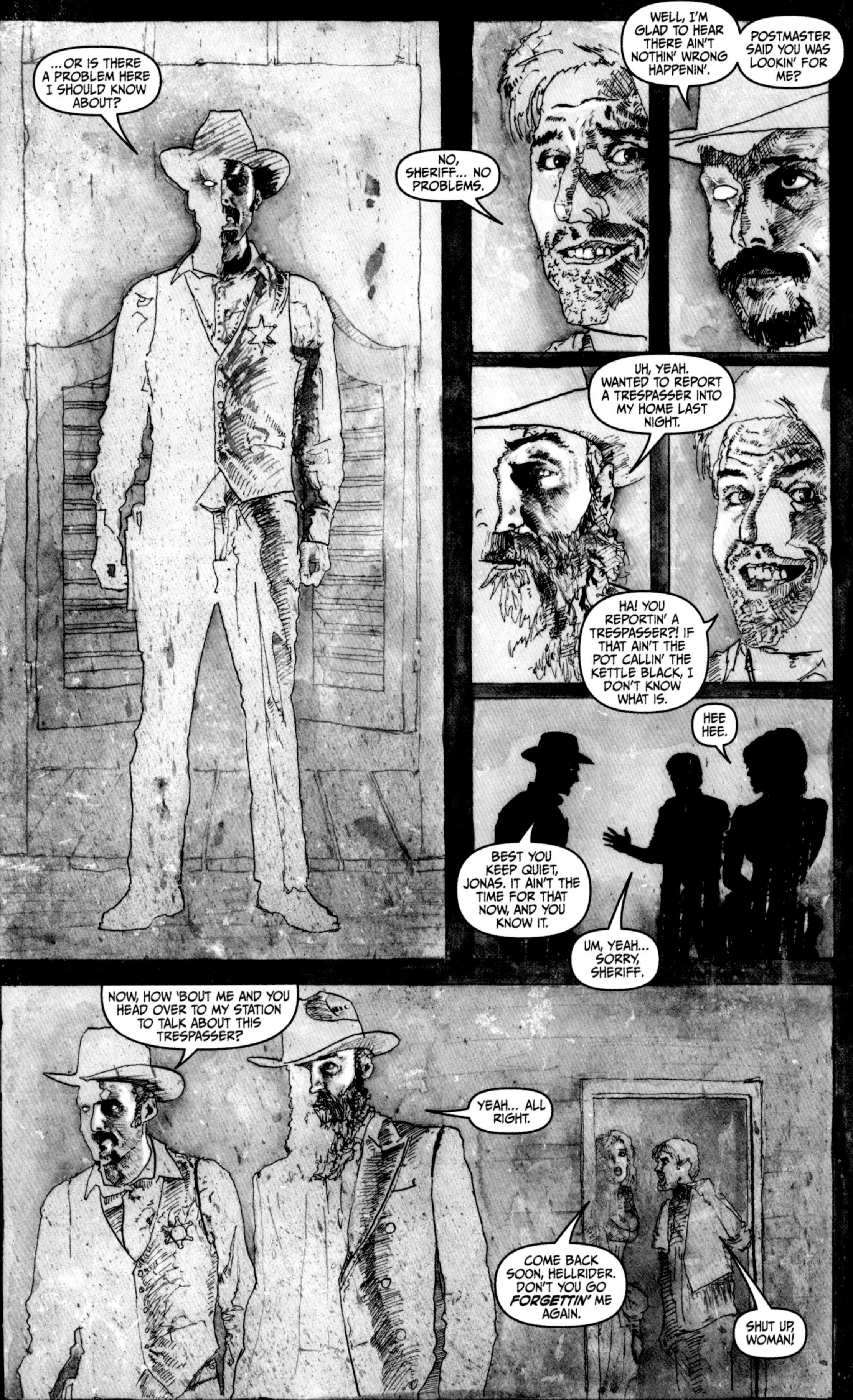
...OR IS THERE A PROBLEM HERE I SHOULD KNOW ABOUT?
NO, SHERIFF... NO PROBLEMS.
WELL, I'M GLAD TO HEAR THERE AIN'T NOTHIN' WRONG HAPPENIN'.
POSTMASTER SAID YOU WAS LOOKIN' FOR ME?
UH, YEAH. WANTED TO REPORT A TRESPASSER INTO MY HOME LAST NIGHT.
HA! YOU REPORTIN' A TRESPASSER?! IF THAT AIN'T THE POT CALLIN' THE KETTLE BLACK, I DON'T KNOW WHAT IS.
HEE HEE.
BEST YOU KEEP QUIET, JONAS. IT AIN'T THE TIME FOR THAT NOW, AND YOU KNOW IT.
UM, YEAH... SORRY, SHERIFF.
NOW, HOW 'BOUT ME AND YOU HEAD OVER TO MY STATION TO TALK ABOUT THIS TRESPASSER?
YEAH... ALL RIGHT.
COME BACK SOON, HELLRIDER. DON'T YOU GO *FORGETTIN'* ME AGAIN.
SHUT UP, WOMAN!

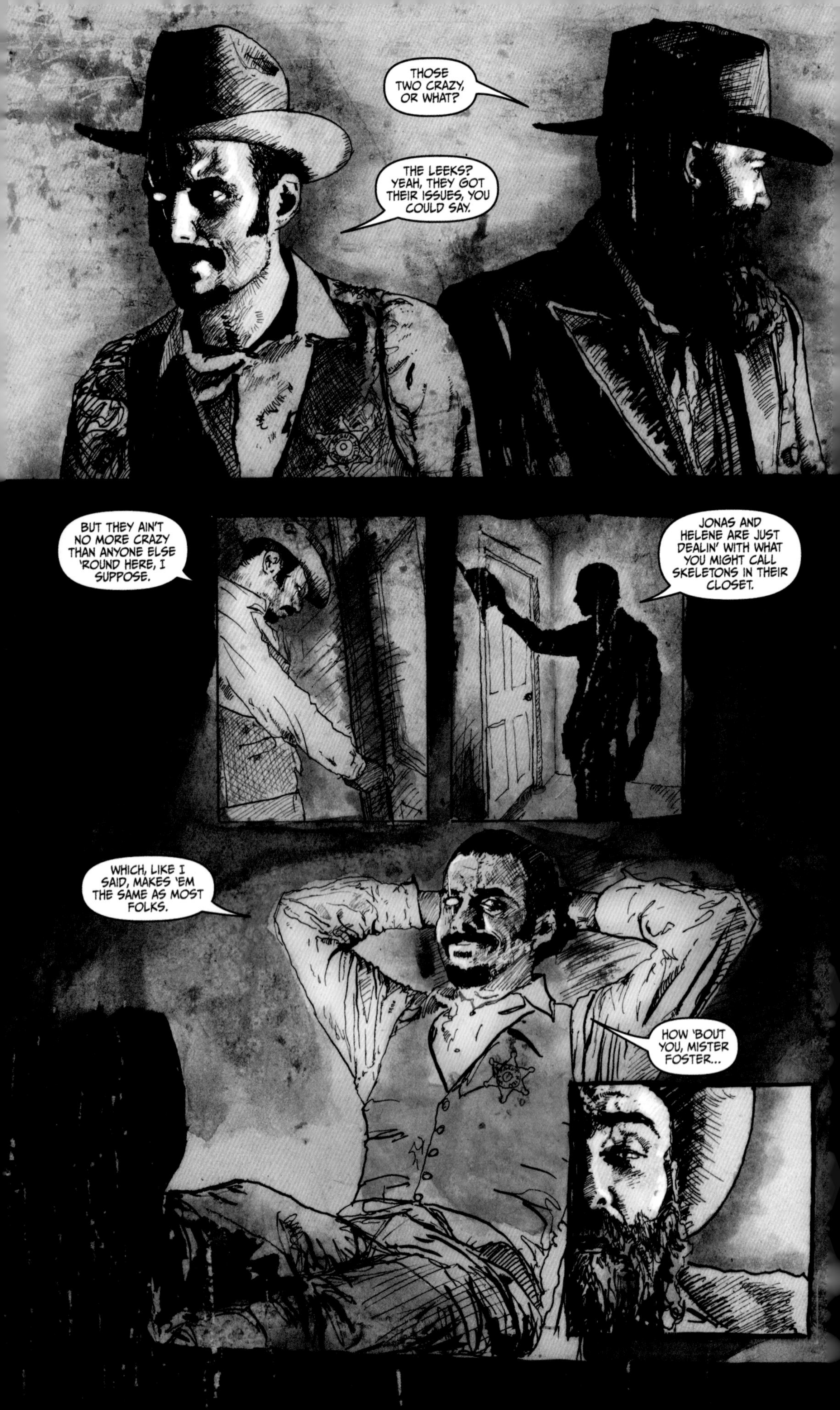
THOSE TWO CRAZY, OR WHAT?
THE LEEKS? YEAH, THEY GOT THEIR ISSUES, YOU COULD SAY.
BUT THEY AIN'T NO MORE CRAZY THAN ANYONE ELSE 'ROUND HERE, I SUPPOSE.
JONAS AND HELENE ARE JUST DEALIN' WITH WHAT YOU MIGHT CALL SKELETONS IN THEIR CLOSET.
WHICH, LIKE I SAID, MAKES 'EM THE SAME AS MOST FOLKS.
HOW 'BOUT YOU, MISTER FOSTER...

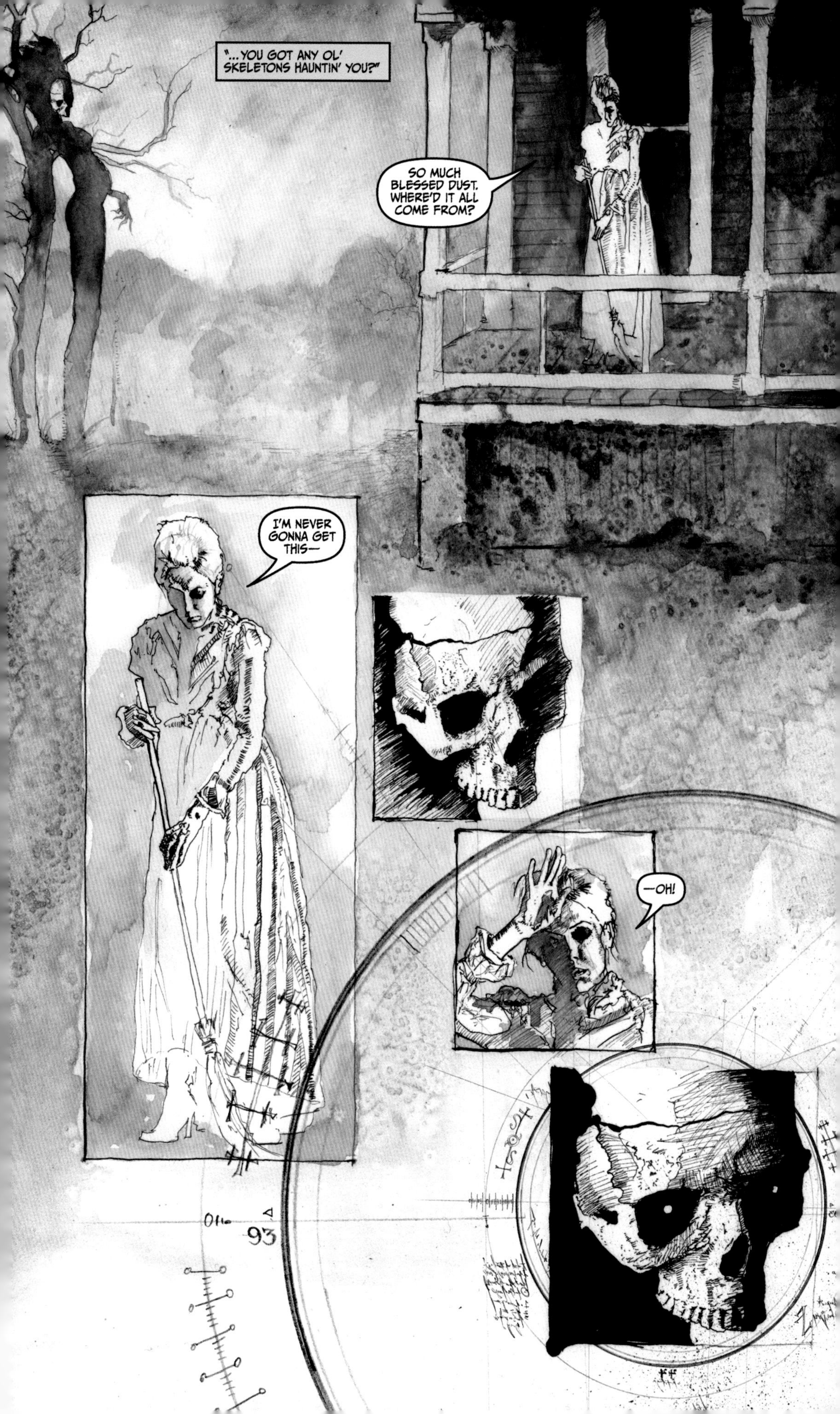
"...YOU GOT ANY OL' SKELETONS HAUNTIN' YOU?"
SO MUCH BLESSED DUST. WHERE'D IT ALL COME FROM?
I'M NEVER GONNA GET THIS—
—OH!

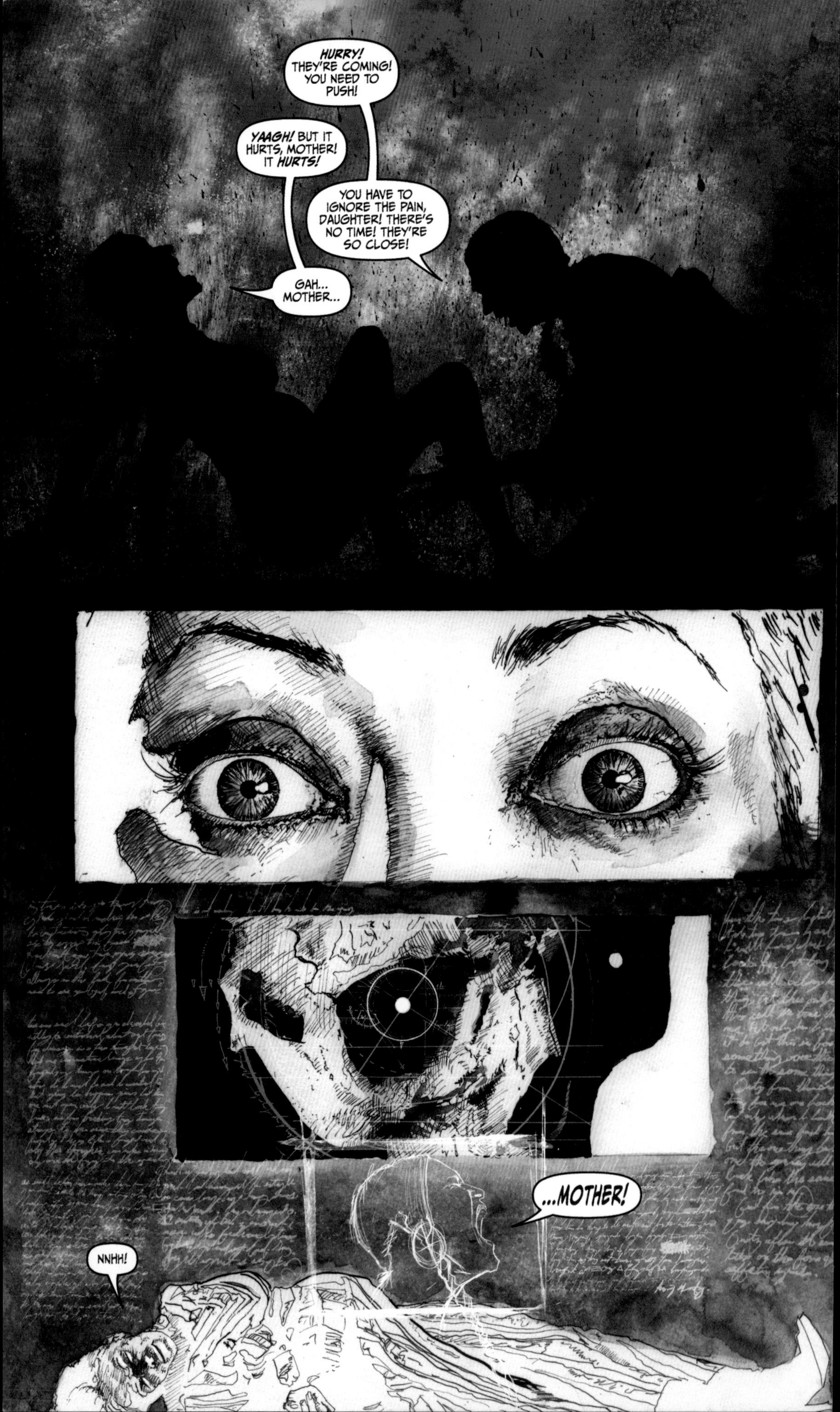
HURRY! THEY'RE COMING! YOU NEED TO PUSH!
YAAGH! BUT IT HURTS, MOTHER! IT HURTS!
YOU HAVE TO IGNORE THE PAIN, DAUGHTER! THERE'S NO TIME! THEY'RE SO CLOSE!
GAH... MOTHER...
...MOTHER!
NNHH!

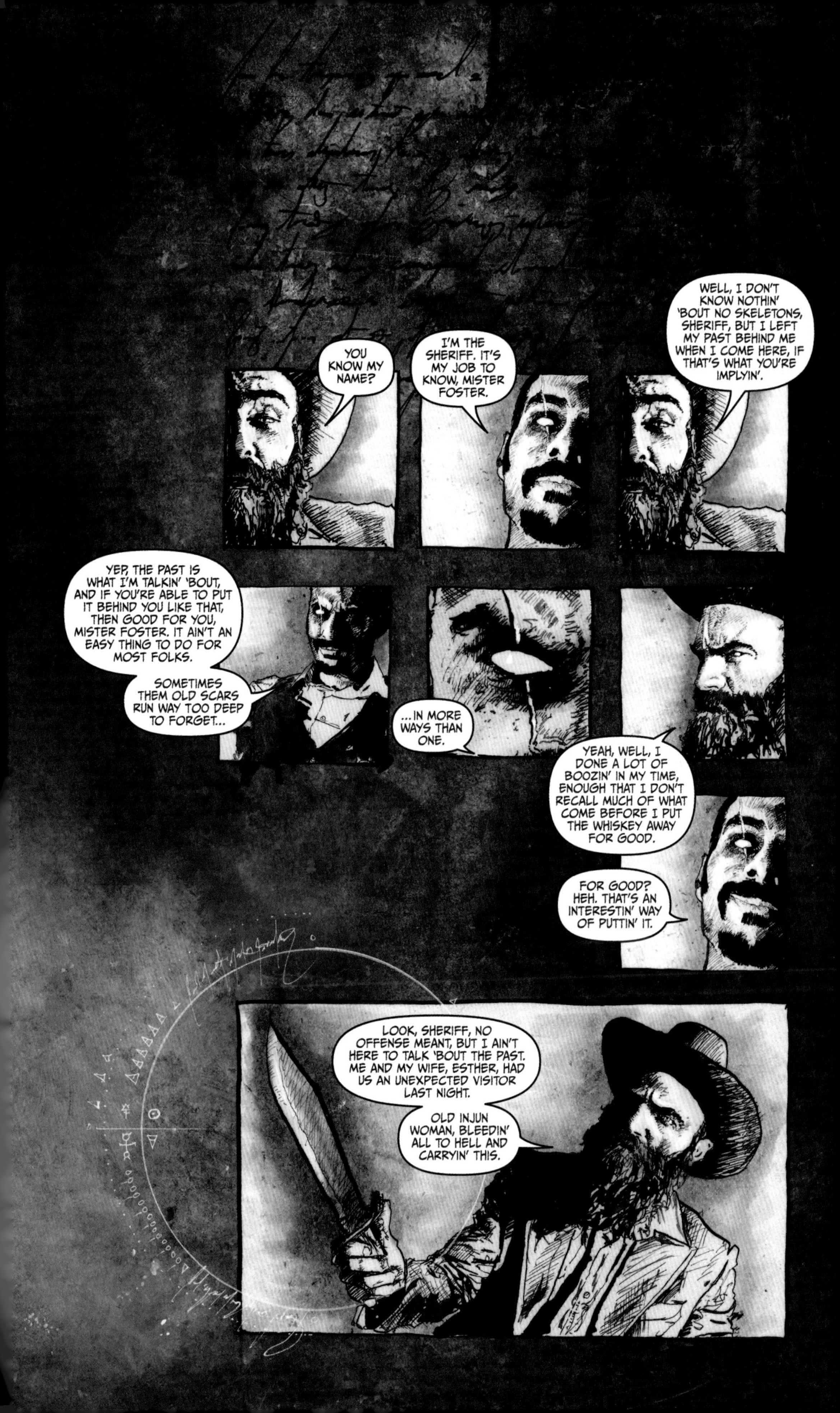
YOU KNOW MY NAME?
I'M THE SHERIFF. IT'S MY JOB TO KNOW, MISTER FOSTER.
WELL, I DON'T KNOW NOTHIN' 'BOUT NO SKELETONS, SHERIFF, BUT I LEFT MY PAST BEHIND ME WHEN I COME HERE, IF THAT'S WHAT YOU'RE IMPLYIN'.
YEP, THE PAST IS WHAT I'M TALKIN' 'BOUT, AND IF YOU'RE ABLE TO PUT IT BEHIND YOU LIKE THAT, THEN GOOD FOR YOU, MISTER FOSTER. IT AIN'T AN EASY THING TO DO FOR MOST FOLKS.
SOMETIMES THEM OLD SCARS RUN WAY TOO DEEP TO FORGET...
...IN MORE WAYS THAN ONE.
YEAH, WELL, I DONE A LOT OF BOOZIN' IN MY TIME, ENOUGH THAT I DON'T RECALL MUCH OF WHAT COME BEFORE I PUT THE WHISKEY AWAY FOR GOOD.
FOR GOOD? HEH. THAT'S AN INTERESTIN' WAY OF PUTTIN' IT.
LOOK, SHERIFF, NO OFFENSE MEANT, BUT I AIN'T HERE TO TALK 'BOUT THE PAST. ME AND MY WIFE, ESTHER, HAD US AN UNEXPECTED VISITOR LAST NIGHT.
OLD INJUN WOMAN, BLEEDIN' ALL TO HELL AND CARRYIN' THIS.

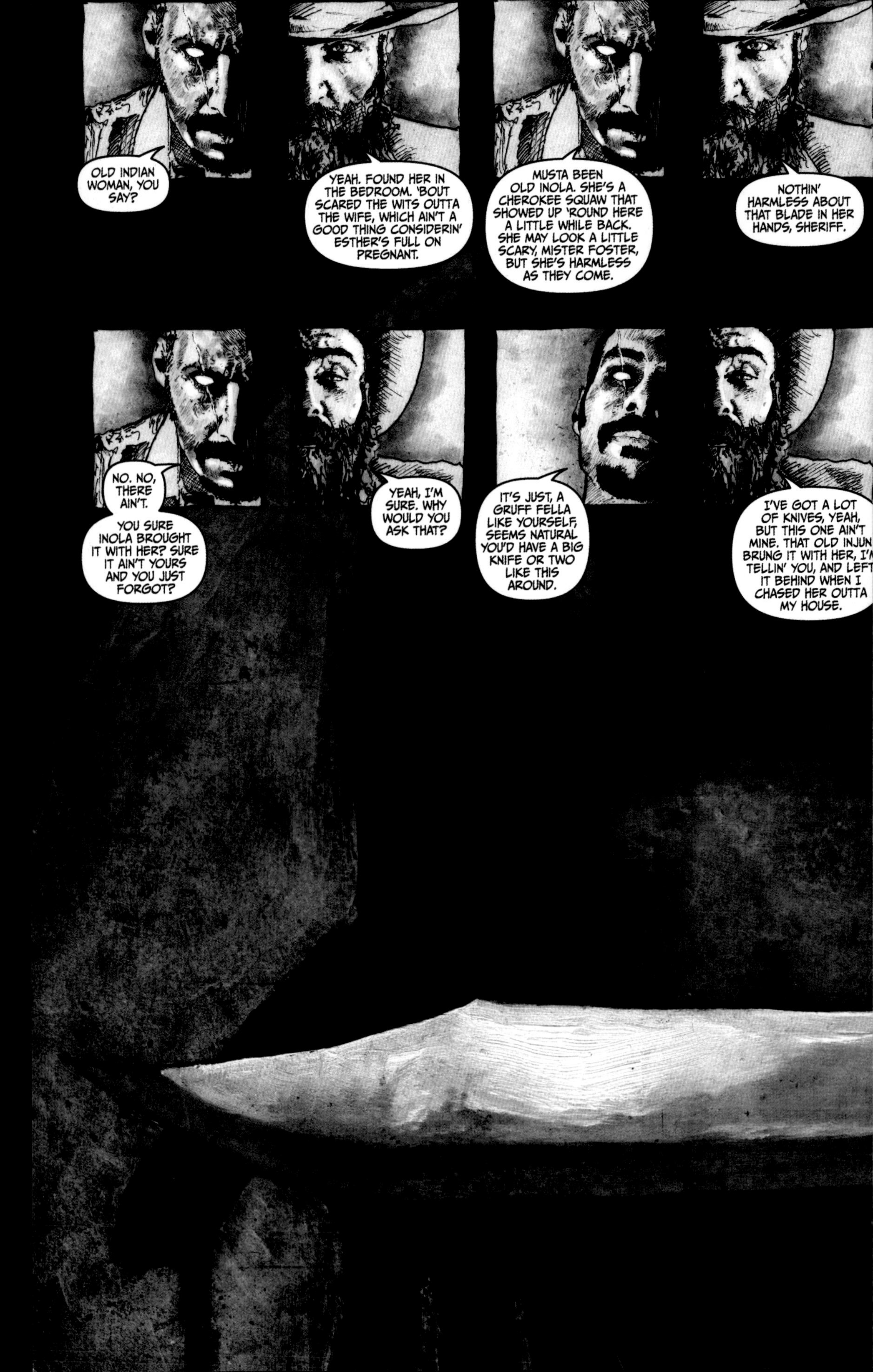
OLD INDIAN WOMAN, YOU SAY?
YEAH. FOUND HER IN THE BEDROOM. 'BOUT SCARED THE WITS OUTTA THE WIFE, WHICH AIN'T A GOOD THING CONSIDERIN' ESTHER'S FULL ON PREGNANT.
MUSTA BEEN OLD INOLA. SHE'S A CHEROKEE SQUAW THAT SHOWED UP 'ROUND HERE A LITTLE WHILE BACK. SHE MAY LOOK A LITTLE SCARY, MISTER FOSTER, BUT SHE'S HARMLESS AS THEY COME.
NOTHIN' HARMLESS ABOUT THAT BLADE IN HER HANDS, SHERIFF.
NO. NO, THERE AIN'T.
YOU SURE INOLA BROUGHT IT WITH HER? SURE IT AIN'T YOURS AND YOU JUST FORGOT?
YEAH, I'M SURE. WHY WOULD YOU ASK THAT?
IT'S JUST, A GRUFF FELLA LIKE YOURSELF, SEEMS NATURAL YOU'D HAVE A BIG KNIFE OR TWO LIKE THIS AROUND.
I'VE GOT A LOT OF KNIVES, YEAH, BUT THIS ONE AIN'T MINE. THAT OLD INJUN BRUNG IT WITH HER, I' TELLIN' YOU, AND LEFT IT BEHIND WHEN I CHASED HER OUTTA MY HOUSE.

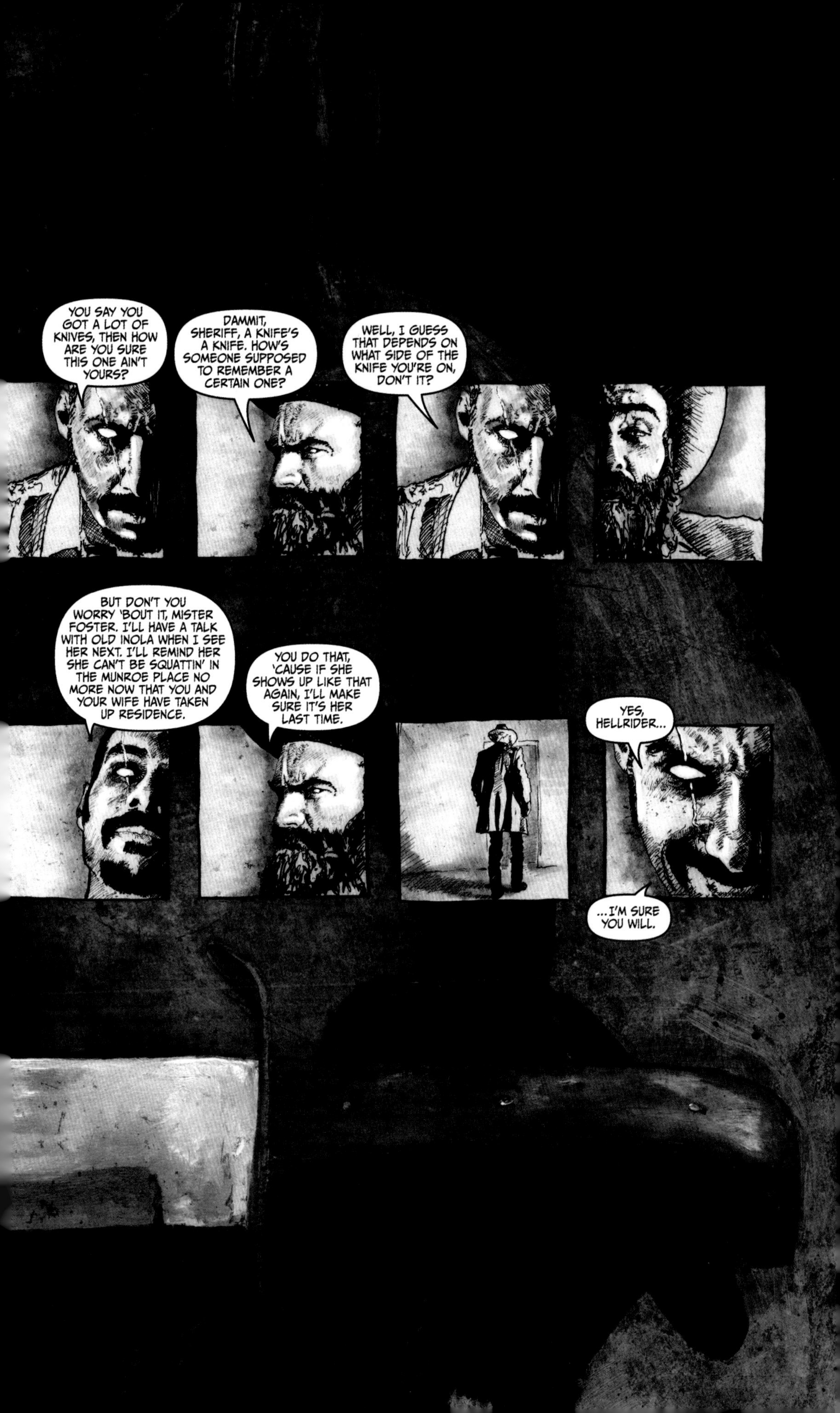
YOU SAY YOU GOT A LOT OF KNIVES, THEN HOW ARE YOU SURE THIS ONE AIN'T YOURS?
DAMMIT, SHERIFF, A KNIFE'S A KNIFE. HOW'S SOMEONE SUPPOSED TO REMEMBER A CERTAIN ONE?
WELL, I GUESS THAT DEPENDS ON WHAT SIDE OF THE KNIFE YOU'RE ON, DON'T IT?
BUT DON'T YOU WORRY 'BOUT IT, MISTER FOSTER. I'LL HAVE A TALK WITH OLD INOLA WHEN I SEE HER NEXT. I'LL REMIND HER SHE CAN'T BE SQUATTIN' IN THE MUNROE PLACE NO MORE NOW THAT YOU AND YOUR WIFE HAVE TAKEN UP RESIDENCE.
YOU DO THAT, 'CAUSE IF SHE SHOWS UP LIKE THAT AGAIN, I'LL MAKE SURE IT'S HER LAST TIME.
YES, HELLRIDER...
...I'M SURE YOU WILL.

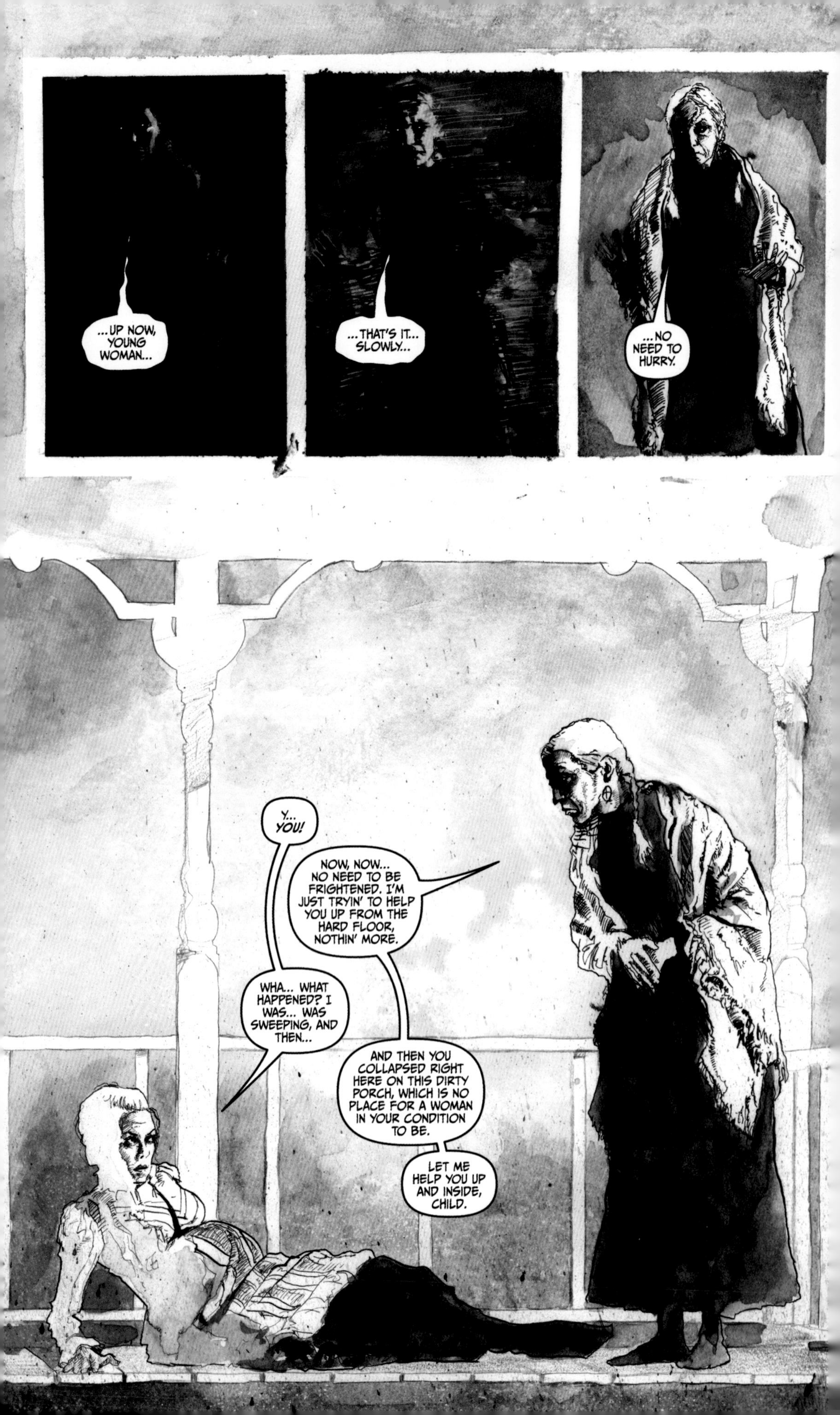
...UP NOW, YOUNG WOMAN...
...THAT'S IT... SLOWLY...
...NO NEED TO HURRY.
Y... YOU!
NOW, NOW... NO NEED TO BE FRIGHTENED. I'M JUST TRYIN' TO HELP YOU UP FROM THE HARD FLOOR, NOTHIN' MORE.
WHA... WHAT HAPPENED? I WAS... WAS SWEEPING, AND THEN...
AND THEN YOU COLLAPSED RIGHT HERE ON THIS DIRTY PORCH, WHICH IS NO PLACE FOR A WOMAN IN YOUR CONDITION TO BE.
LET ME HELP YOU UP AND INSIDE, CHILD.

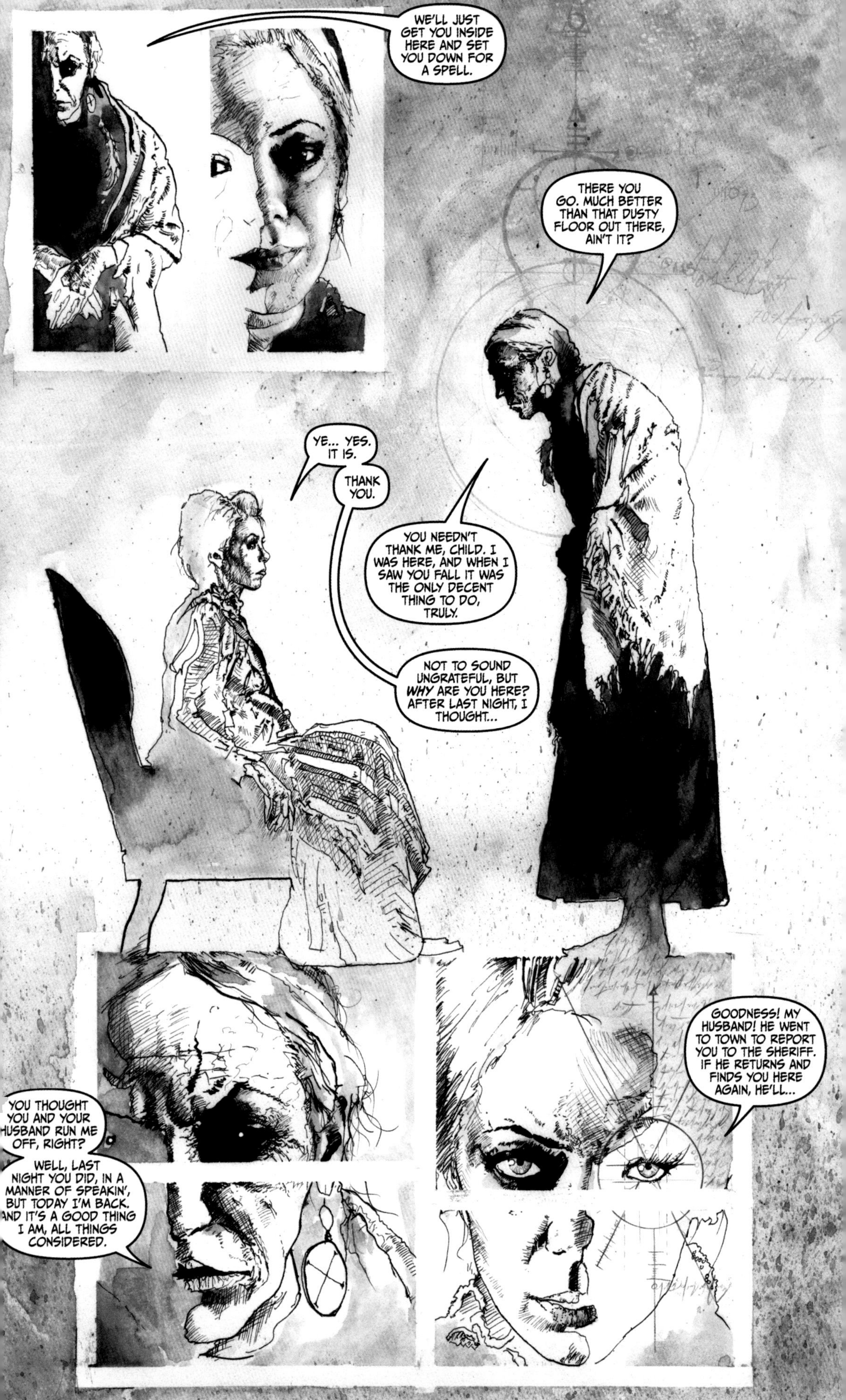
WE'LL JUST GET YOU INSIDE HERE AND SET YOU DOWN FOR A SPELL.
THERE YOU GO. MUCH BETTER THAN THAT DUSTY FLOOR OUT THERE, AIN'T IT?
YE... YES. IT IS.
THANK YOU.
YOU NEEDN'T THANK ME, CHILD. I WAS HERE, AND WHEN I SAW YOU FALL IT WAS THE ONLY DECENT THING TO DO, TRULY.
NOT TO SOUND UNGRATEFUL, BUT *WHY* ARE YOU HERE? AFTER LAST NIGHT, I THOUGHT...
YOU THOUGHT YOU AND YOUR HUSBAND RUN ME OFF, RIGHT?
WELL, LAST NIGHT YOU DID, IN A MANNER OF SPEAKIN', BUT TODAY I'M BACK. AND IT'S A GOOD THING I AM, ALL THINGS CONSIDERED.
GOODNESS! MY HUSBAND! HE WENT TO TOWN TO REPORT YOU TO THE SHERIFF. IF HE RETURNS AND FINDS YOU HERE AGAIN, HE'LL...

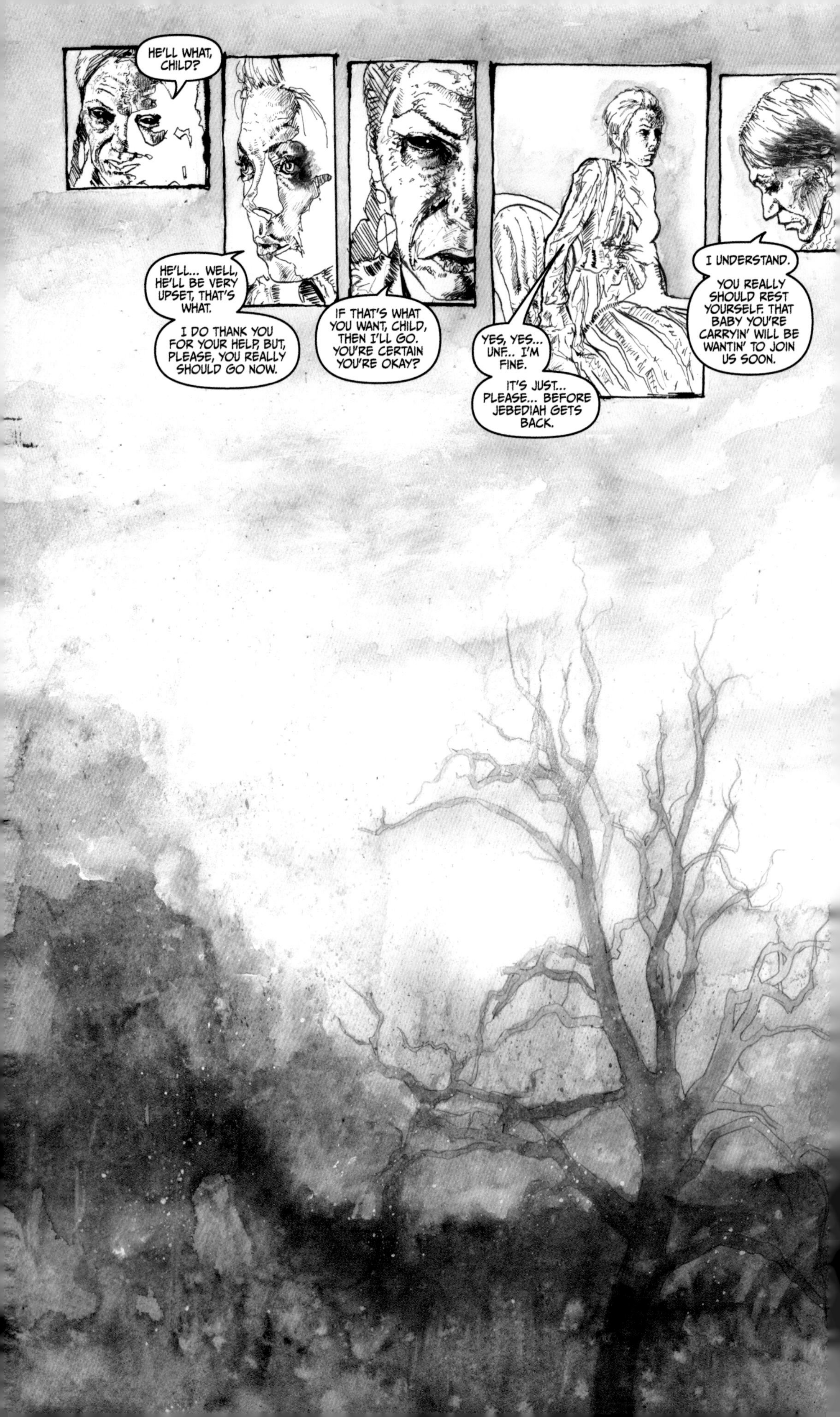
HE'LL WHAT, CHILD?
HE'LL... WELL, HE'LL BE VERY UPSET, THAT'S WHAT.
I DO THANK YOU FOR YOUR HELP, BUT, PLEASE, YOU REALLY SHOULD GO NOW.
IF THAT'S WHAT YOU WANT, CHILD, THEN I'LL GO. YOU'RE CERTAIN YOU'RE OKAY?
YES, YES... UNF... I'M FINE.
IT'S JUST... PLEASE... BEFORE JEBEDIAH GETS BACK.
I UNDERSTAND.
YOU REALLY SHOULD REST YOURSELF. THAT BABY YOU'RE CARRYIN' WILL BE WANTIN' TO JOIN US SOON.

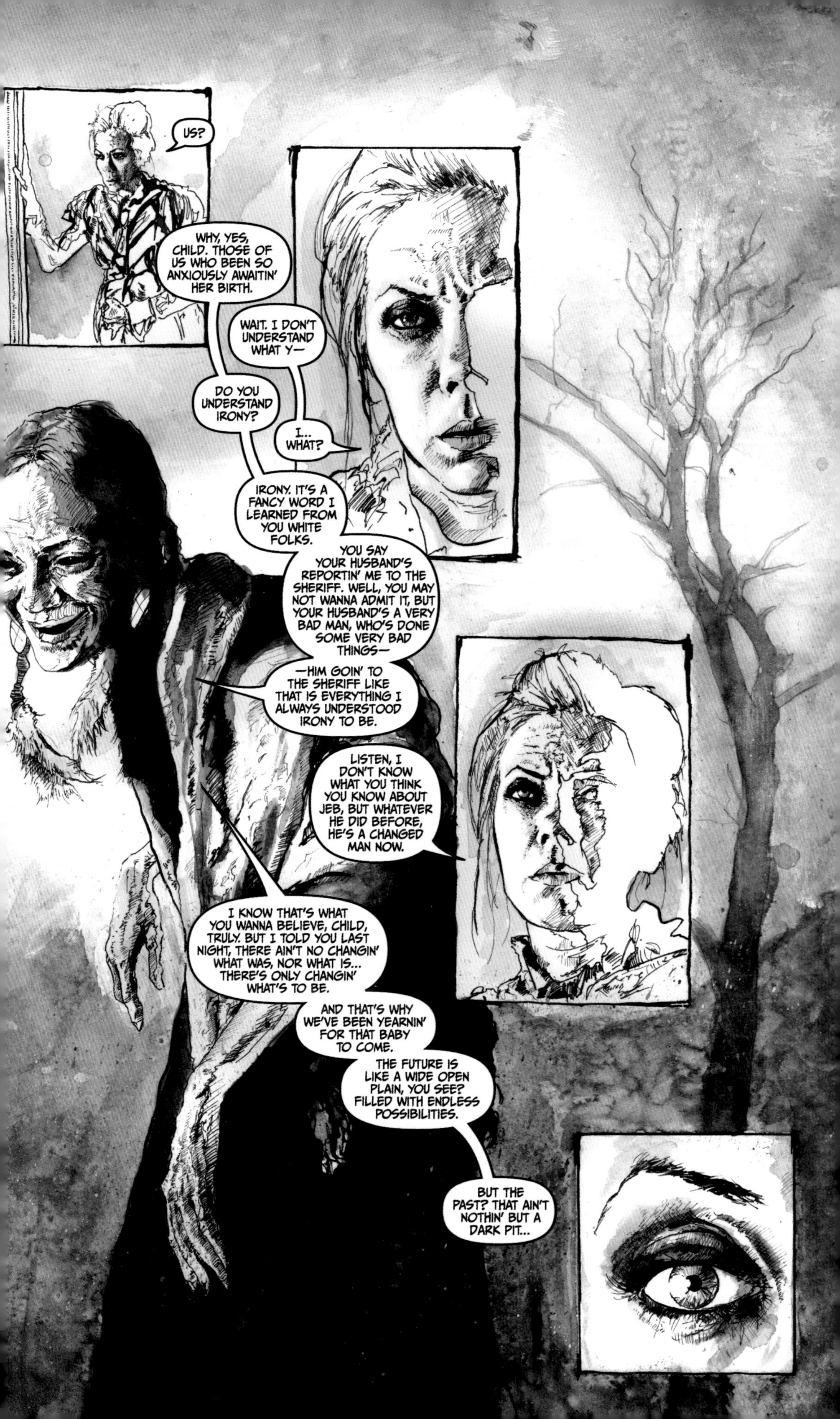
US?
WHY, YES, CHILD. THOSE OF US WHO BEEN SO ANXIOUSLY AWAITIN' HER BIRTH.
WAIT. I DON'T UNDERSTAND WHAT Y—
DO YOU UNDERSTAND IRONY?
I... WHAT?
IRONY. IT'S A FANCY WORD I LEARNED FROM YOU WHITE FOLKS.
YOU SAY YOUR HUSBAND'S REPORTIN' ME TO THE SHERIFF. WELL, YOU MAY NOT WANNA ADMIT IT, BUT YOUR HUSBAND'S A VERY BAD MAN, WHO'S DONE SOME VERY BAD THINGS—
—HIM GOIN' TO THE SHERIFF LIKE THAT IS EVERYTHING I ALWAYS UNDERSTOOD IRONY TO BE.
LISTEN, I DON'T KNOW WHAT YOU THINK YOU KNOW ABOUT JEB, BUT WHATEVER HE DID BEFORE, HE'S A CHANGED MAN NOW.
I KNOW THAT'S WHAT YOU WANNA BELIEVE, CHILD, TRULY. BUT I TOLD YOU LAST NIGHT, THERE AIN'T NO CHANGIN' WHAT WAS, NOR WHAT IS... THERE'S ONLY CHANGIN' WHAT'S TO BE.
AND THAT'S WHY WE'VE BEEN YEARNIN' FOR THAT BABY TO COME.
THE FUTURE IS LIKE A WIDE OPEN PLAIN, YOU SEE? FILLED WITH ENDLESS POSSIBILITIES.
BUT THE PAST? THAT AIN'T NOTHIN' BUT A DARK PIT...

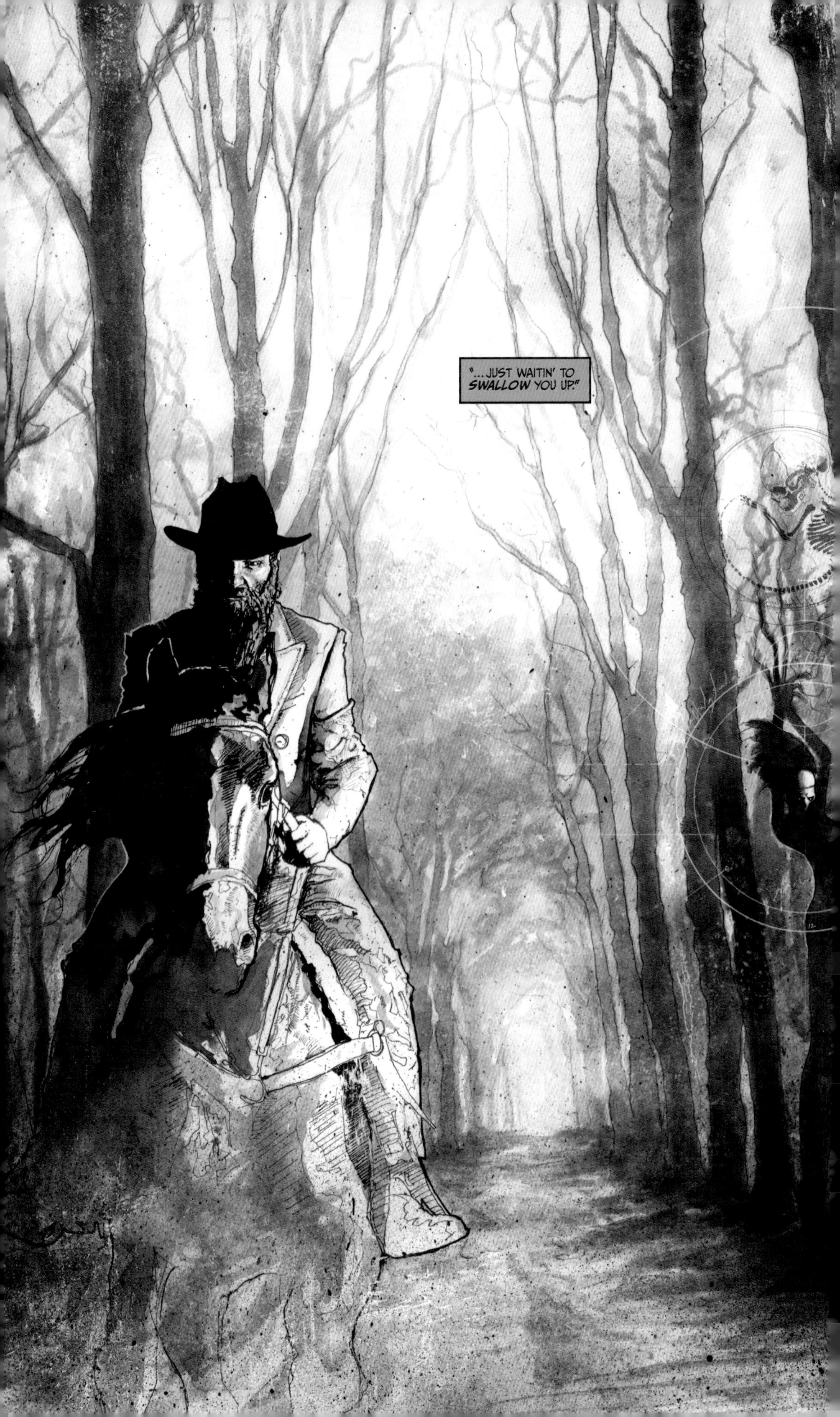
"...JUST WAITIN' TO SWALLOW YOU UP."

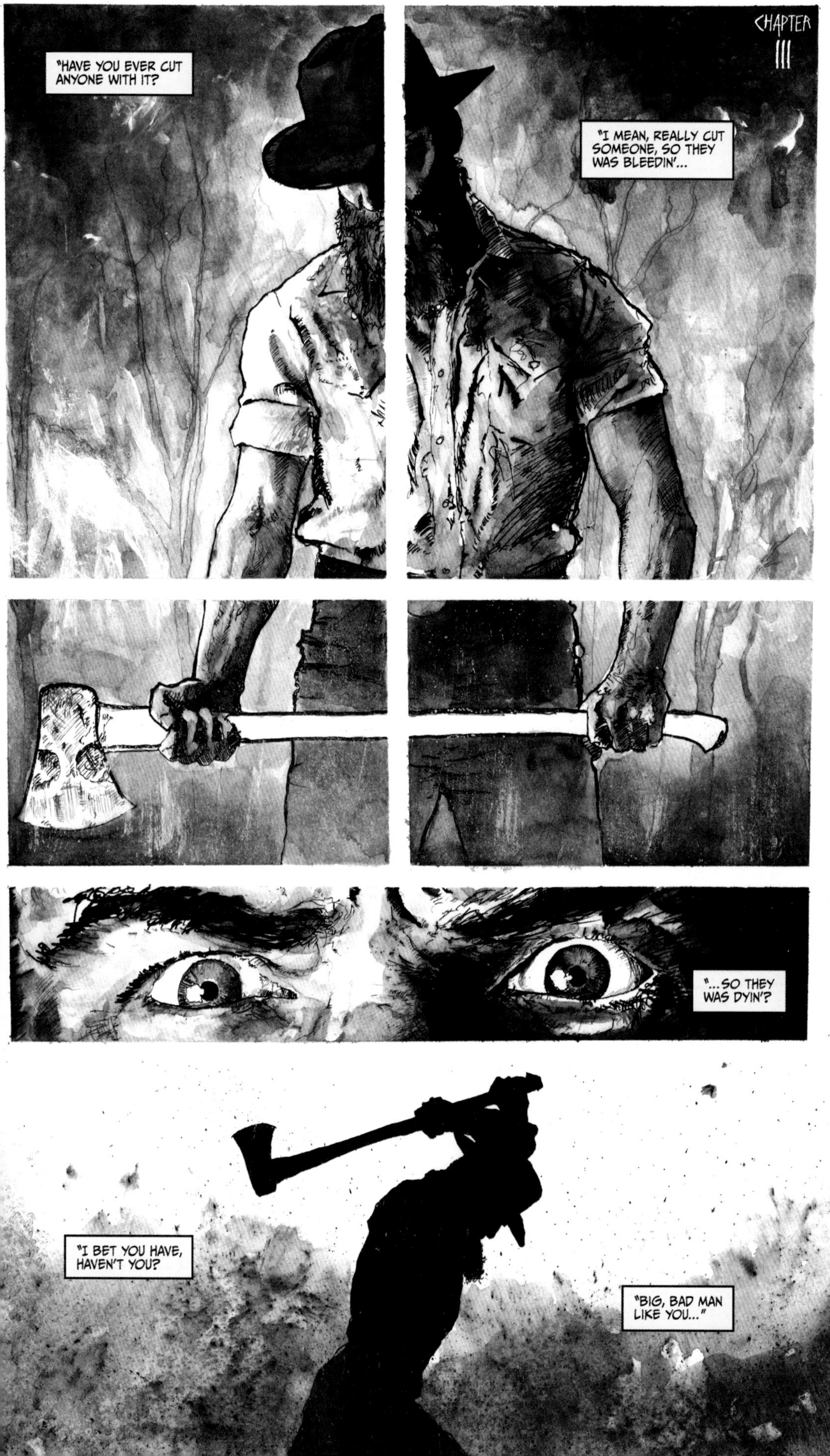
CHAPTER III
"HAVE YOU EVER CUT ANYONE WITH IT?
"I MEAN, REALLY CUT SOMEONE, SO THEY WAS BLEEDIN'...
"...SO THEY WAS DYIN'?
"I BET YOU HAVE, HAVEN'T YOU?
"BIG, BAD MAN LIKE YOU..."

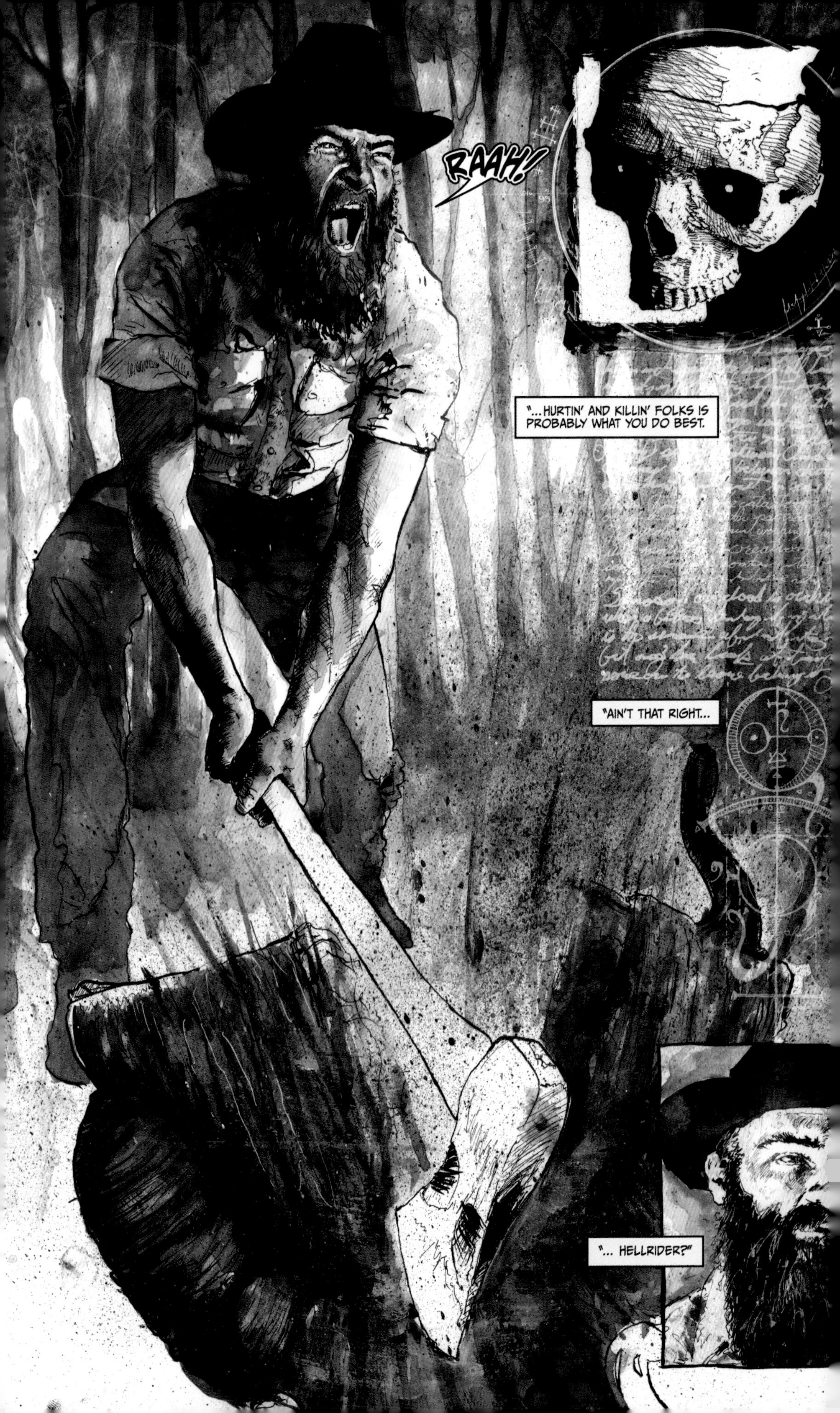
RAAH!
"...HURTIN' AND KILLIN' FOLKS IS PROBABLY WHAT YOU DO BEST.
"AIN'T THAT RIGHT...
"... HELLRIDER?"

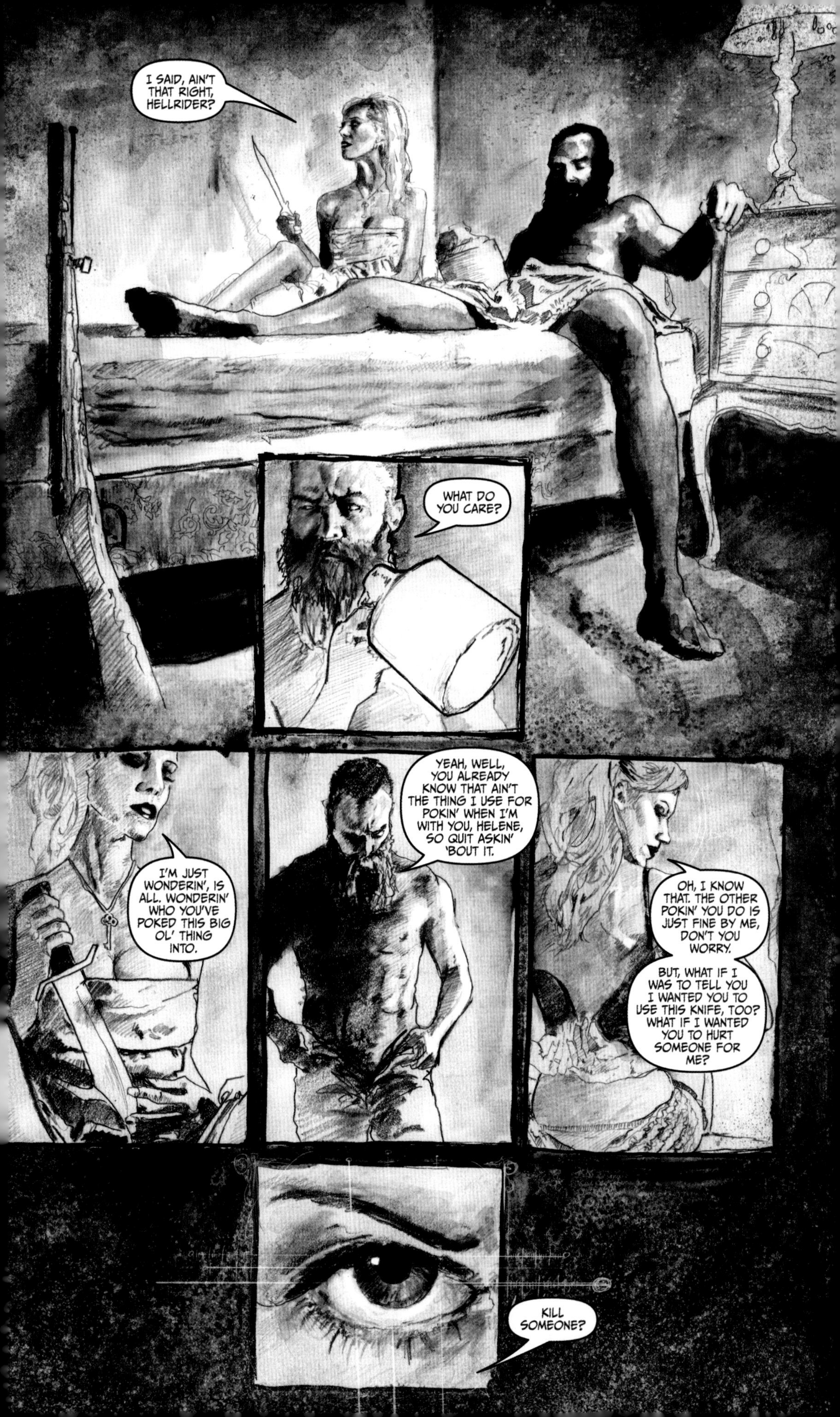
I SAID, AIN'T THAT RIGHT, HELLRIDER?
WHAT DO YOU CARE?
I'M JUST WONDERIN', IS ALL. WONDERIN' WHO YOU'VE POKED THIS BIG OL' THING INTO.
YEAH, WELL, YOU ALREADY KNOW THAT AIN'T THE THING I USE FOR POKIN' WHEN I'M WITH YOU, HELENE, SO QUIT ASKIN' 'BOUT IT.
OH, I KNOW THAT. THE OTHER POKIN' YOU DO IS JUST FINE BY ME, DON'T YOU WORRY.
BUT, WHAT IF I WAS TO TELL YOU I WANTED YOU TO USE THIS KNIFE, TOO? WHAT IF I WANTED YOU TO HURT SOMEONE FOR ME?
KILL SOMEONE?

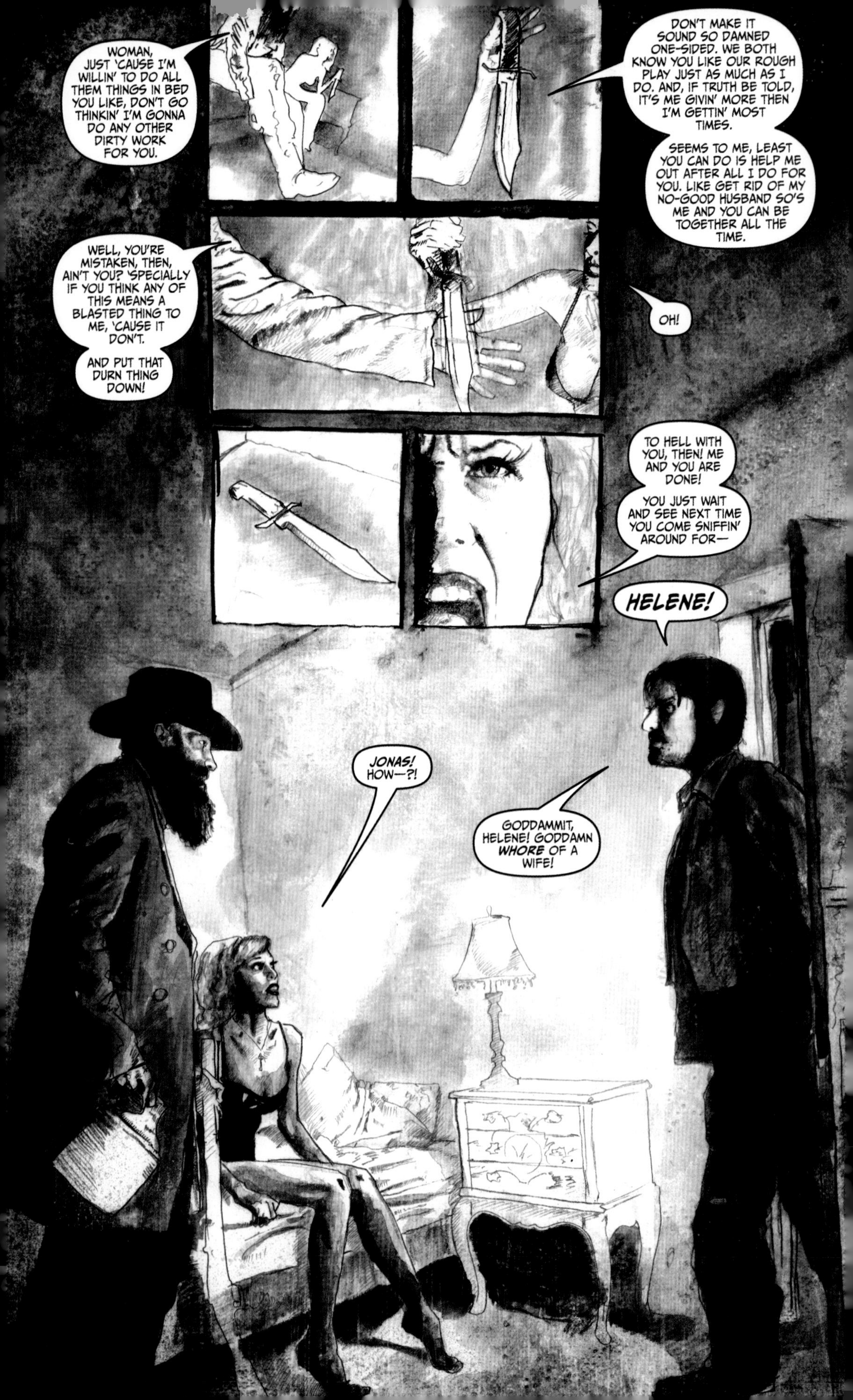
WOMAN, JUST 'CAUSE I'M WILLIN' TO DO ALL THEM THINGS IN BED YOU LIKE, DON'T GO THINKIN' I'M GONNA DO ANY OTHER DIRTY WORK FOR YOU.
DON'T MAKE IT SOUND SO DAMNED ONE-SIDED. WE BOTH KNOW YOU LIKE OUR ROUGH PLAY JUST AS MUCH AS I DO. AND, IF TRUTH BE TOLD, IT'S ME GIVIN' MORE THEN I'M GETTIN' MOST TIMES.
SEEMS TO ME, LEAST YOU CAN DO IS HELP ME OUT AFTER ALL I DO FOR YOU. LIKE GET RID OF MY NO-GOOD HUSBAND SO'S ME AND YOU CAN BE TOGETHER ALL THE TIME.
WELL, YOU'RE MISTAKEN, THEN, AIN'T YOU? 'SPECIALLY IF YOU THINK ANY OF THIS MEANS A BLASTED THING TO ME, 'CAUSE IT DON'T.
AND PUT THAT DURN THING DOWN!
OH!
TO HELL WITH YOU, THEN! ME AND YOU ARE DONE!
YOU JUST WAIT AND SEE NEXT TIME YOU COME SNIFFIN' AROUND FOR—
HELENE!
JONAS! HOW—?!
GODDAMMIT, HELENE! GODDAMN WHORE OF A WIFE!

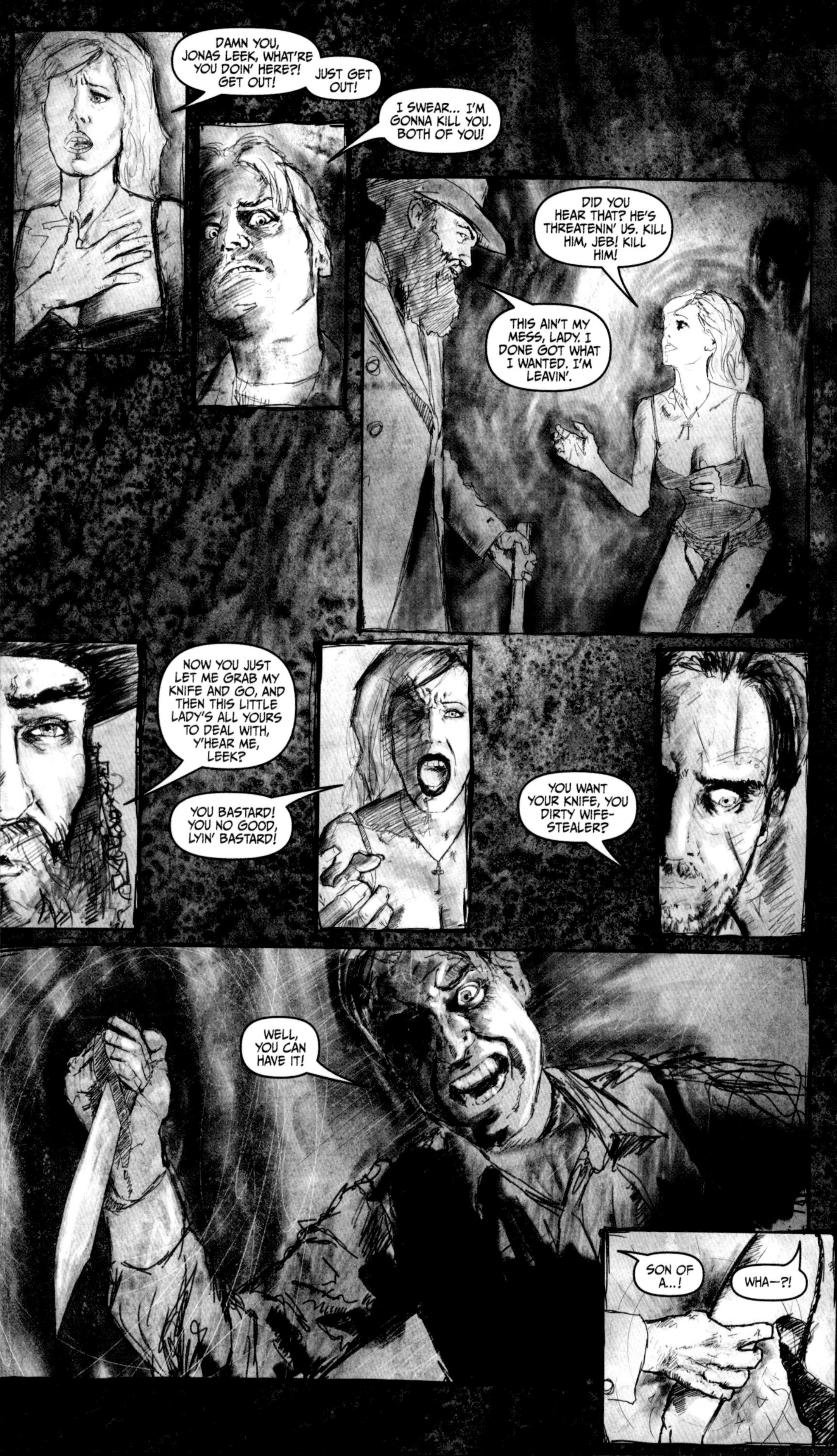
DAMN YOU, JONAS LEEK, WHAT'RE YOU DOIN' HERE?! GET OUT!
JUST GET OUT!
I SWEAR... I'M GONNA KILL YOU. BOTH OF YOU!
DID YOU HEAR THAT? HE'S THREATENIN' US. KILL HIM, JEB! KILL HIM!
THIS AIN'T MY MESS, LADY. I DONE GOT WHAT I WANTED. I'M LEAVIN'.
NOW YOU JUST LET ME GRAB MY KNIFE AND GO, AND THEN THIS LITTLE LADY'S ALL YOURS TO DEAL WITH, Y'HEAR ME, LEEK?
YOU BASTARD! YOU NO GOOD, LYIN' BASTARD!
YOU WANT YOUR KNIFE, YOU DIRTY WIFE-STEALER?
WELL, YOU CAN HAVE IT!
SON OF A...!
WHA--?!

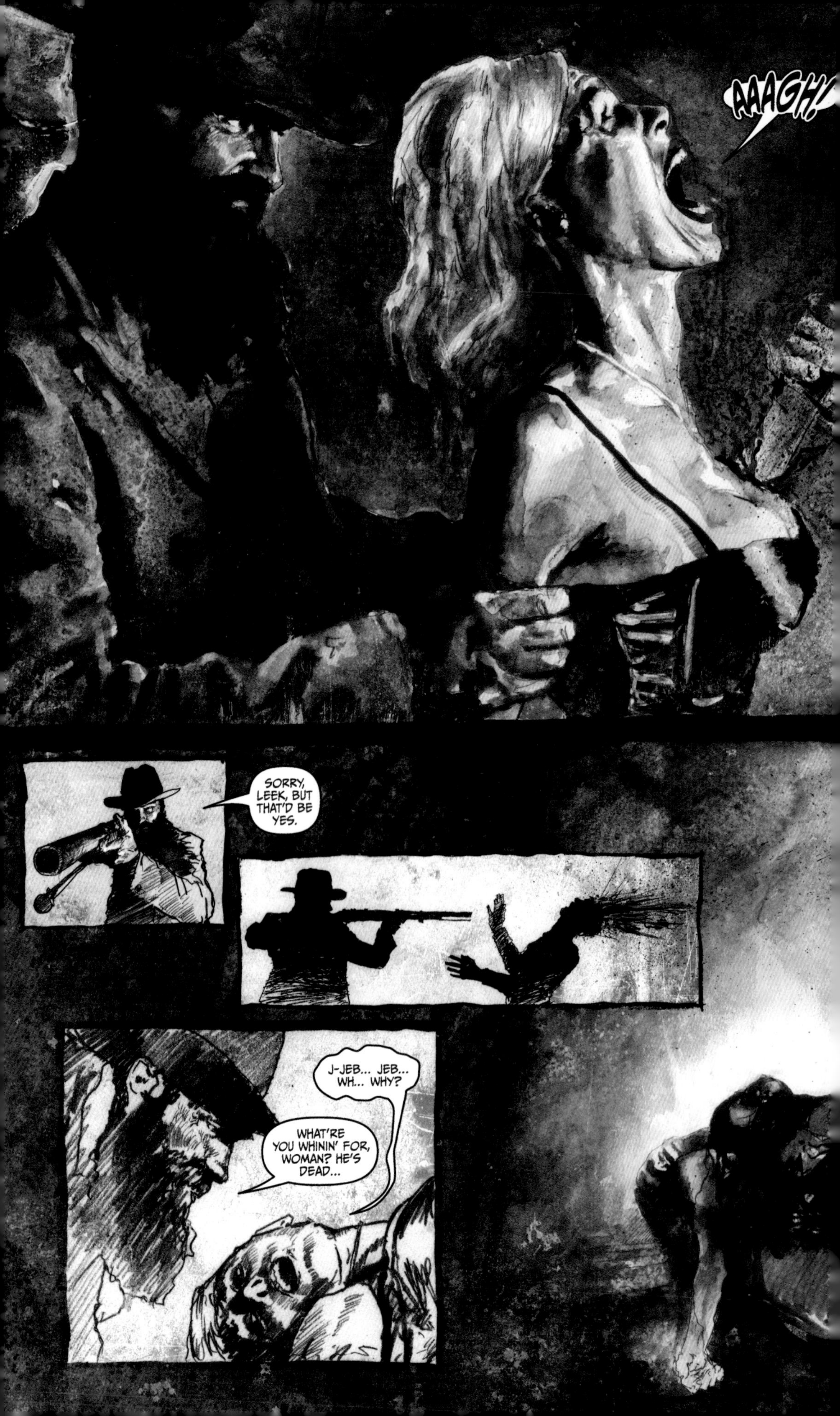
AAAGH!
SORRY, LEEK, BUT THAT'D BE YES.
J-JEB... JEB... WH... WHY?
WHAT'RE YOU WHININ' FOR, WOMAN? HE'S DEAD...

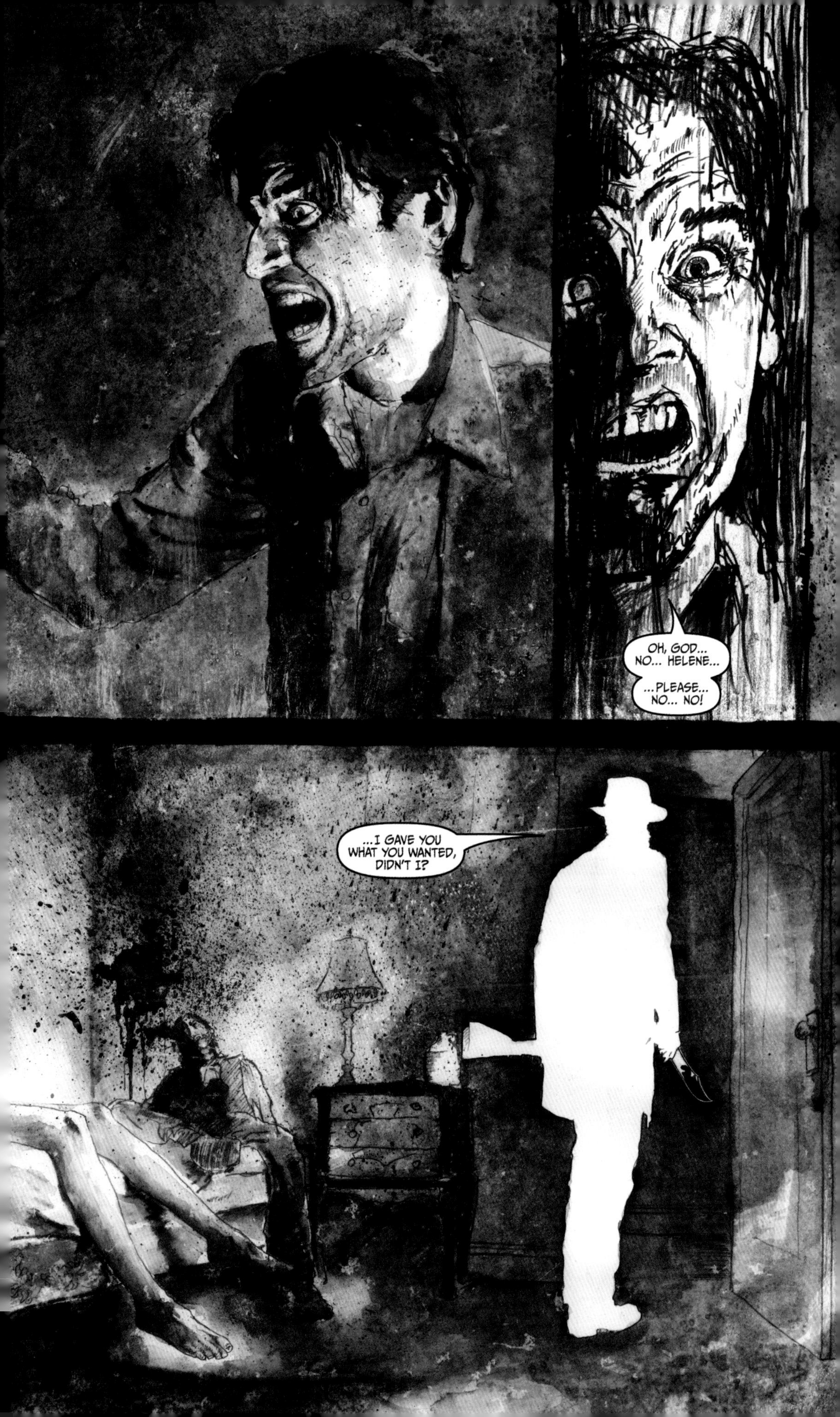
OH, GOD... NO... HELENE...
...PLEASE... NO... NO!
...I GAVE YOU WHAT YOU WANTED, DIDN'T I?

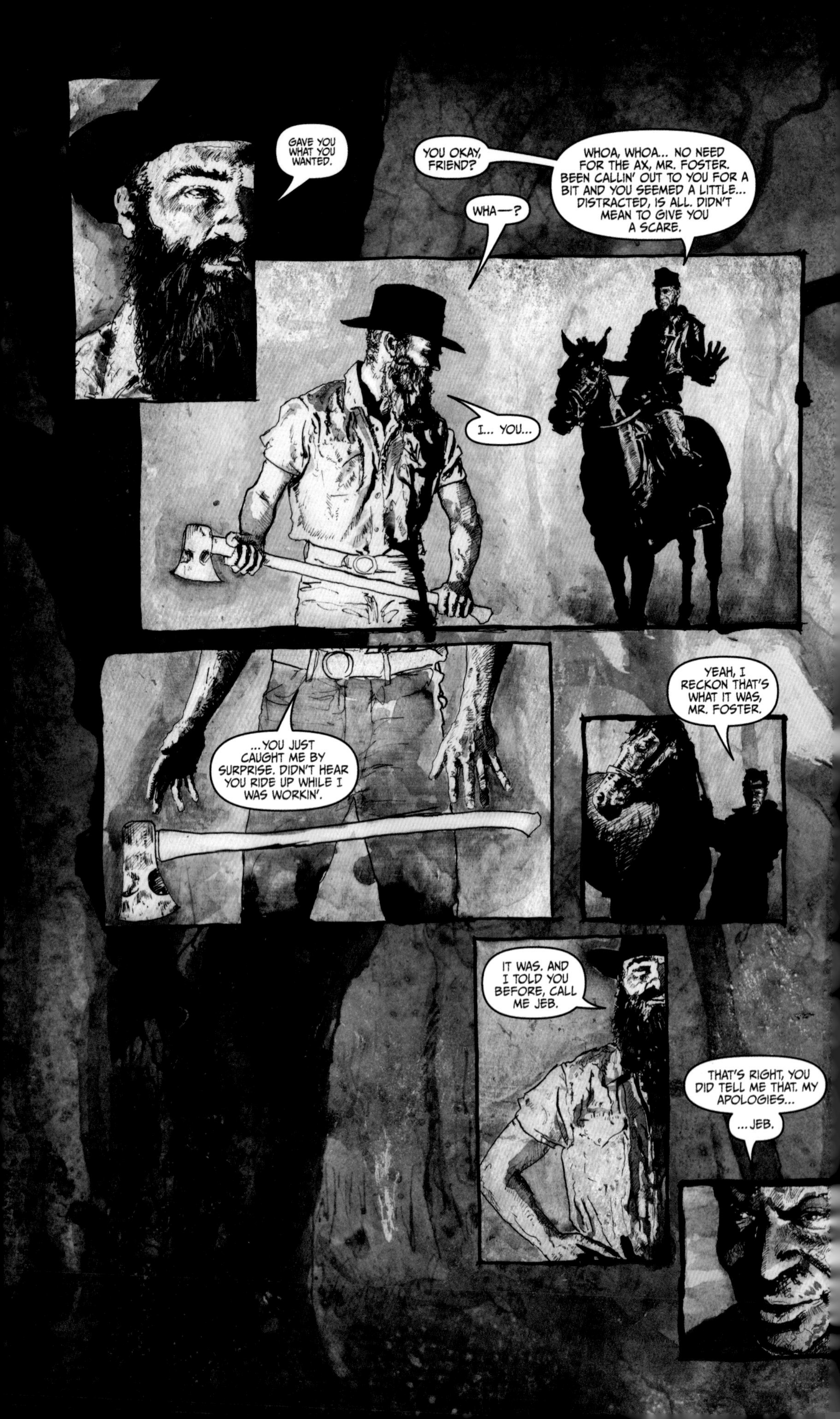
GAVE YOU WHAT YOU WANTED.
YOU OKAY, FRIEND?
WHOA, WHOA... NO NEED FOR THE AX, MR. FOSTER. BEEN CALLIN' OUT TO YOU FOR A BIT AND YOU SEEMED A LITTLE... DISTRACTED, IS ALL. DIDN'T MEAN TO GIVE YOU A SCARE.
WHA—?
I... YOU...
...YOU JUST CAUGHT ME BY SURPRISE. DIDN'T HEAR YOU RIDE UP WHILE I WAS WORKIN'.
YEAH, I RECKON THAT'S WHAT IT WAS, MR. FOSTER.
IT WAS. AND I TOLD YOU BEFORE, CALL ME JEB.
THAT'S RIGHT, YOU DID TELL ME THAT. MY APOLOGIES...
...JEB.

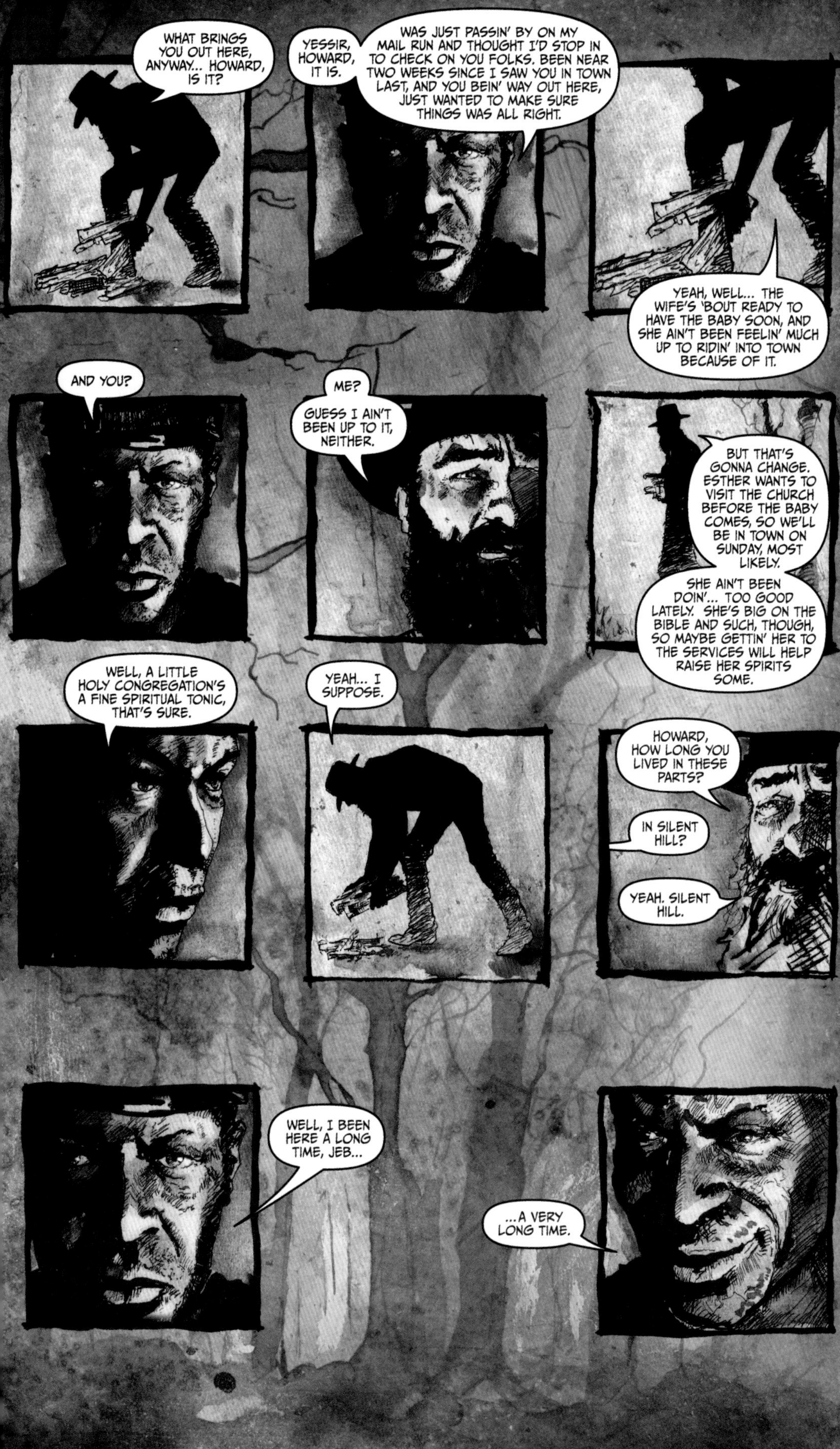
WHAT BRINGS YOU OUT HERE, ANYWAY... HOWARD, IS IT?
YESSIR, HOWARD, IT IS.
WAS JUST PASSIN' BY ON MY MAIL RUN AND THOUGHT I'D STOP IN TO CHECK ON YOU FOLKS. BEEN NEAR TWO WEEKS SINCE I SAW YOU IN TOWN LAST, AND YOU BEIN' WAY OUT HERE, JUST WANTED TO MAKE SURE THINGS WAS ALL RIGHT.
YEAH, WELL... THE WIFE'S 'BOUT READY TO HAVE THE BABY SOON, AND SHE AIN'T BEEN FEELIN' MUCH UP TO RIDIN' INTO TOWN BECAUSE OF IT.
AND YOU?
ME?
GUESS I AIN'T BEEN UP TO IT, NEITHER.
BUT THAT'S GONNA CHANGE. ESTHER WANTS TO VISIT THE CHURCH BEFORE THE BABY COMES, SO WE'LL BE IN TOWN ON SUNDAY, MOST LIKELY.
SHE AIN'T BEEN DOIN'... TOO GOOD LATELY. SHE'S BIG ON THE BIBLE AND SUCH, THOUGH, SO MAYBE GETTIN' HER TO THE SERVICES WILL HELP RAISE HER SPIRITS SOME.
WELL, A LITTLE HOLY CONGREGATION'S A FINE SPIRITUAL TONIC, THAT'S SURE.
YEAH... I SUPPOSE.
HOWARD, HOW LONG YOU LIVED IN THESE PARTS?
IN SILENT HILL?
YEAH. SILENT HILL.
WELL, I BEEN HERE A LONG TIME, JEB...
...A VERY LONG TIME.

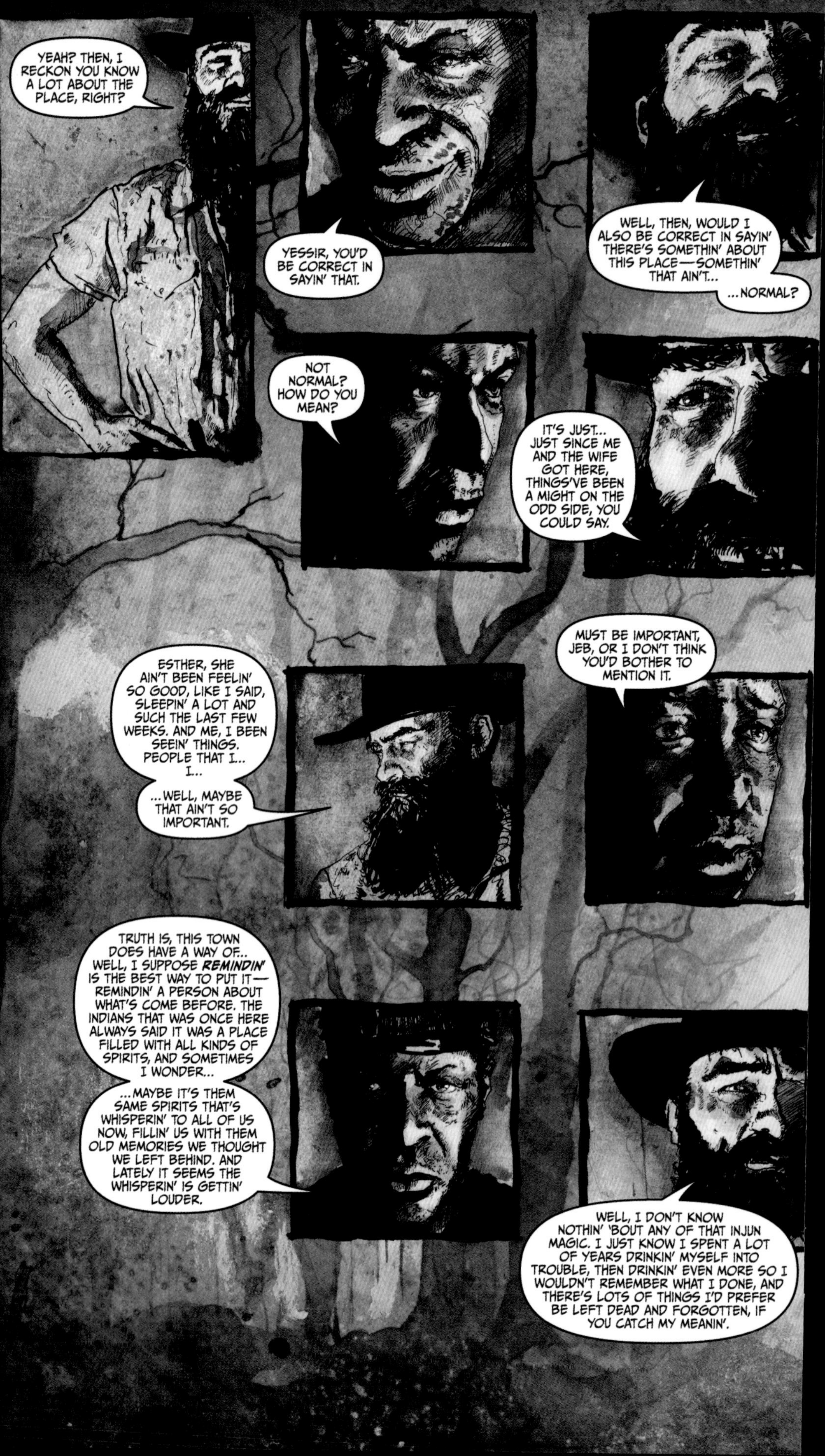

YEAH? THEN, I RECKON YOU KNOW A LOT ABOUT THE PLACE, RIGHT?
YESSIR, YOU'D BE CORRECT IN SAYIN' THAT.
WELL, THEN, WOULD I ALSO BE CORRECT IN SAYIN' THERE'S SOMETHIN' ABOUT THIS PLACE—SOMETHIN' THAT AIN'T... ...NORMAL?
NOT NORMAL? HOW DO YOU MEAN?
IT'S JUST... JUST SINCE ME AND THE WIFE GOT HERE, THINGS'VE BEEN A MIGHT ON THE ODD SIDE, YOU COULD SAY.
ESTHER, SHE AIN'T BEEN FEELIN' SO GOOD, LIKE I SAID, SLEEPIN' A LOT AND SUCH THE LAST FEW WEEKS. AND ME, I BEEN SEEIN' THINGS. PEOPLE THAT I... I...
...WELL, MAYBE THAT AIN'T SO IMPORTANT.
MUST BE IMPORTANT, JEB, OR I DON'T THINK YOU'D BOTHER TO MENTION IT.
TRUTH IS, THIS TOWN DOES HAVE A WAY OF... WELL, I SUPPOSE REMINDIN' IS THE BEST WAY TO PUT IT—REMINDIN' A PERSON ABOUT WHAT'S COME BEFORE. THE INDIANS THAT WAS ONCE HERE ALWAYS SAID IT WAS A PLACE FILLED WITH ALL KINDS OF SPIRITS, AND SOMETIMES I WONDER...
...MAYBE IT'S THEM SAME SPIRITS THAT'S WHISPERIN' TO ALL OF US NOW, FILLIN' US WITH THEM OLD MEMORIES WE THOUGHT WE LEFT BEHIND. AND LATELY IT SEEMS THE WHISPERIN' IS GETTIN' LOUDER.
WELL, I DON'T KNOW NOTHIN' 'BOUT ANY OF THAT INJUN MAGIC. I JUST KNOW I SPENT A LOT OF YEARS DRINKIN' MYSELF INTO TROUBLE, THEN DRINKIN' EVEN MORE SO I WOULDN'T REMEMBER WHAT I DONE, AND THERE'S LOTS OF THINGS I'D PREFER BE LEFT DEAD AND FORGOTTEN, IF YOU CATCH MY MEANIN'.

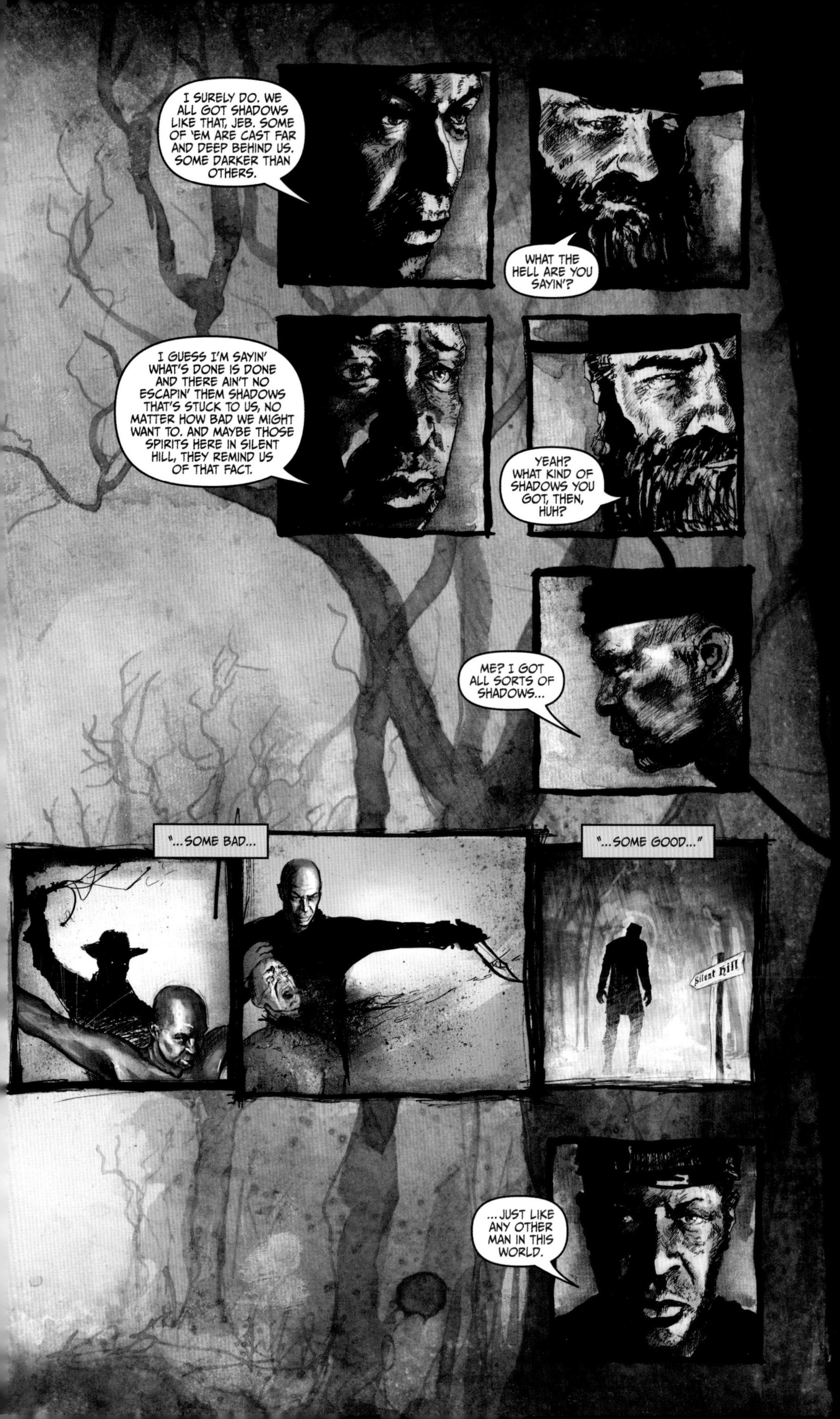
I SURELY DO. WE ALL GOT SHADOWS LIKE THAT, JEB. SOME OF 'EM ARE CAST FAR AND DEEP BEHIND US. SOME DARKER THAN OTHERS.
WHAT THE HELL ARE YOU SAYIN'?
I GUESS I'M SAYIN' WHAT'S DONE IS DONE AND THERE AIN'T NO ESCAPIN' THEM SHADOWS THAT'S STUCK TO US, NO MATTER HOW BAD WE MIGHT WANT TO. AND MAYBE THOSE SPIRITS HERE IN SILENT HILL, THEY REMIND US OF THAT FACT.
YEAH? WHAT KIND OF SHADOWS YOU GOT, THEN, HUH?
ME? I GOT ALL SORTS OF SHADOWS...
"...SOME BAD...
"...SOME GOOD..."
Silent Hill
...JUST LIKE ANY OTHER MAN IN THIS WORLD.

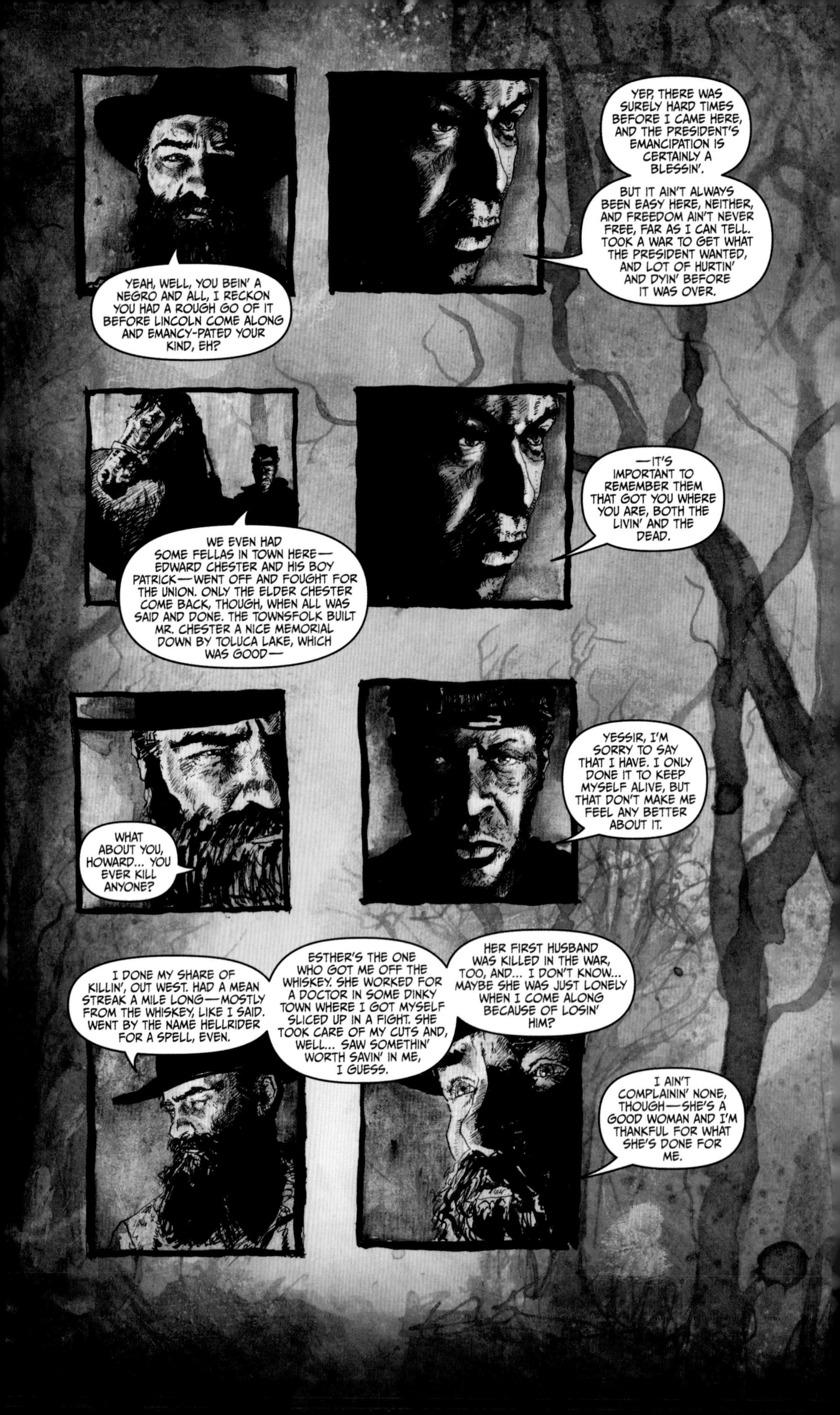
YEAH, WELL, YOU BEIN' A NEGRO AND ALL, I RECKON YOU HAD A ROUGH GO OF IT BEFORE LINCOLN COME ALONG AND EMANCY-PATED YOUR KIND, EH?
YEP, THERE WAS SURELY HARD TIMES BEFORE I CAME HERE, AND THE PRESIDENT'S EMANCIPATION IS CERTAINLY A BLESSIN'.
BUT IT AIN'T ALWAYS BEEN EASY HERE, NEITHER, AND FREEDOM AIN'T NEVER FREE, FAR AS I CAN TELL. TOOK A WAR TO GET WHAT THE PRESIDENT WANTED, AND LOT OF HURTIN' AND DYIN' BEFORE IT WAS OVER.
WE EVEN HAD SOME FELLAS IN TOWN HERE—EDWARD CHESTER AND HIS BOY PATRICK—WENT OFF AND FOUGHT FOR THE UNION. ONLY THE ELDER CHESTER COME BACK, THOUGH, WHEN ALL WAS SAID AND DONE. THE TOWNSFOLK BUILT MR. CHESTER A NICE MEMORIAL DOWN BY TOLUCA LAKE, WHICH WAS GOOD—
—IT'S IMPORTANT TO REMEMBER THEM THAT GOT YOU WHERE YOU ARE, BOTH THE LIVIN' AND THE DEAD.
WHAT ABOUT YOU, HOWARD... YOU EVER KILL ANYONE?
YESSIR, I'M SORRY TO SAY THAT I HAVE. I ONLY DONE IT TO KEEP MYSELF ALIVE, BUT THAT DON'T MAKE ME FEEL ANY BETTER ABOUT IT.
I DONE MY SHARE OF KILLIN', OUT WEST. HAD A MEAN STREAK A MILE LONG—MOSTLY FROM THE WHISKEY, LIKE I SAID. WENT BY THE NAME HELLRIDER FOR A SPELL, EVEN.
ESTHER'S THE ONE WHO GOT ME OFF THE WHISKEY. SHE WORKED FOR A DOCTOR IN SOME DINKY TOWN WHERE I GOT MYSELF SLICED UP IN A FIGHT. SHE TOOK CARE OF MY CUTS AND, WELL... SAW SOMETHIN' WORTH SAVIN' IN ME, I GUESS.
HER FIRST HUSBAND WAS KILLED IN THE WAR, TOO, AND... I DON'T KNOW... MAYBE SHE WAS JUST LONELY WHEN I COME ALONG BECAUSE OF LOSIN' HIM?
I AIN'T COMPLAININ' NONE, THOUGH—SHE'S A GOOD WOMAN AND I'M THANKFUL FOR WHAT SHE'S DONE FOR ME.

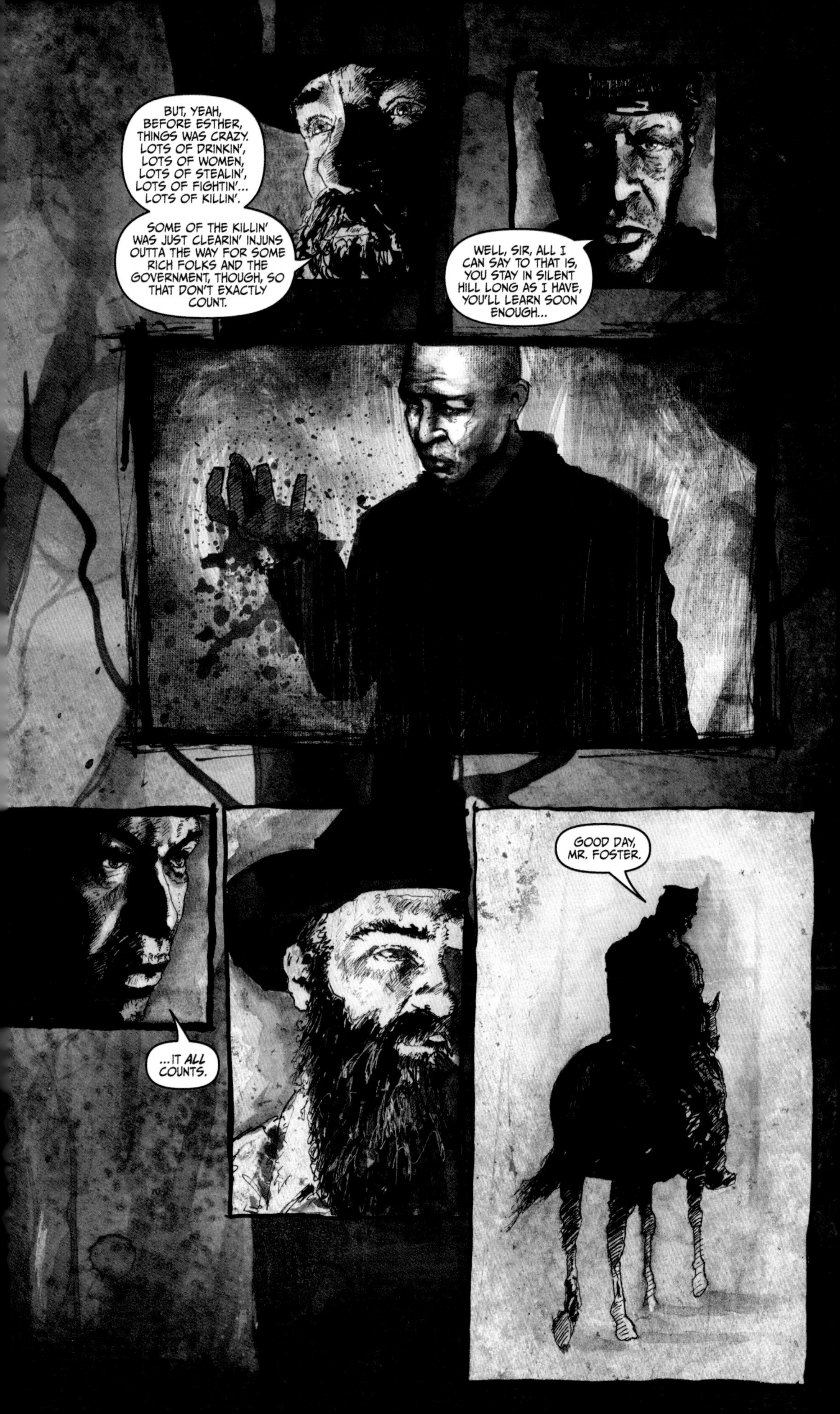
BUT, YEAH, BEFORE ESTHER, THINGS WAS CRAZY. LOTS OF DRINKIN', LOTS OF WOMEN, LOTS OF STEALIN', LOTS OF FIGHTIN'... LOTS OF KILLIN'.
SOME OF THE KILLIN' WAS JUST CLEARIN' INJUNS OUTTA THE WAY FOR SOME RICH FOLKS AND THE GOVERNMENT, THOUGH, SO THAT DON'T EXACTLY COUNT.
WELL, SIR, ALL I CAN SAY TO THAT IS, YOU STAY IN SILENT HILL LONG AS I HAVE, YOU'LL LEARN SOON ENOUGH...
...IT *ALL* COUNTS.
GOOD DAY, MR. FOSTER.

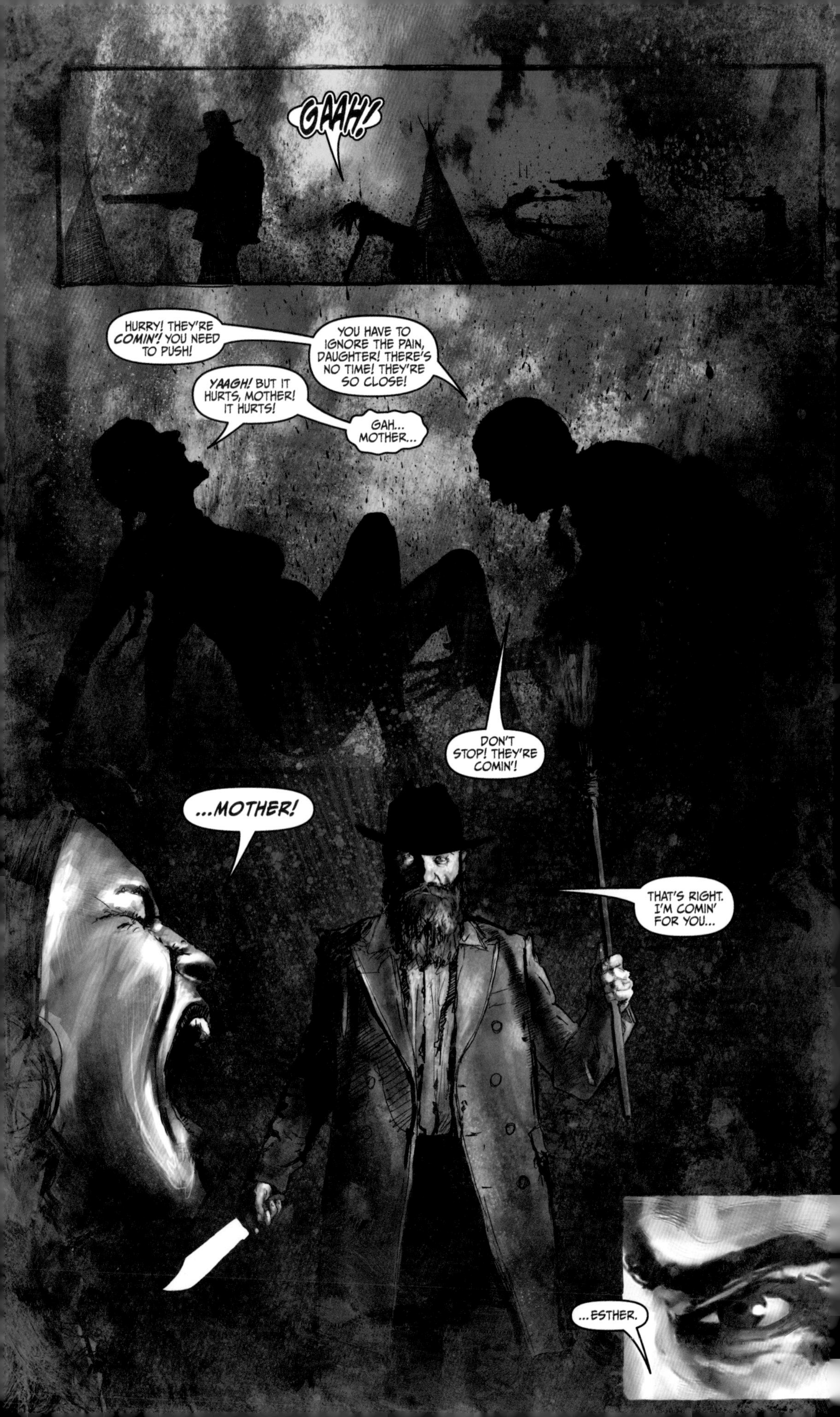
GAAH!
HURRY! THEY'RE *COMIN'!* YOU NEED TO PUSH!
YOU HAVE TO IGNORE THE PAIN, DAUGHTER! THERE'S NO TIME! THEY'RE SO CLOSE!
YAAGH! BUT IT HURTS, MOTHER! IT HURTS!
GAH... MOTHER...
DON'T STOP! THEY'RE COMIN'!
...MOTHER!
THAT'S RIGHT. I'M COMIN' FOR YOU...
...ESTHER.

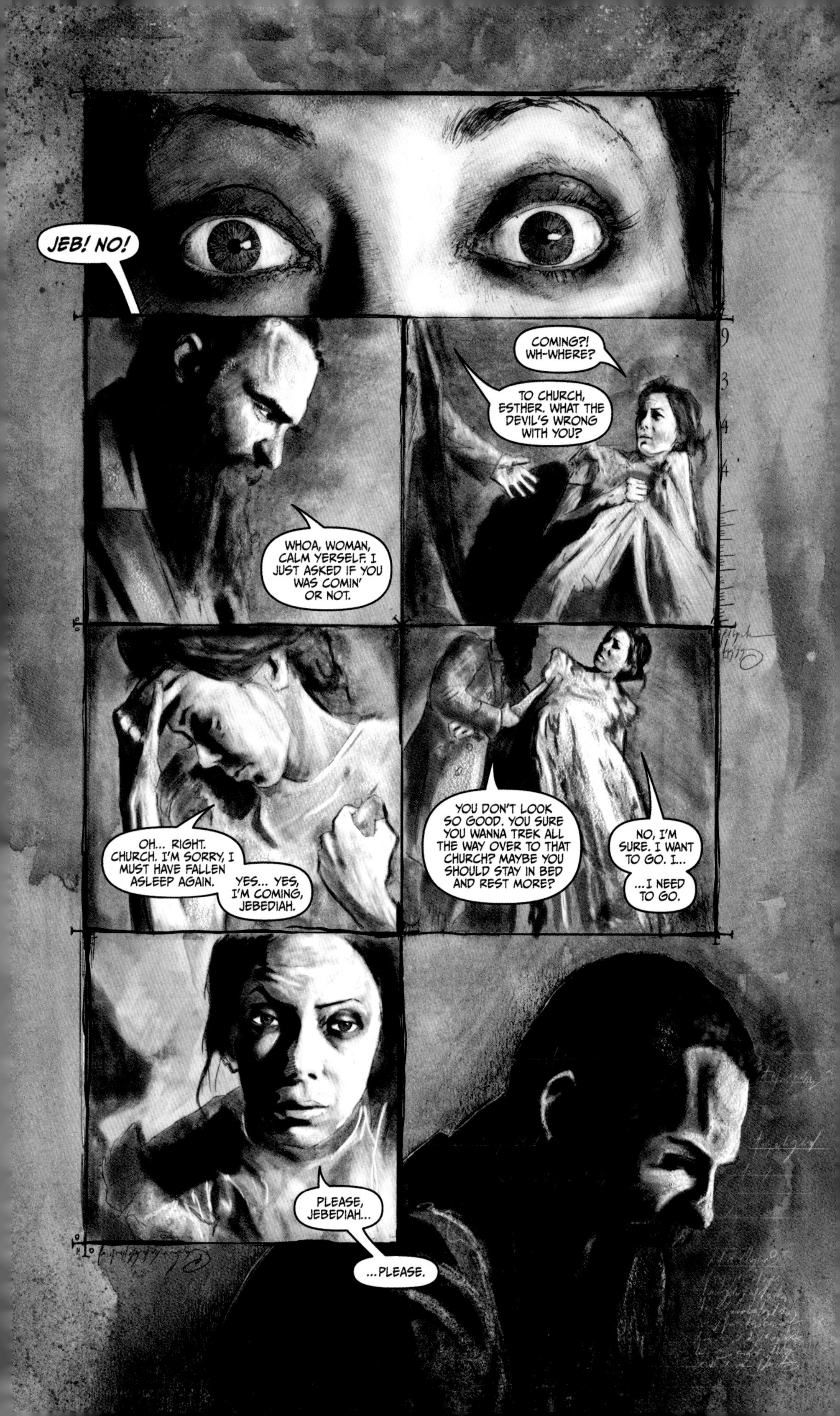
JEB! NO!
WHOA, WOMAN, CALM YERSELF. I JUST ASKED IF YOU WAS COMIN' OR NOT.
COMING?! WH-WHERE?
TO CHURCH, ESTHER. WHAT THE DEVIL'S WRONG WITH YOU?
OH... RIGHT. CHURCH. I'M SORRY, I MUST HAVE FALLEN ASLEEP AGAIN.
YES... YES, I'M COMING, JEBEDIAH.
YOU DON'T LOOK SO GOOD. YOU SURE YOU WANNA TREK ALL THE WAY OVER TO THAT CHURCH? MAYBE YOU SHOULD STAY IN BED AND REST MORE?
NO, I'M SURE. I WANT TO GO. I...
...I NEED TO GO.
PLEASE, JEBEDIAH...
...PLEASE.

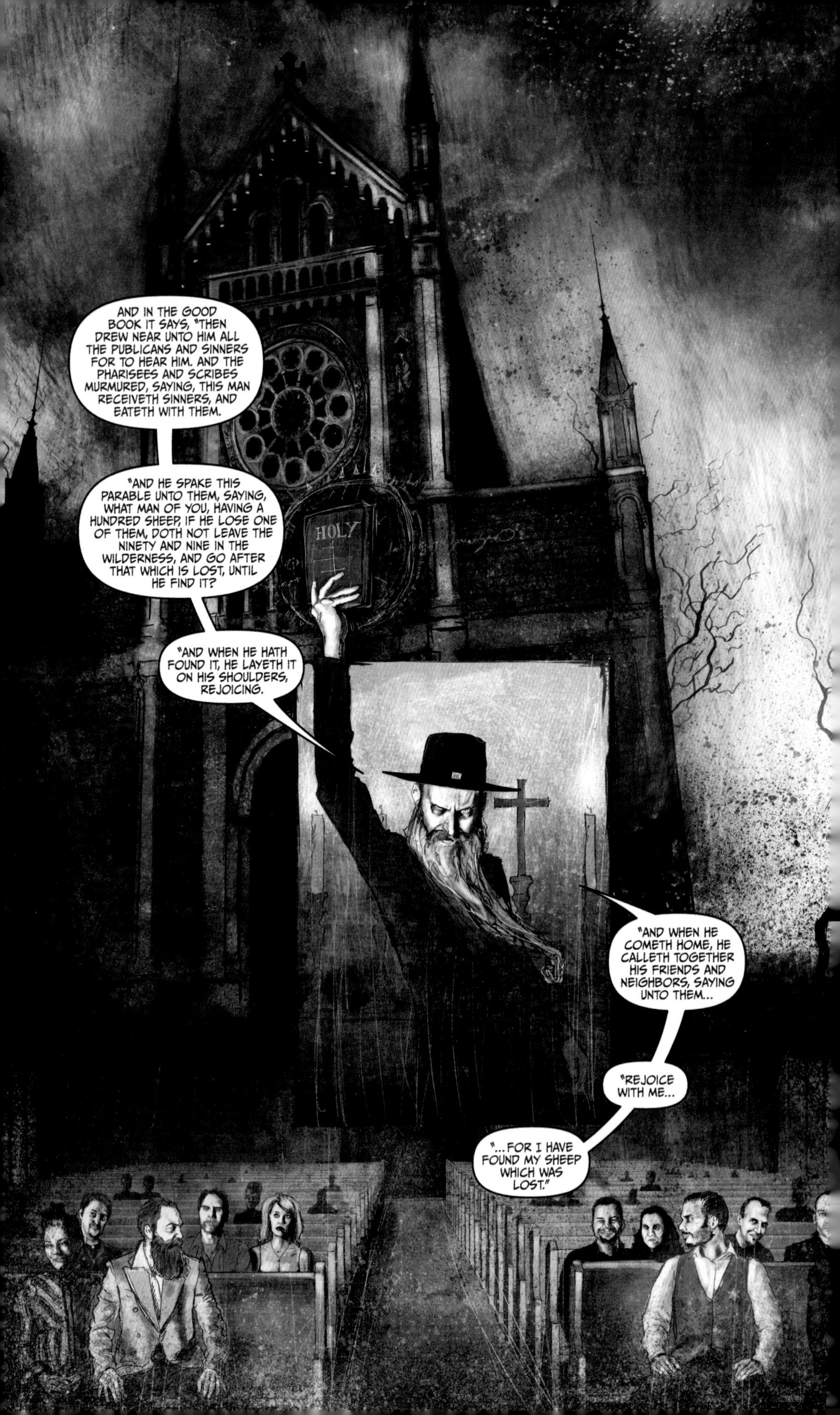
AND IN THE GOOD BOOK IT SAYS, "THEN DREW NEAR UNTO HIM ALL THE PUBLICANS AND SINNERS FOR TO HEAR HIM. AND THE PHARISEES AND SCRIBES MURMURED, SAYING, THIS MAN RECEIVETH SINNERS, AND EATETH WITH THEM.
"AND HE SPAKE THIS PARABLE UNTO THEM, SAYING, WHAT MAN OF YOU, HAVING A HUNDRED SHEEP, IF HE LOSE ONE OF THEM, DOTH NOT LEAVE THE NINETY AND NINE IN THE WILDERNESS, AND GO AFTER THAT WHICH IS LOST, UNTIL HE FIND IT?
"AND WHEN HE HATH FOUND IT, HE LAYETH IT ON HIS SHOULDERS, REJOICING.
"AND WHEN HE COMETH HOME, HE CALLETH TOGETHER HIS FRIENDS AND NEIGHBORS, SAYING UNTO THEM...
"REJOICE WITH ME...
"...FOR I HAVE FOUND MY SHEEP WHICH WAS LOST."
HOLY

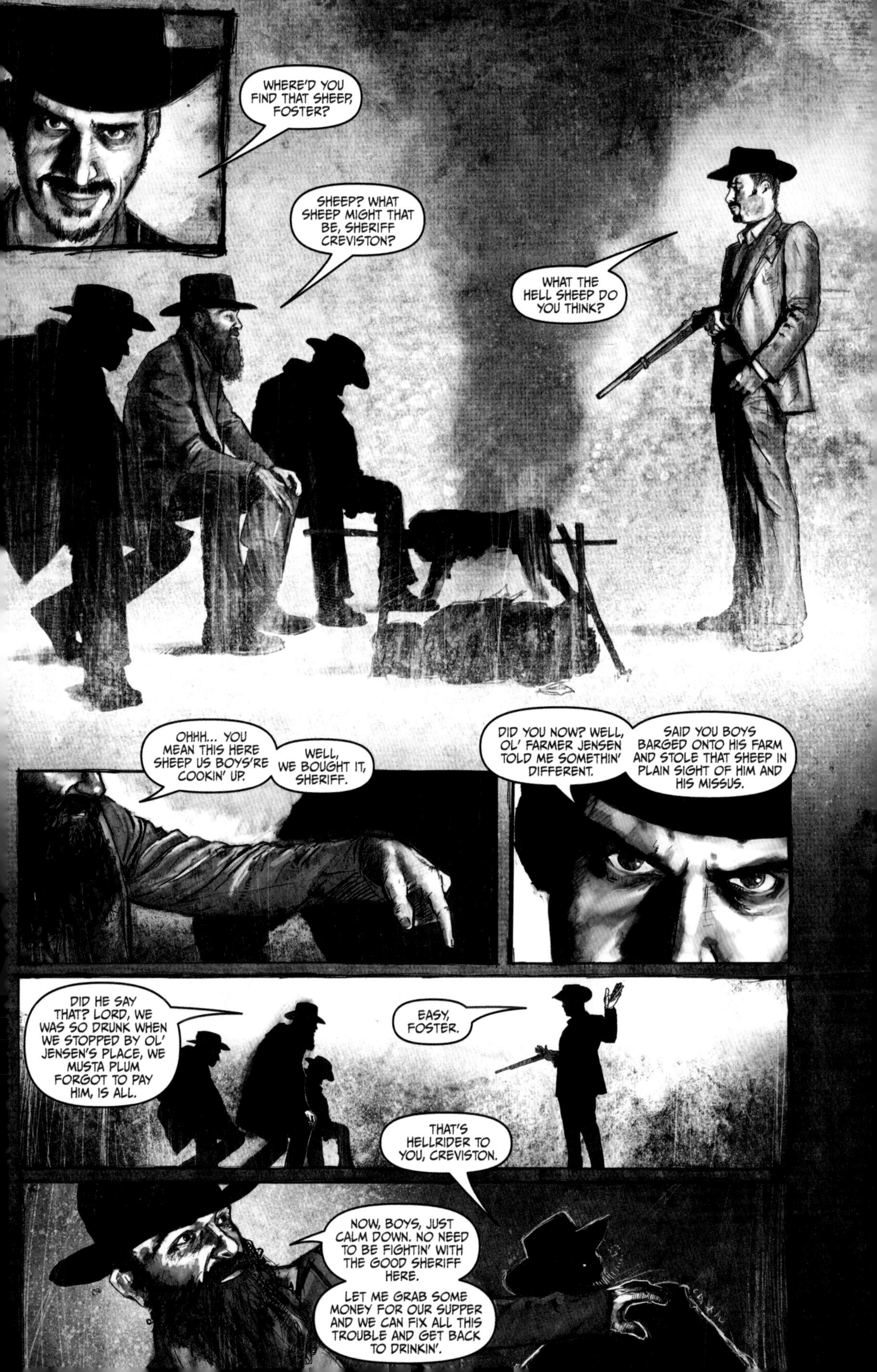
WHERE'D YOU FIND THAT SHEEP, FOSTER?
SHEEP? WHAT SHEEP MIGHT THAT BE, SHERIFF CREVISTON?
WHAT THE HELL SHEEP DO YOU THINK?
OHHH... YOU MEAN THIS HERE SHEEP US BOYS'RE COOKIN' UP.
WELL, WE BOUGHT IT, SHERIFF.
DID YOU NOW? WELL, OL' FARMER JENSEN TOLD ME SOMETHIN' DIFFERENT.
SAID YOU BOYS BARGED ONTO HIS FARM AND STOLE THAT SHEEP IN PLAIN SIGHT OF HIM AND HIS MISSUS.
DID HE SAY THAT? LORD, WE WAS SO DRUNK WHEN WE STOPPED BY OL' JENSEN'S PLACE, WE MUSTA PLUM FORGOT TO PAY HIM, IS ALL.
EASY, FOSTER.
THAT'S HELLRIDER TO YOU, CREVISTON.
NOW, BOYS, JUST CALM DOWN. NO NEED TO BE FIGHTIN' WITH THE GOOD SHERIFF HERE.
LET ME GRAB SOME MONEY FOR OUR SUPPER AND WE CAN FIX ALL THIS TROUBLE AND GET BACK TO DRINKIN'.

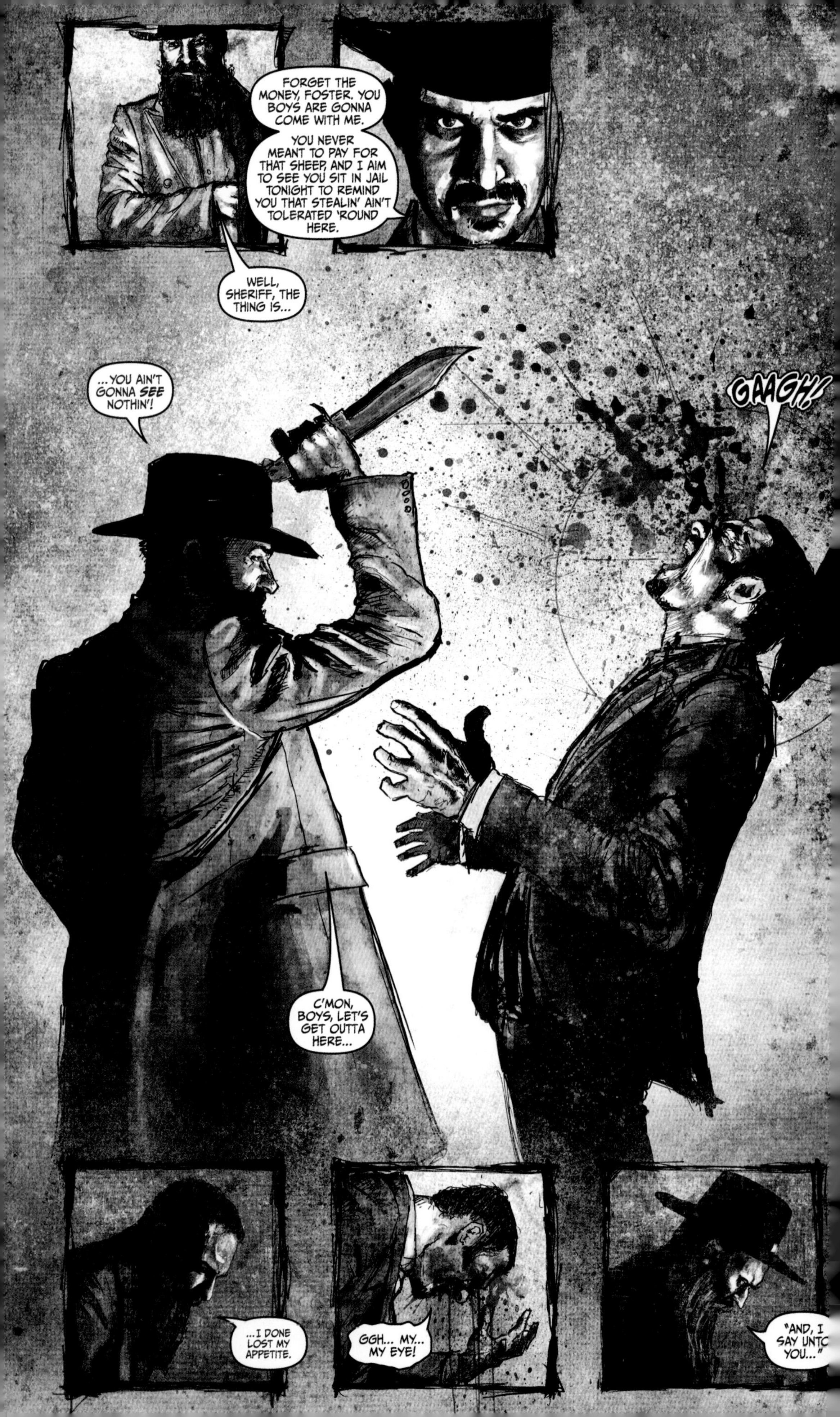
FORGET THE MONEY, FOSTER. YOU BOYS ARE GONNA COME WITH ME.
YOU NEVER MEANT TO PAY FOR THAT SHEEP, AND I AIM TO SEE YOU SIT IN JAIL TONIGHT TO REMIND YOU THAT STEALIN' AIN'T TOLERATED 'ROUND HERE.
WELL, SHERIFF, THE THING IS...
...YOU AIN'T GONNA *SEE* NOTHIN'!
GAAGH!
C'MON, BOYS, LET'S GET OUTTA HERE...
...I DONE LOST MY APPETITE.
GGH... MY... MY EYE!
"AND, I SAY UNTO YOU..."

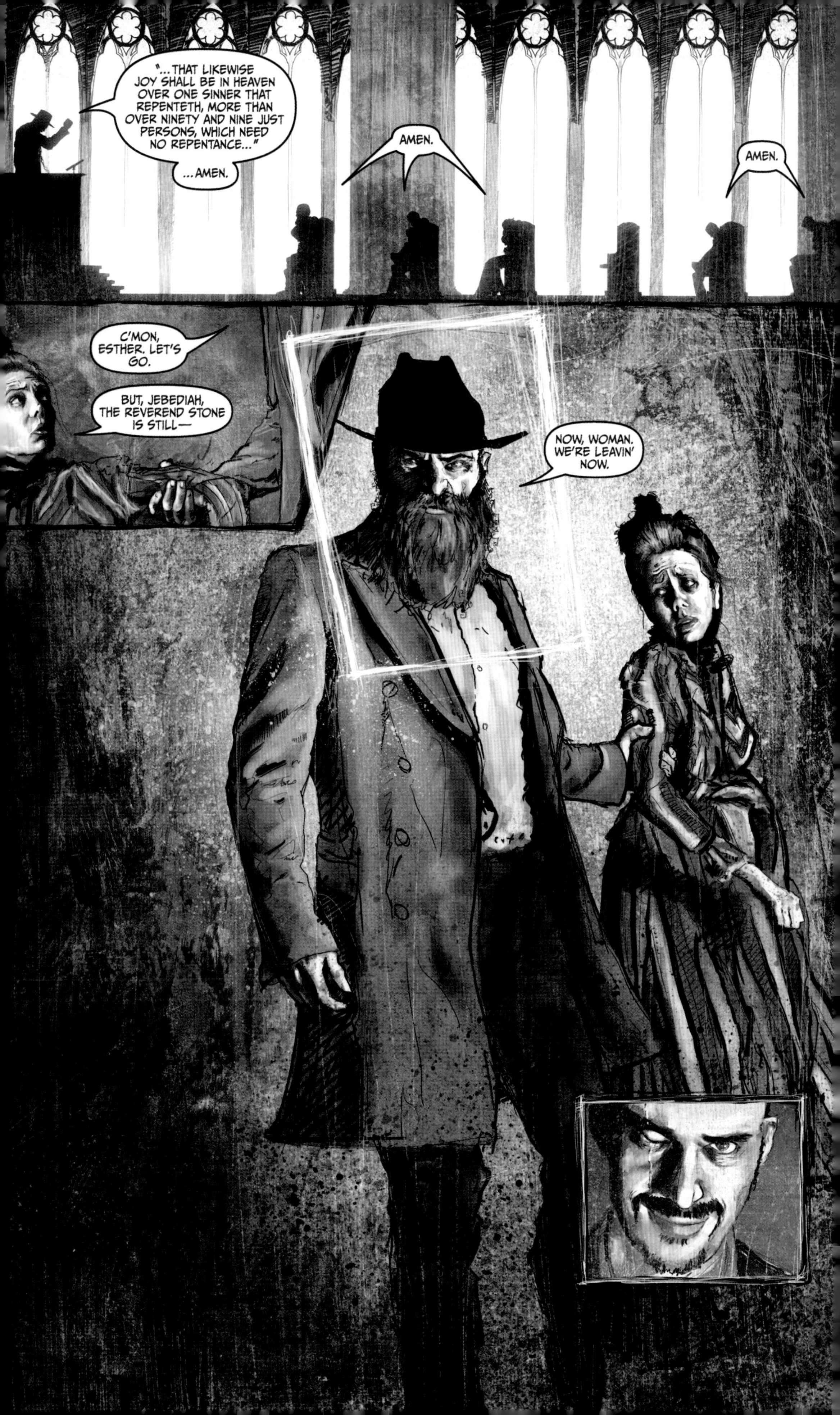
"...THAT LIKEWISE JOY SHALL BE IN HEAVEN OVER ONE SINNER THAT REPENTETH, MORE THAN OVER NINETY AND NINE JUST PERSONS, WHICH NEED NO REPENTANCE..."
...AMEN.
AMEN.
AMEN.
C'MON, ESTHER. LET'S GO.
BUT, JEBEDIAH, THE REVEREND STONE IS STILL—
NOW, WOMAN. WE'RE LEAVIN' NOW.

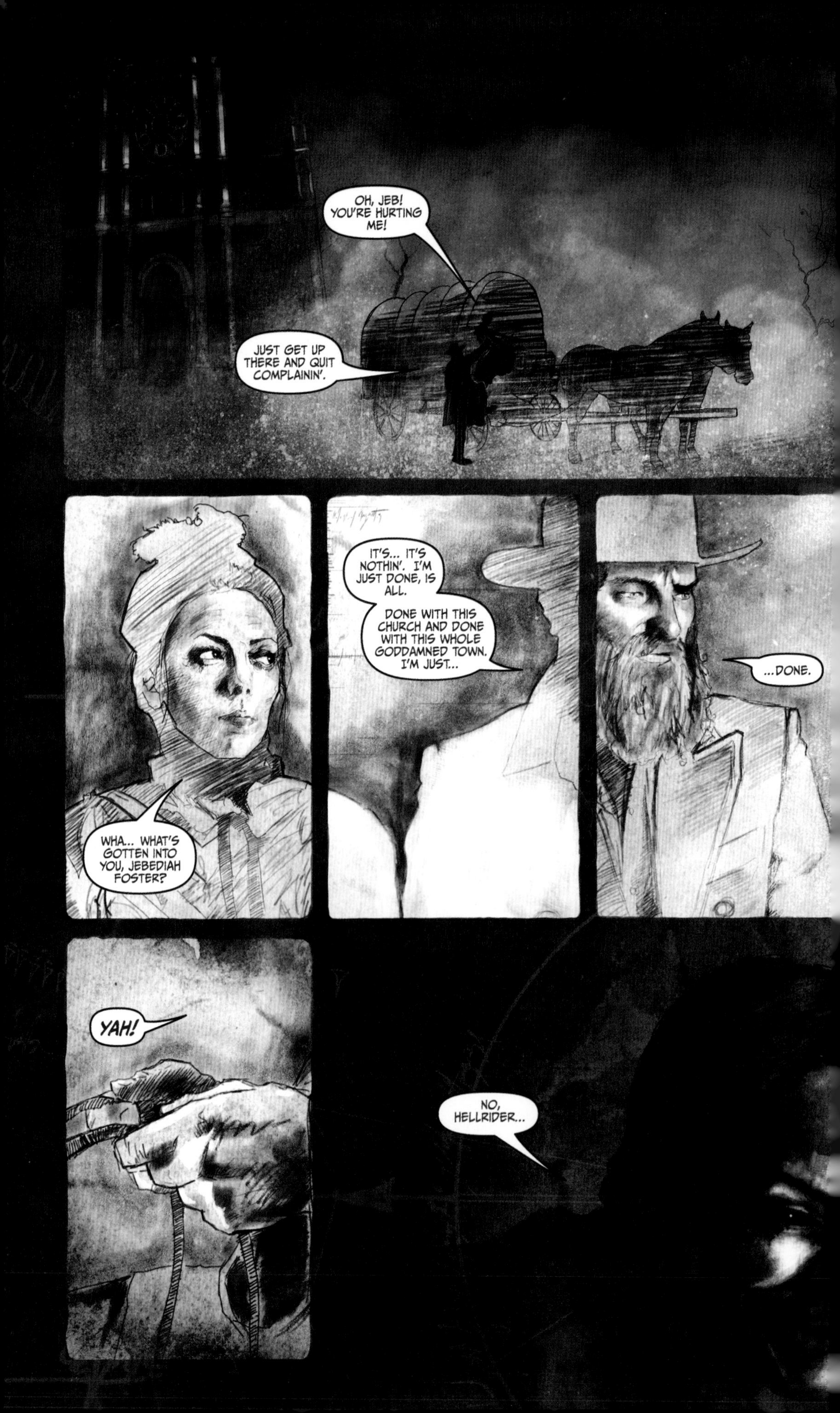
OH, JEB! YOU'RE HURTING ME!
JUST GET UP THERE AND QUIT COMPLAININ'.
WHA... WHAT'S GOTTEN INTO YOU, JEBEDIAH FOSTER?
IT'S... IT'S NOTHIN'. I'M JUST DONE, IS ALL.
DONE WITH THIS CHURCH AND DONE WITH THIS WHOLE GODDAMNED TOWN. I'M JUST...
...DONE.
YAH!
NO, HELLRIDER...

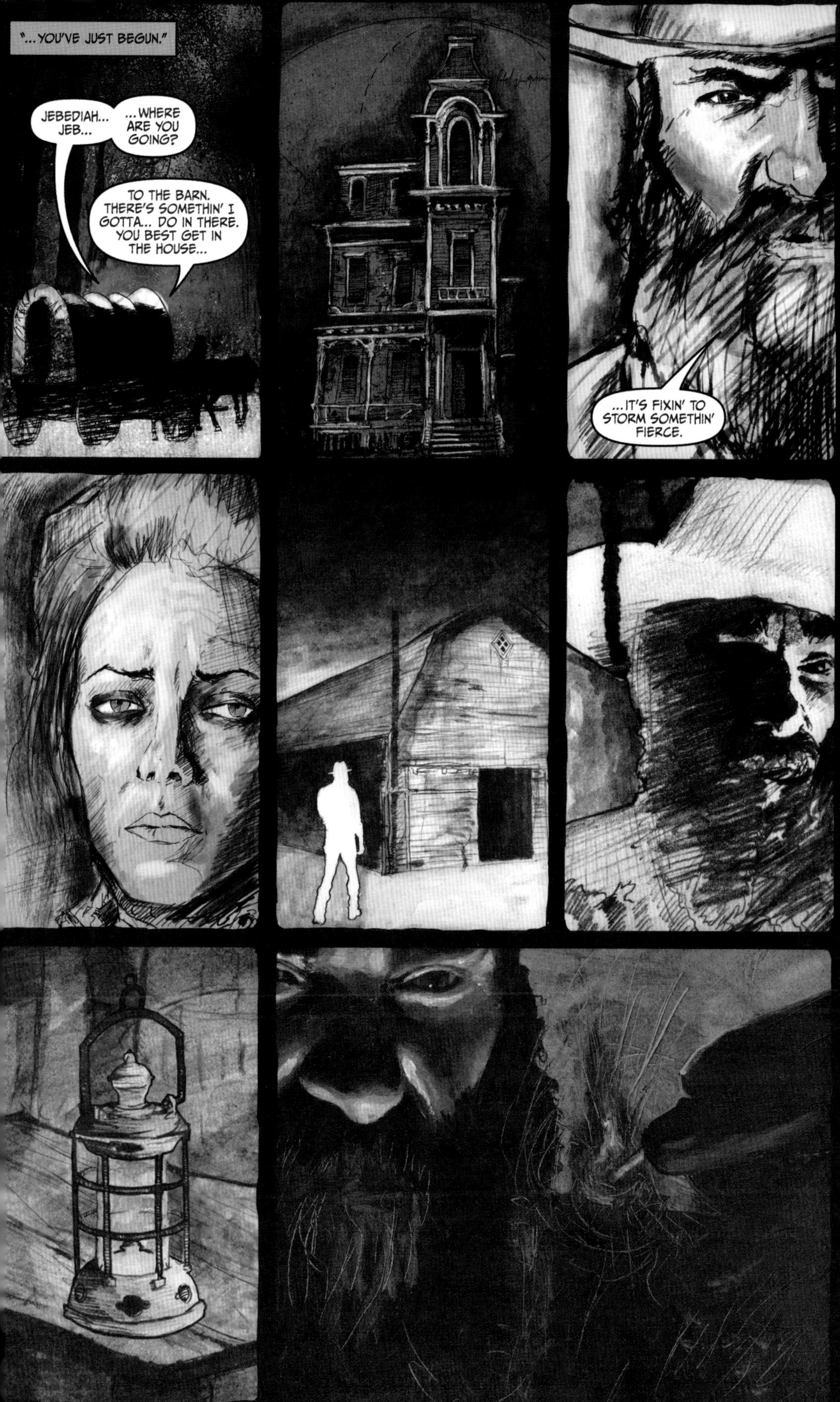
"...YOU'VE JUST BEGUN."
JEBEDIAH... JEB...
...WHERE ARE YOU GOING?
TO THE BARN. THERE'S SOMETHIN' I GOTTA... DO IN THERE. YOU BEST GET IN THE HOUSE...
...IT'S FIXIN' TO STORM SOMETHIN' FIERCE.

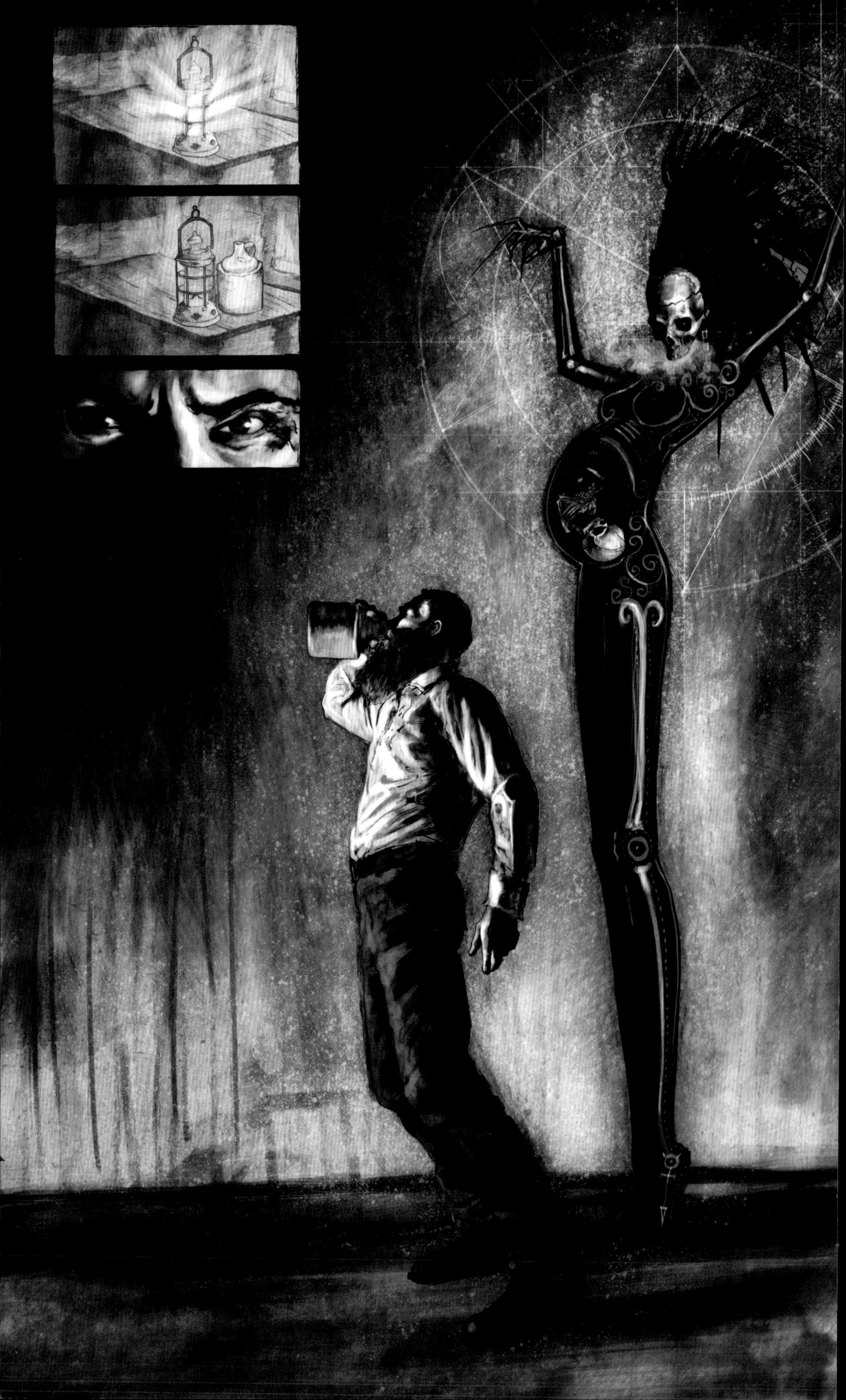

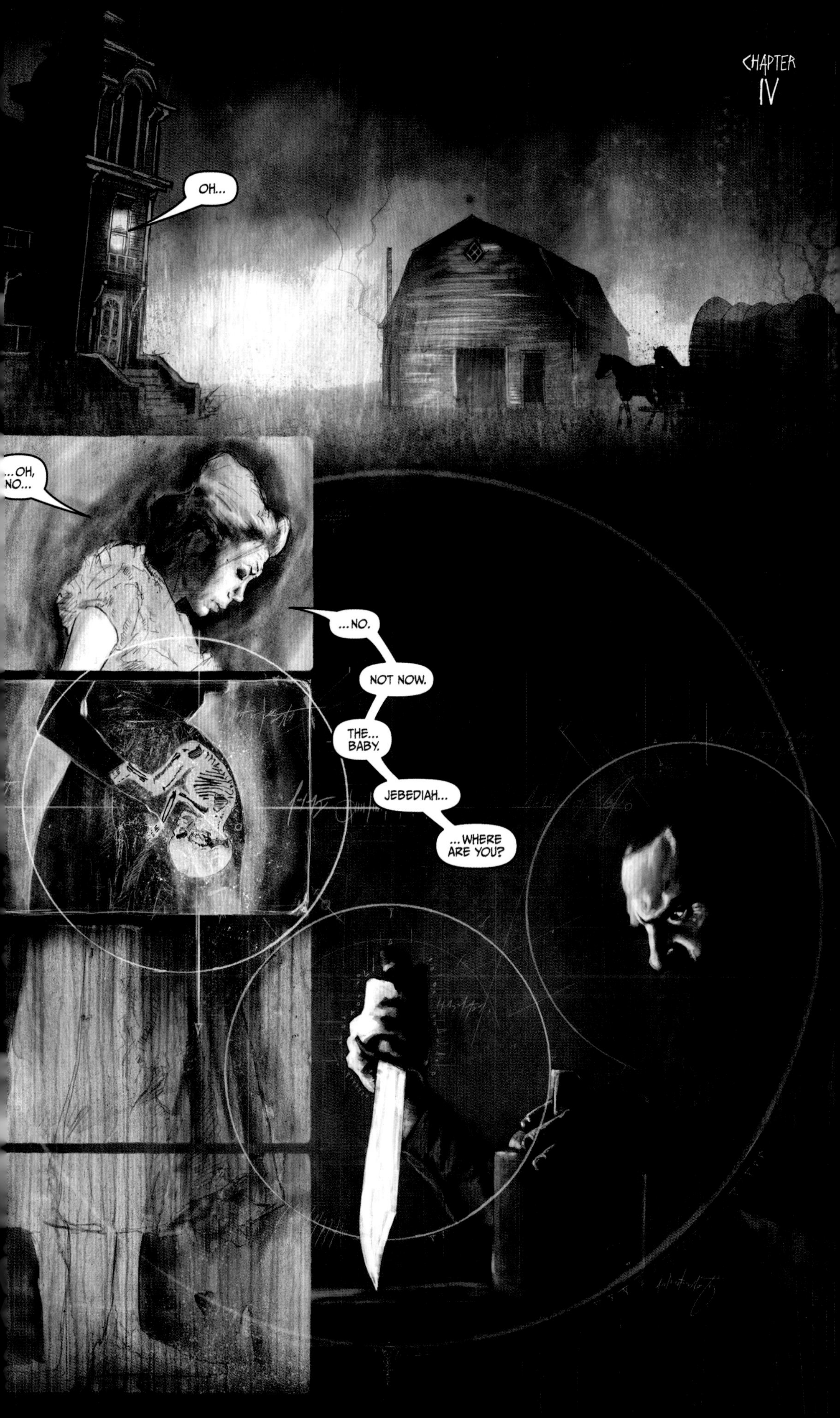
CHAPTER
IV
OH...
...OH, NO...
...NO.
NOT NOW.
THE... BABY.
JEBEDIAH...
...WHERE ARE YOU?

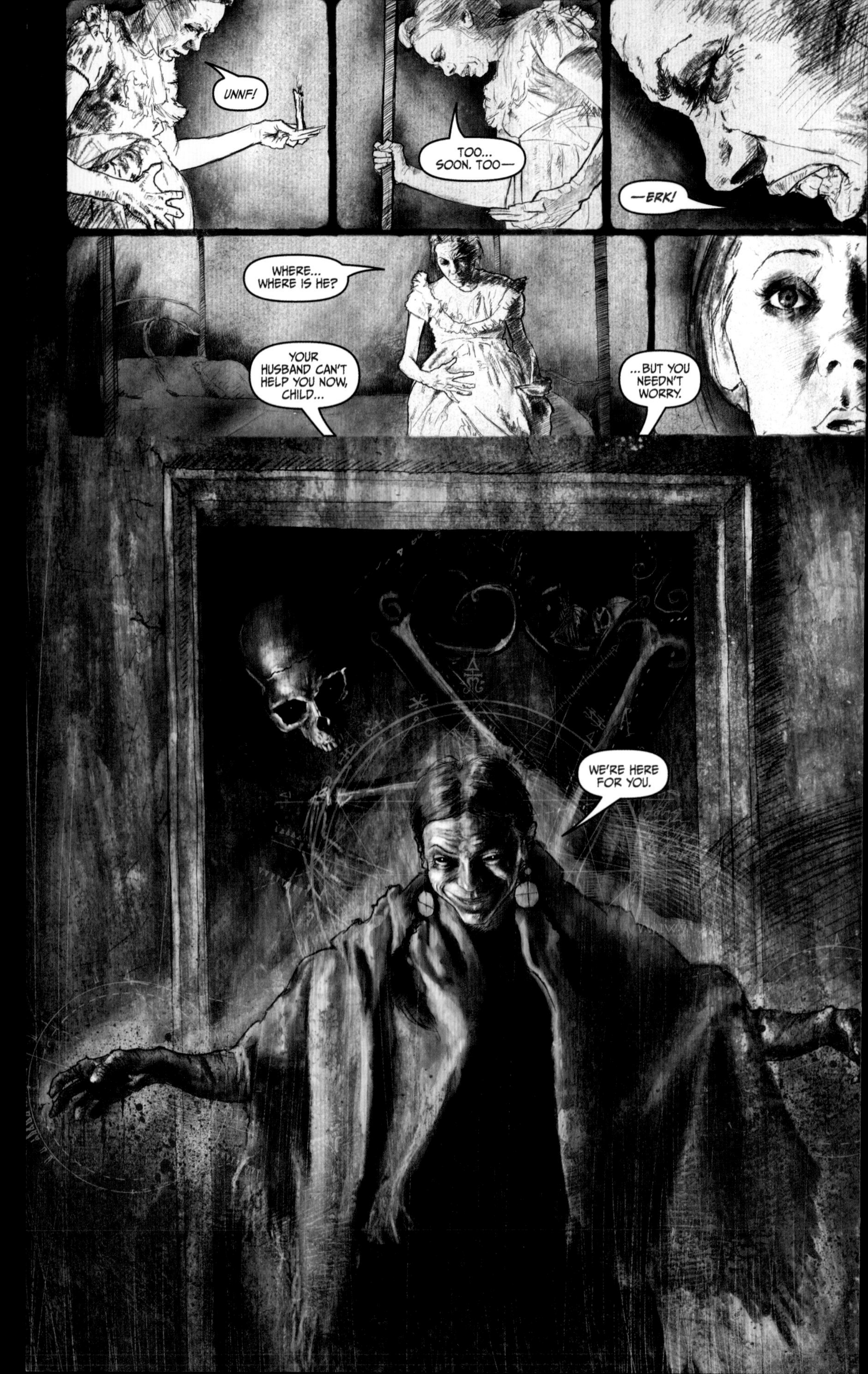

UNNF!
TOO... SOON. TOO—
—ERK!
WHERE... WHERE IS HE?
YOUR HUSBAND CAN'T HELP YOU NOW, CHILD...
...BUT YOU NEEDN'T WORRY.
WE'RE HERE FOR YOU.

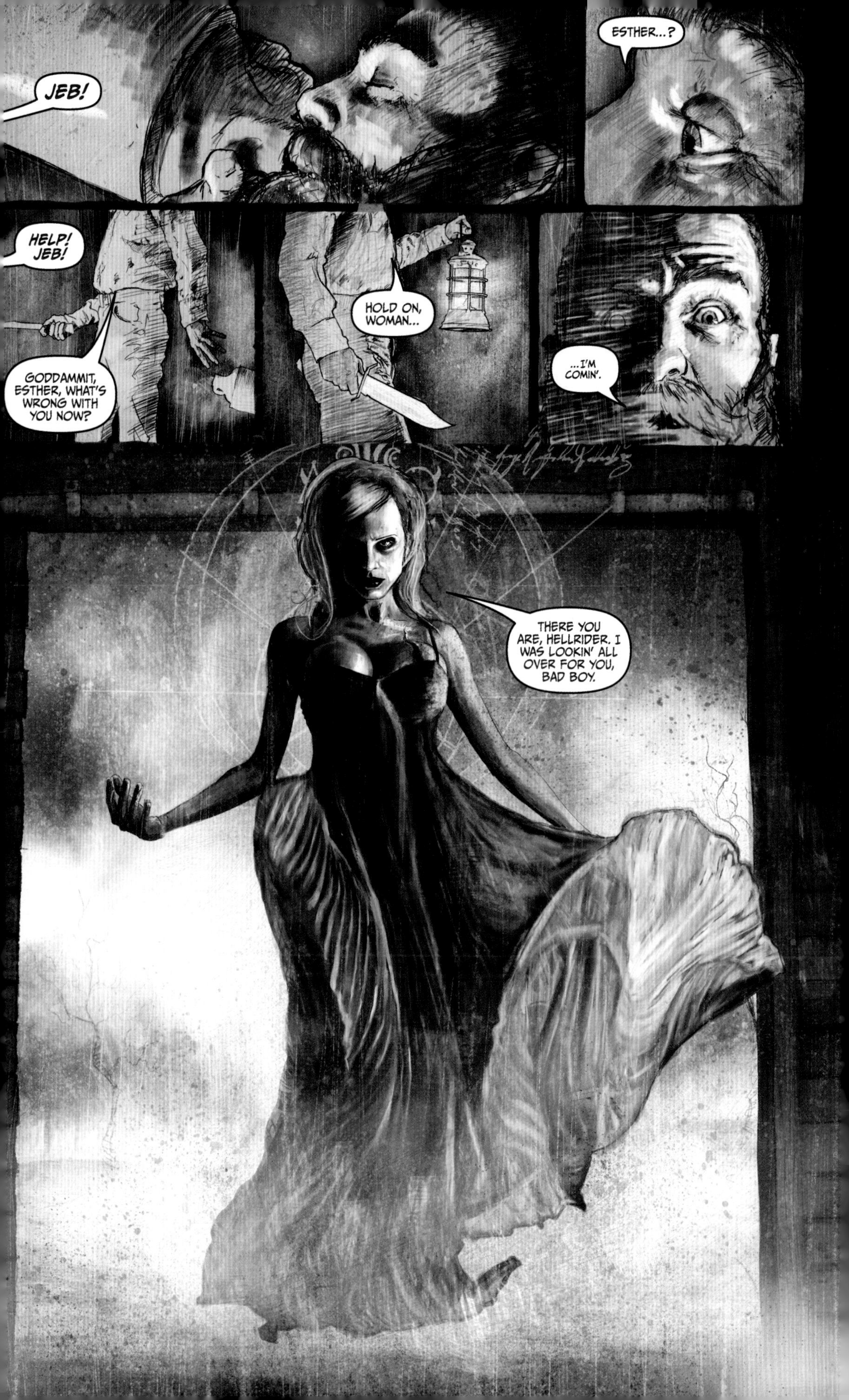
JEB!
ESTHER...?
HELP! JEB!
GODDAMMIT, ESTHER, WHAT'S WRONG WITH YOU NOW?
HOLD ON, WOMAN...
...I'M COMIN'.
THERE YOU ARE, HELLRIDER. I WAS LOOKIN' ALL OVER FOR YOU, BAD BOY.

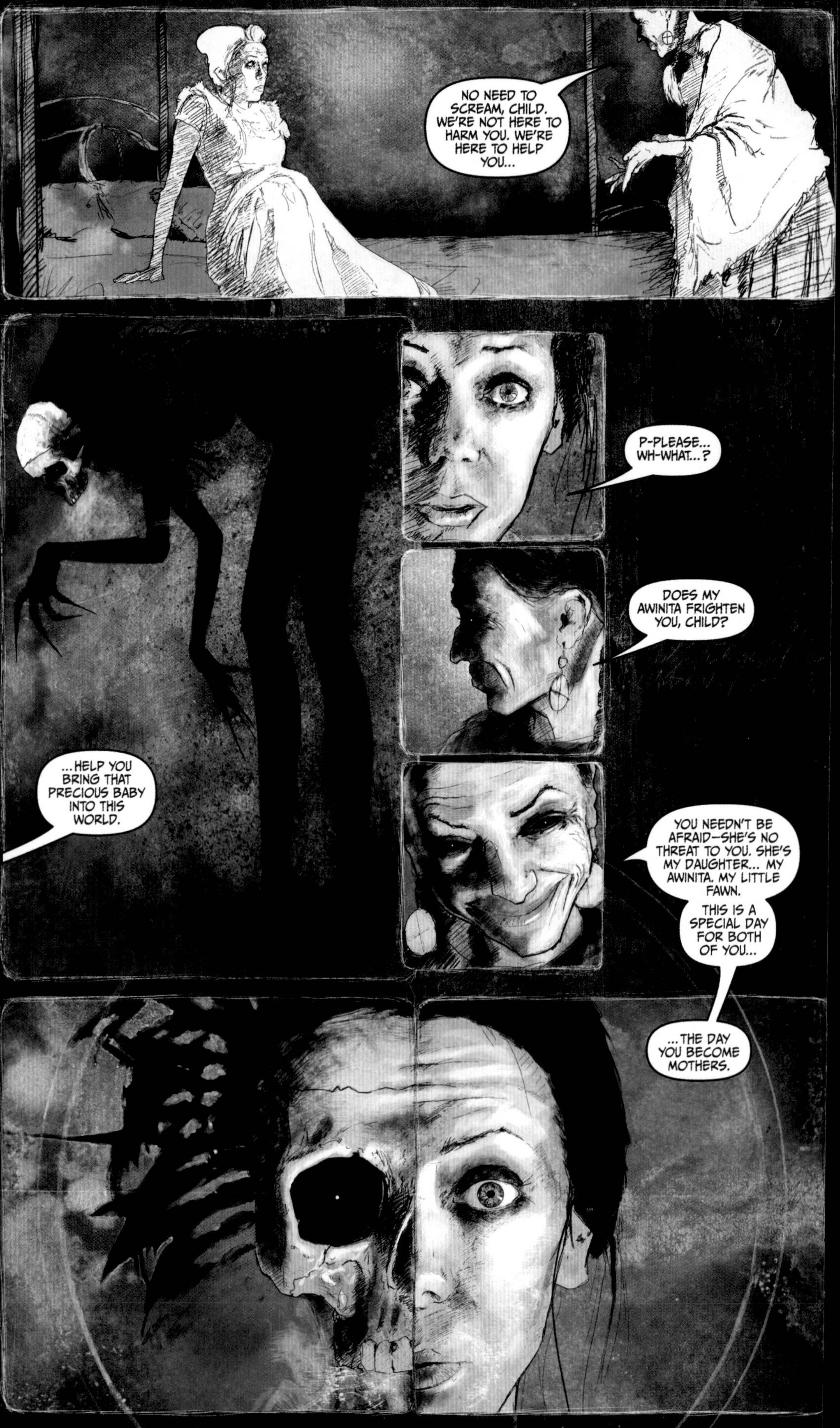
NO NEED TO SCREAM, CHILD. WE'RE NOT HERE TO HARM YOU. WE'RE HERE TO HELP YOU...
...HELP YOU BRING THAT PRECIOUS BABY INTO THIS WORLD.
P-PLEASE... WH-WHAT...?
DOES MY AWINITA FRIGHTEN YOU, CHILD?
YOU NEEDN'T BE AFRAID—SHE'S NO THREAT TO YOU. SHE'S MY DAUGHTER... MY AWINITA. MY LITTLE FAWN.
THIS IS A SPECIAL DAY FOR BOTH OF YOU...
...THE DAY YOU BECOME MOTHERS.

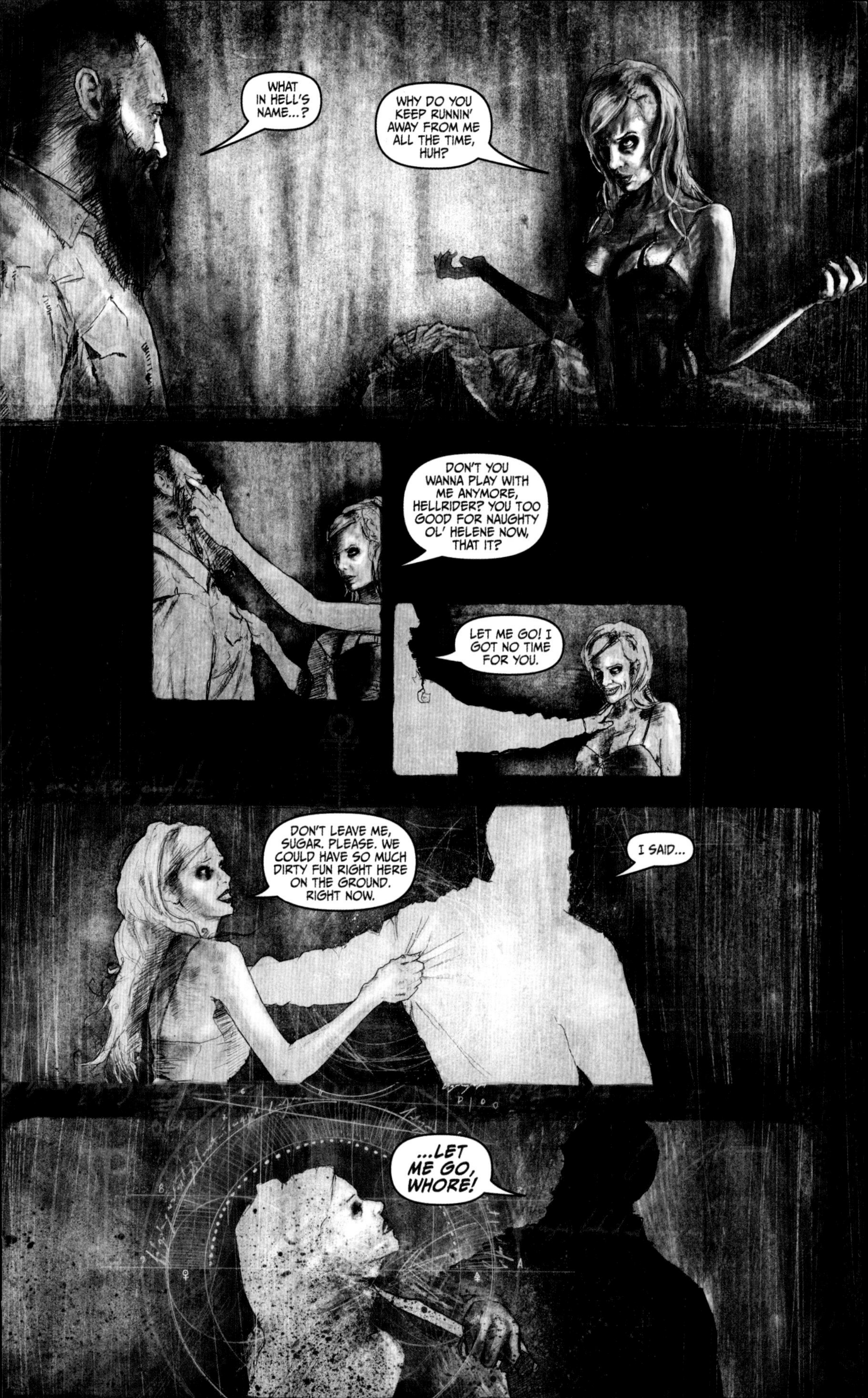
WHAT IN HELL'S NAME...?
WHY DO YOU KEEP RUNNIN' AWAY FROM ME ALL THE TIME, HUH?
DON'T YOU WANNA PLAY WITH ME ANYMORE, HELLRIDER? YOU TOO GOOD FOR NAUGHTY OL' HELENE NOW, THAT IT?
LET ME GO! I GOT NO TIME FOR YOU.
DON'T LEAVE ME, SUGAR. PLEASE. WE COULD HAVE SO MUCH DIRTY FUN RIGHT HERE ON THE GROUND. RIGHT NOW.
I SAID...
...LET ME GO, WHORE!

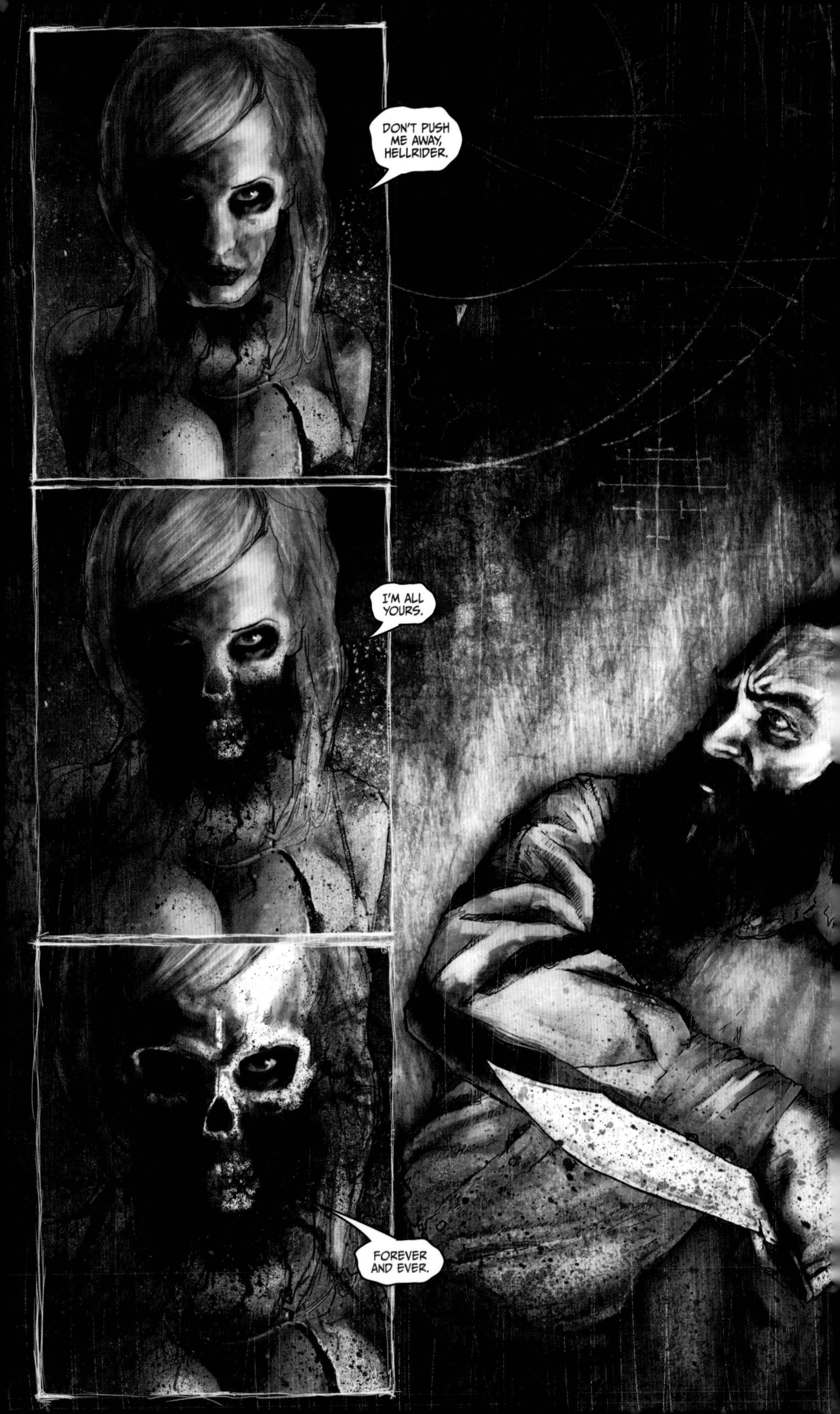
DON'T PUSH ME AWAY, HELLRIDER.
I'M ALL YOURS.
FOREVER AND EVER.

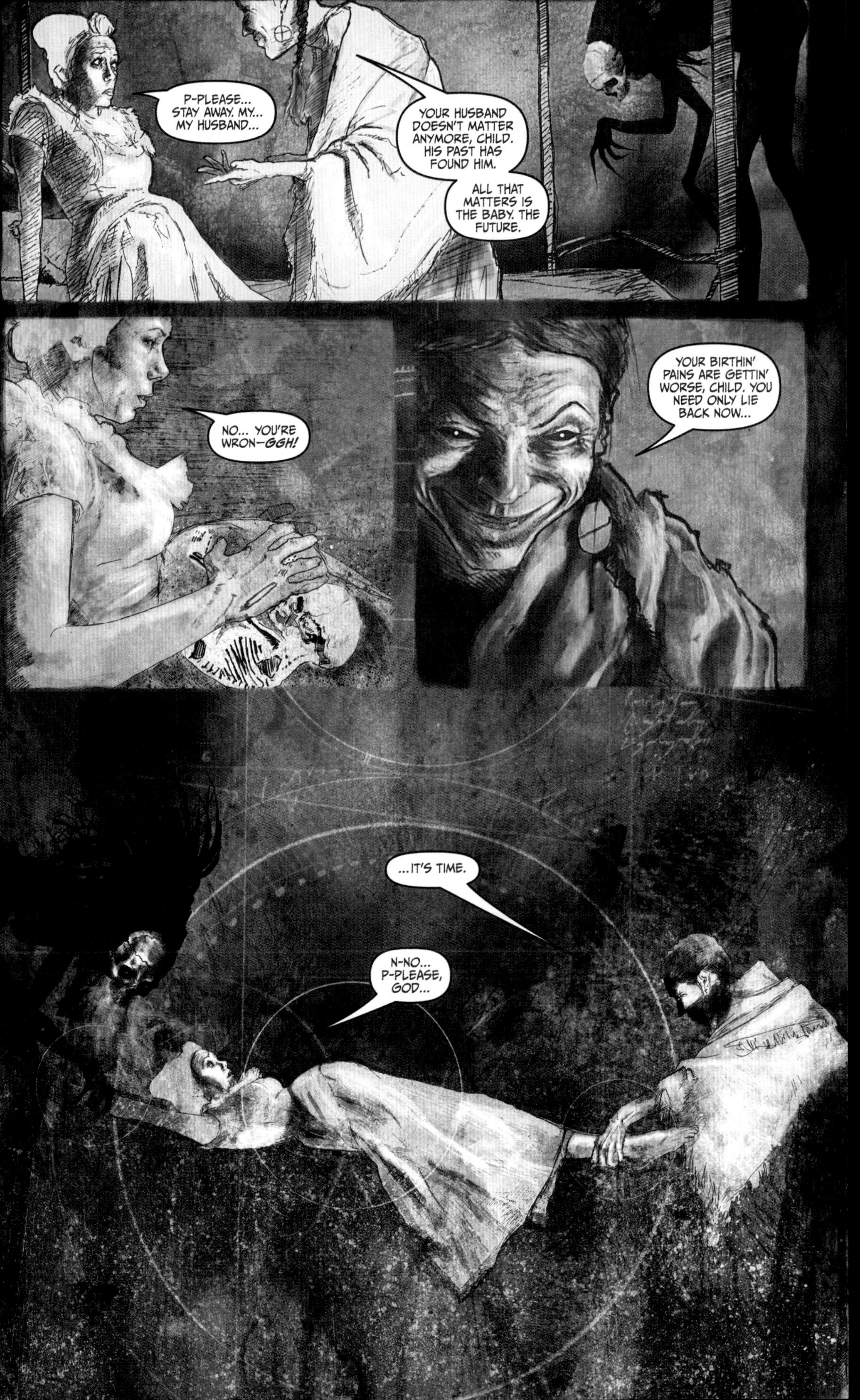
P-PLEASE... STAY AWAY. MY... MY HUSBAND...
YOUR HUSBAND DOESN'T MATTER ANYMORE, CHILD. HIS PAST HAS FOUND HIM.
ALL THAT MATTERS IS THE BABY. THE FUTURE.
NO... YOU'RE WRON—GGH!
YOUR BIRTHIN' PAINS ARE GETTIN' WORSE, CHILD. YOU NEED ONLY LIE BACK NOW...
...IT'S TIME.
N-NO... P-PLEASE, GOD...

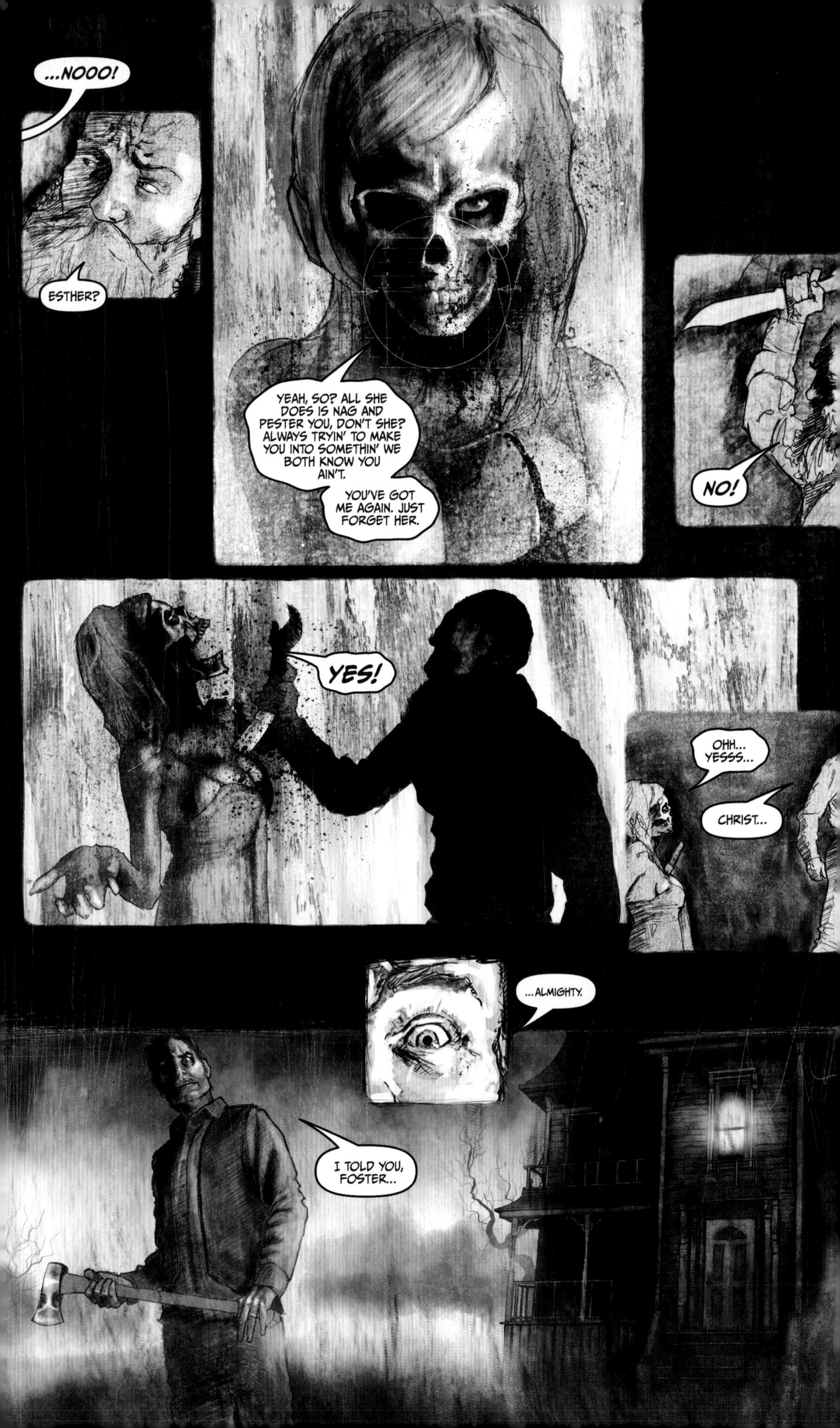
...NOOO!
ESTHER?
YEAH, SO? ALL SHE DOES IS NAG AND PESTER YOU, DON'T SHE? ALWAYS TRYIN' TO MAKE YOU INTO SOMETHIN' WE BOTH KNOW YOU AIN'T.
YOU'VE GOT ME AGAIN. JUST FORGET HER.
NO!
YES!
OHH... YESSS...
CHRIST...
...ALMIGHTY.
I TOLD YOU, FOSTER...

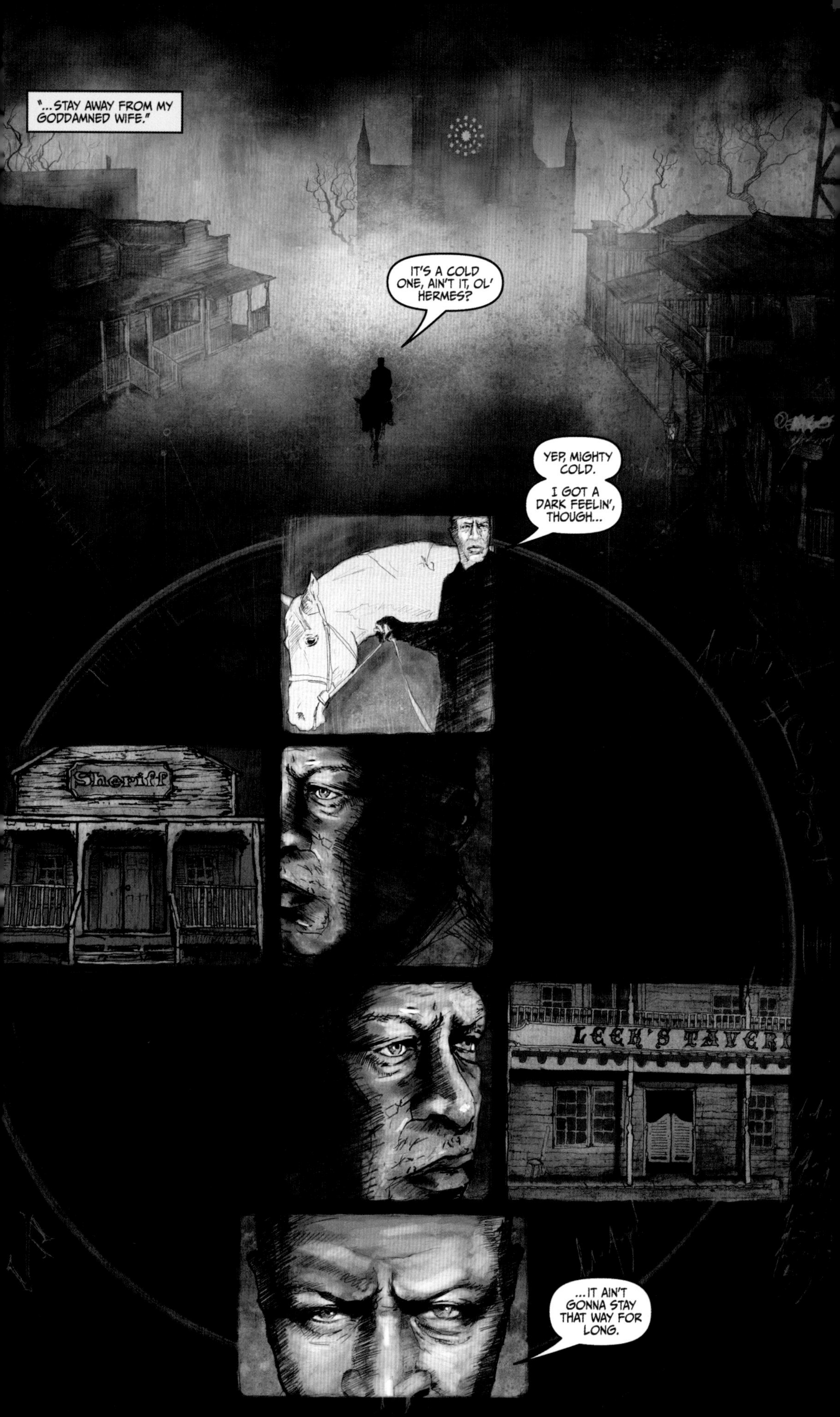
"...STAY AWAY FROM MY GODDAMNED WIFE."
IT'S A COLD ONE, AIN'T IT, OL' HERMES?
YEP, MIGHTY COLD.
I GOT A DARK FEELIN', THOUGH...
Sheriff
LEEK'S TAVER
...IT AIN'T GONNA STAY THAT WAY FOR LONG.

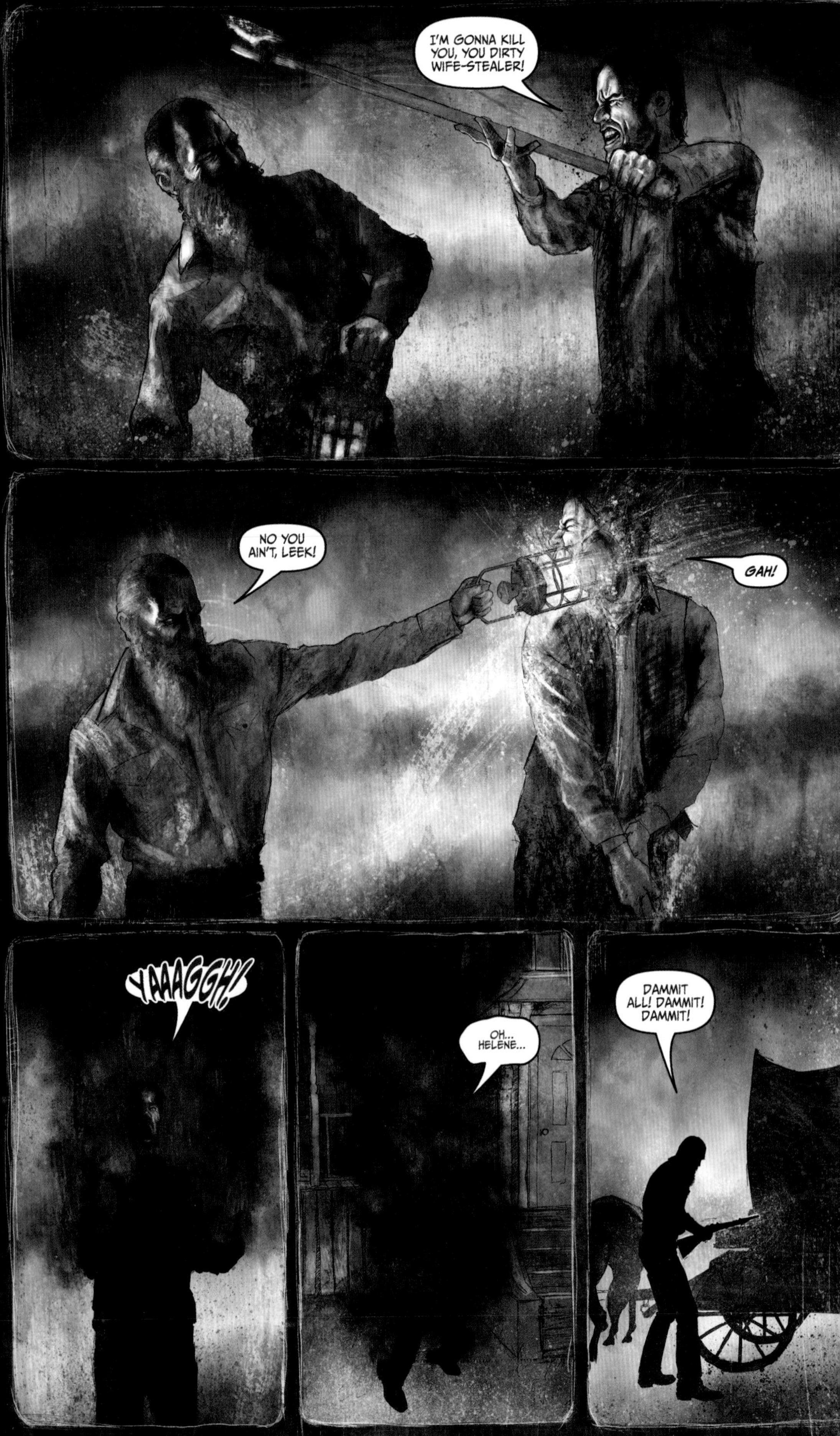
I'M GONNA KILL YOU, YOU DIRTY WIFE-STEALER!
NO YOU AIN'T, LEEK!
GAH!
YAAAGGH!
OH... HELENE...
DAMMIT ALL! DAMMIT! DAMMIT!

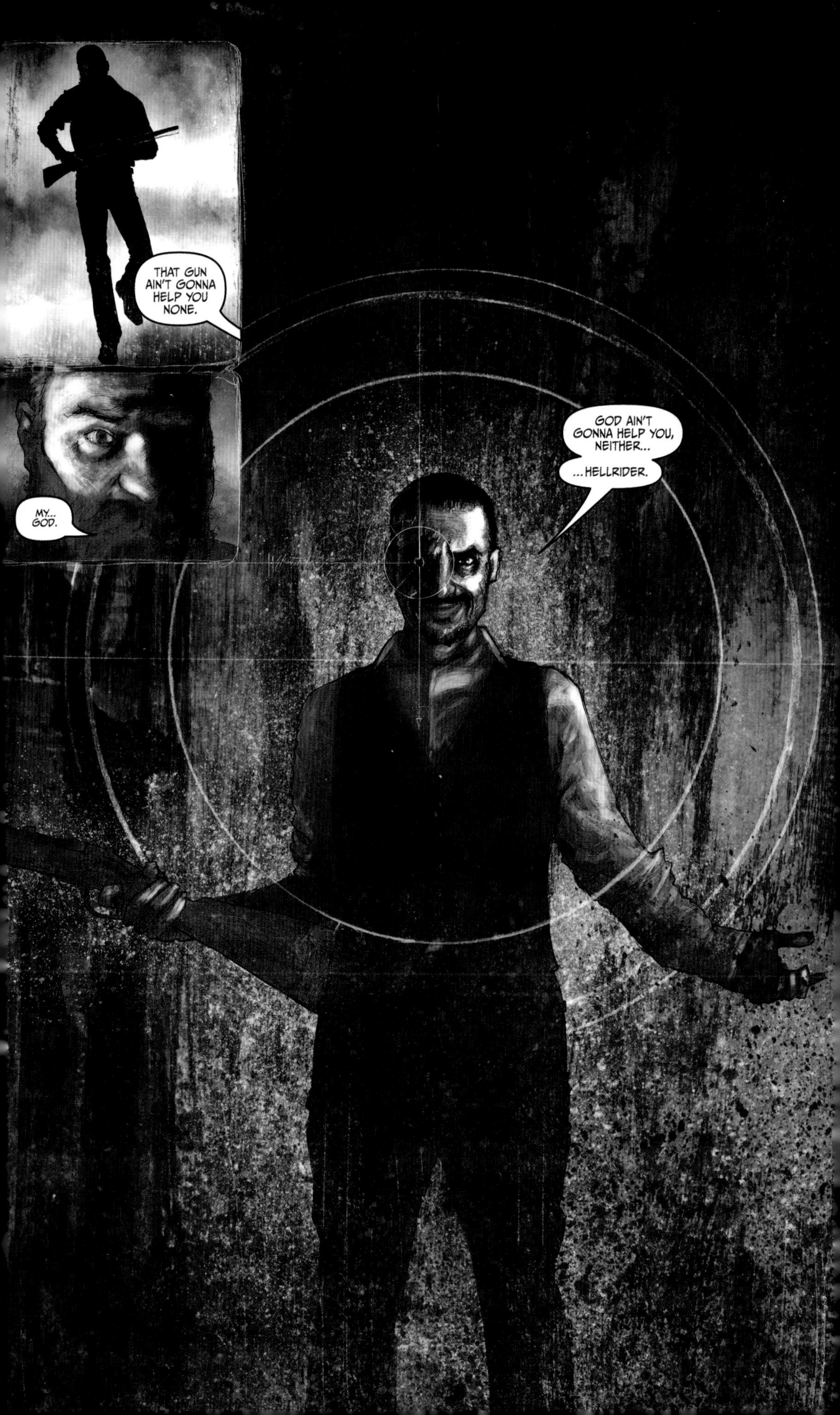
THAT GUN AIN'T GONNA HELP YOU NONE.
MY... GOD.
GOD AIN'T GONNA HELP YOU, NEITHER...
...HELLRIDER.

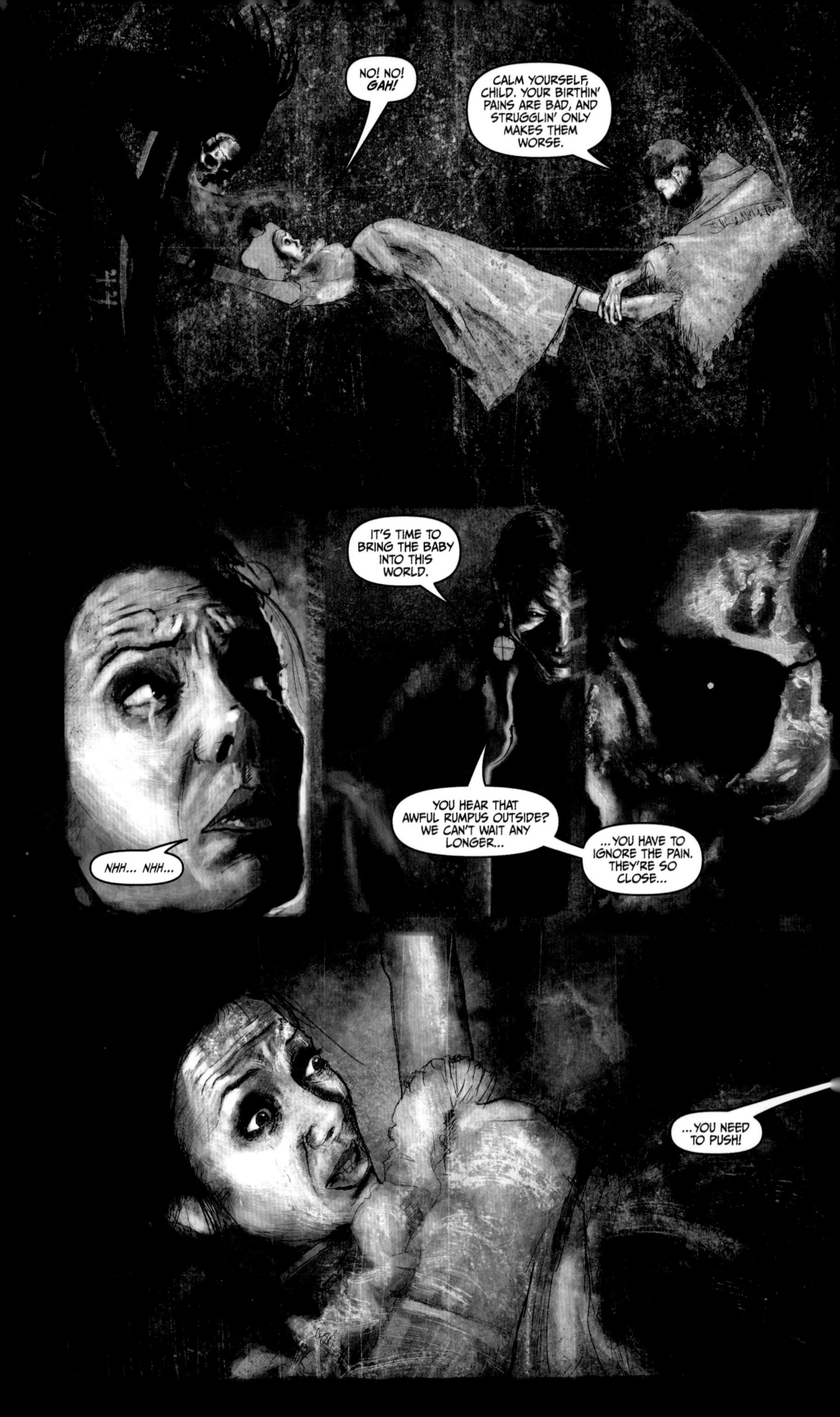
NO! NO! GAH!
CALM YOURSELF, CHILD. YOUR BIRTHIN' PAINS ARE BAD, AND STRUGGLIN' ONLY MAKES THEM WORSE.
NHH... NHH...
IT'S TIME TO BRING THE BABY INTO THIS WORLD.
YOU HEAR THAT AWFUL RUMPUS OUTSIDE? WE CAN'T WAIT ANY LONGER...
...YOU HAVE TO IGNORE THE PAIN. THEY'RE SO CLOSE...
...YOU NEED TO PUSH!

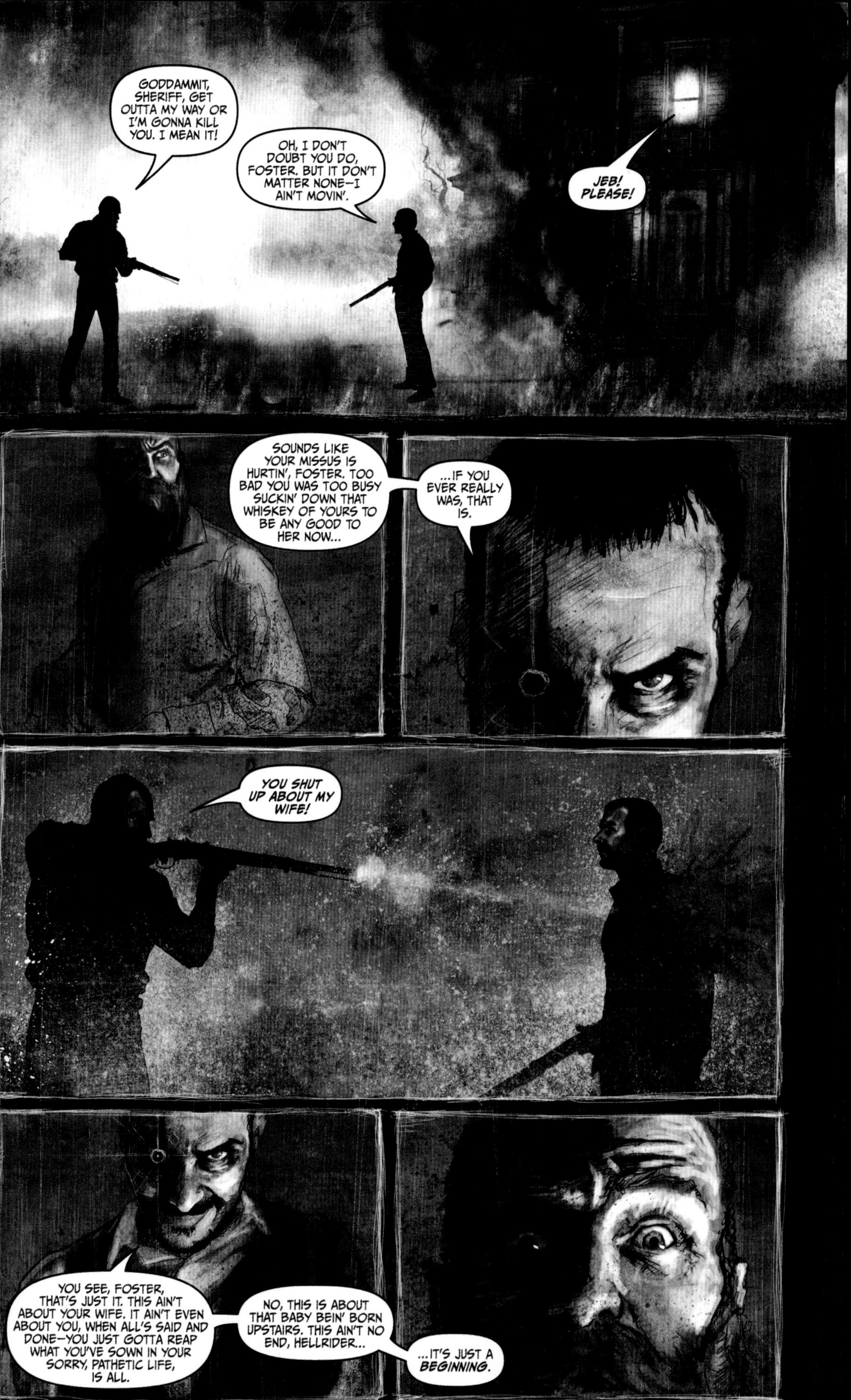
GODDAMMIT, SHERIFF, GET OUTTA MY WAY OR I'M GONNA KILL YOU. I MEAN IT!
OH, I DON'T DOUBT YOU DO, FOSTER. BUT IT DON'T MATTER NONE—I AIN'T MOVIN'.
JEB! PLEASE!
SOUNDS LIKE YOUR MISSUS IS HURTIN', FOSTER. TOO BAD YOU WAS TOO BUSY SUCKIN' DOWN THAT WHISKEY OF YOURS TO BE ANY GOOD TO HER NOW...
...IF YOU EVER REALLY WAS, THAT IS.
YOU SHUT UP ABOUT MY WIFE!
YOU SEE, FOSTER, THAT'S JUST IT. THIS AIN'T ABOUT YOUR WIFE. IT AIN'T EVEN ABOUT YOU, WHEN ALL'S SAID AND DONE—YOU JUST GOTTA REAP WHAT YOU'VE SOWN IN YOUR SORRY, PATHETIC LIFE, IS ALL.
NO, THIS IS ABOUT THAT BABY BEIN' BORN UPSTAIRS. THIS AIN'T NO END, HELLRIDER...
...IT'S JUST A BEGINNING.

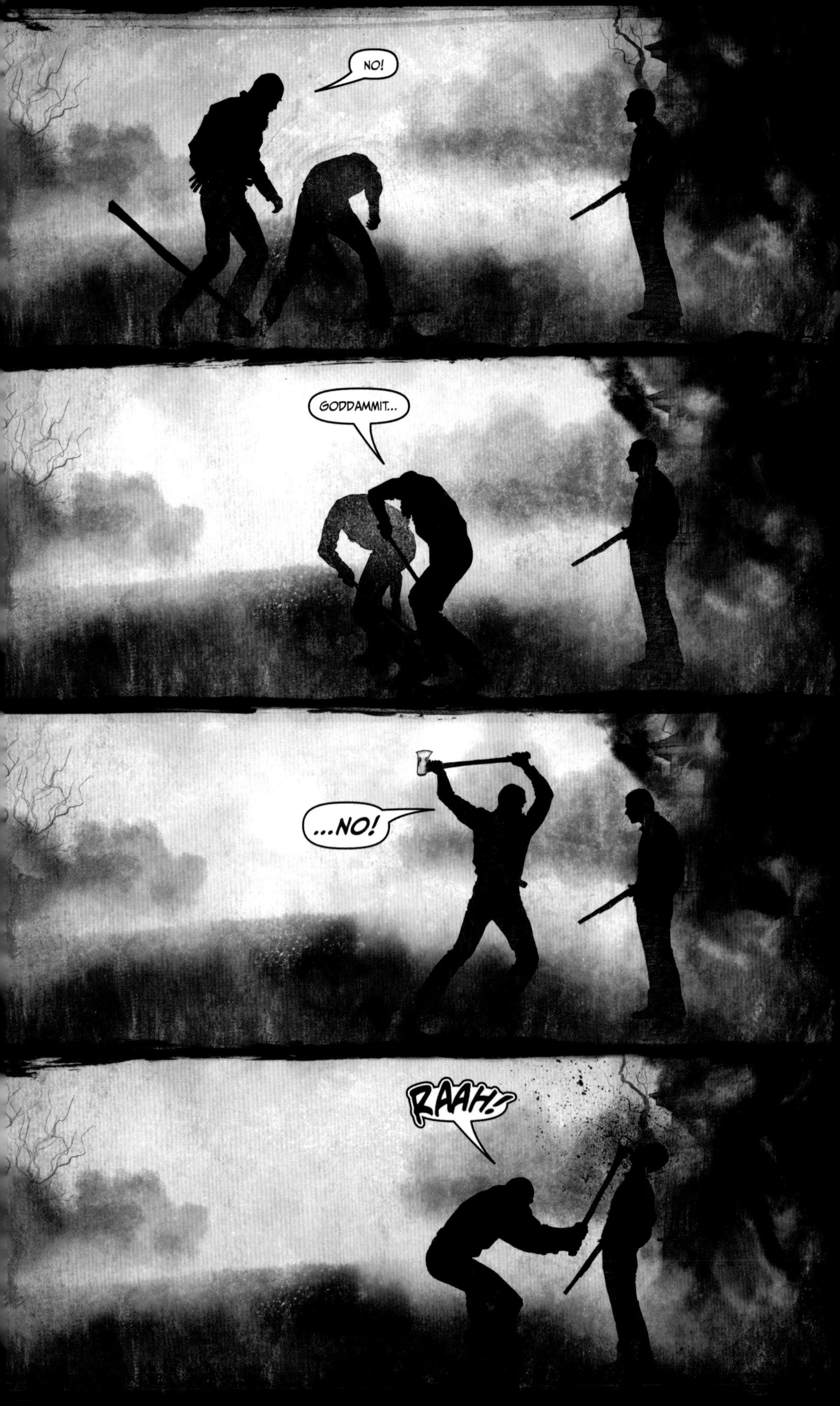
NO!
GODDAMMIT...
...NO!
RAAH!

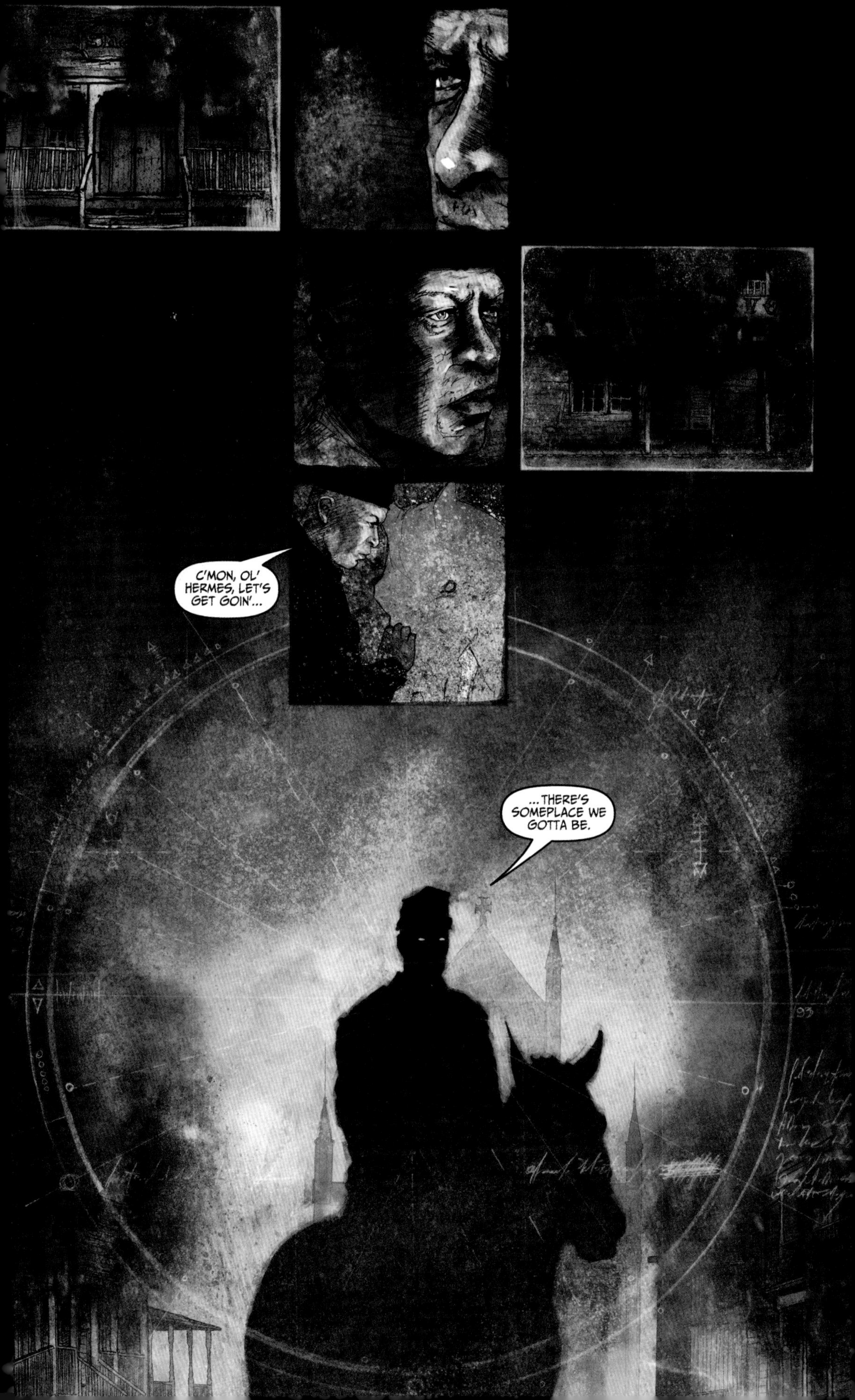
C'MON, OL' HERMES, LET'S GET GOIN'...
...THERE'S SOMEPLACE WE GOTTA BE.

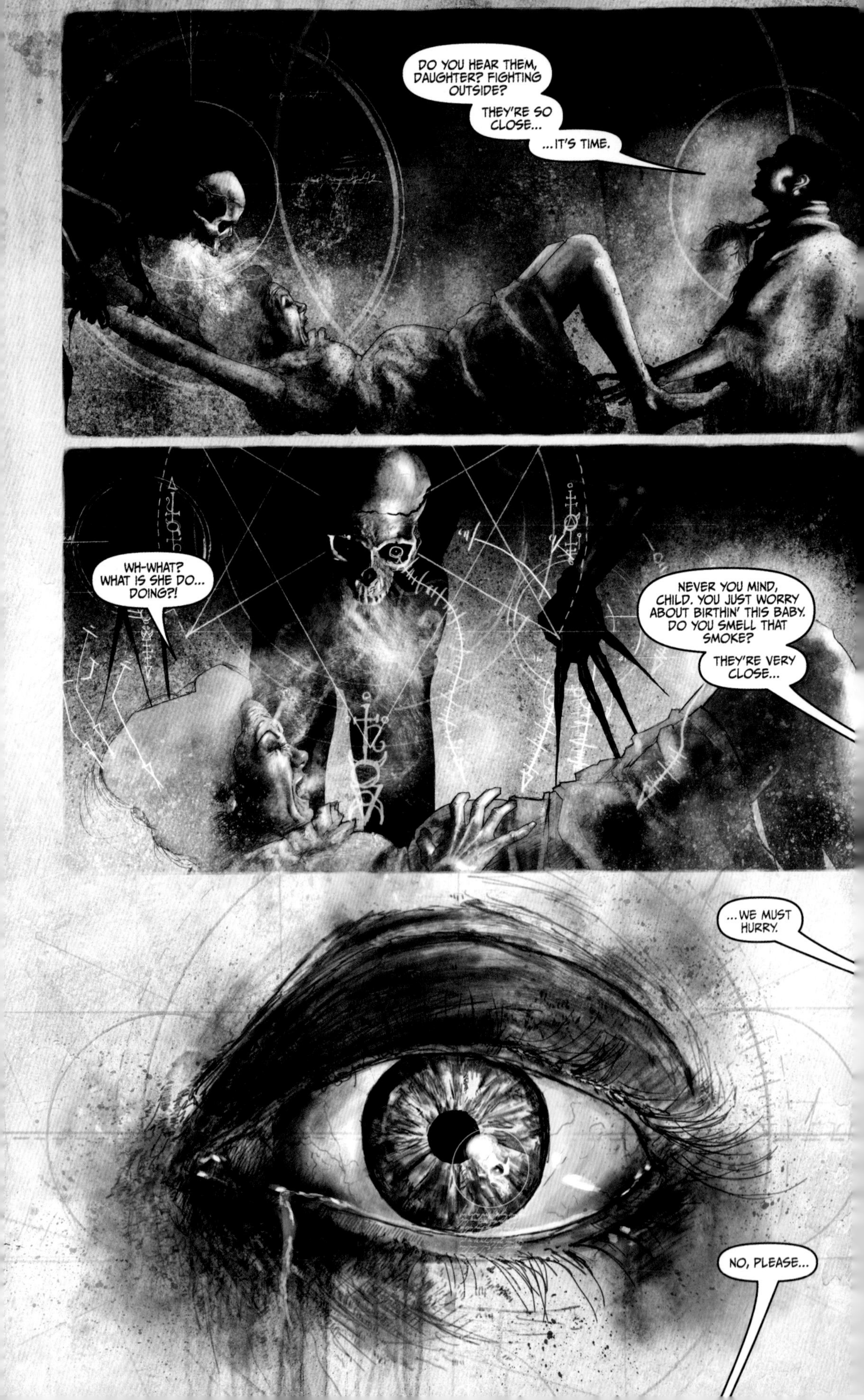
DO YOU HEAR THEM, DAUGHTER? FIGHTING OUTSIDE?
THEY'RE SO CLOSE...
...IT'S TIME.
WH-WHAT? WHAT IS SHE DO... DOING?!
NEVER YOU MIND, CHILD. YOU JUST WORRY ABOUT BIRTHIN' THIS BABY. DO YOU SMELL THAT SMOKE?
THEY'RE VERY CLOSE...
...WE MUST HURRY.
NO, PLEASE...

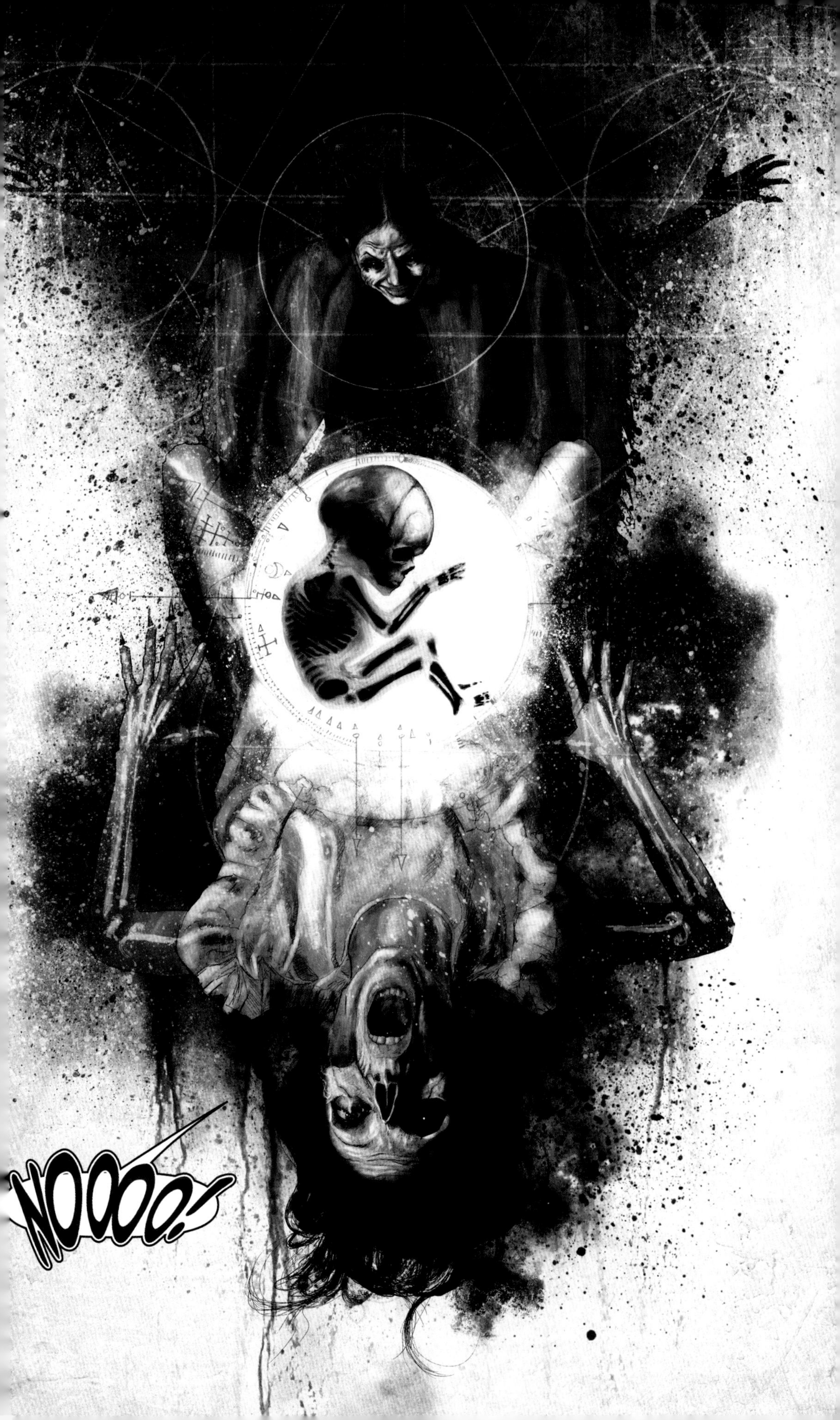
NOOOO!

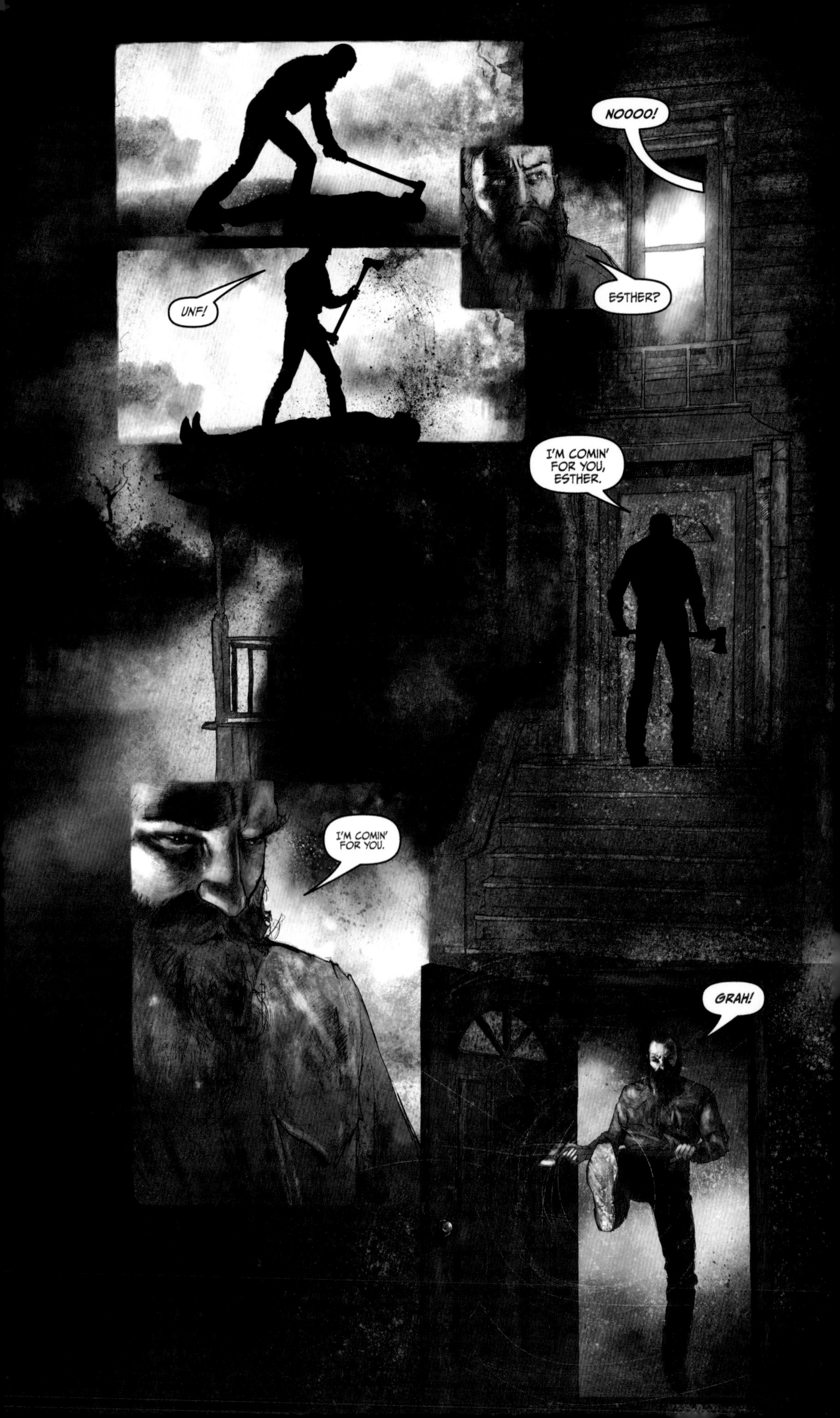
NOOOO!
UNF!
ESTHER?
I'M COMIN' FOR YOU, ESTHER.
I'M COMIN' FOR YOU.
GRAH!

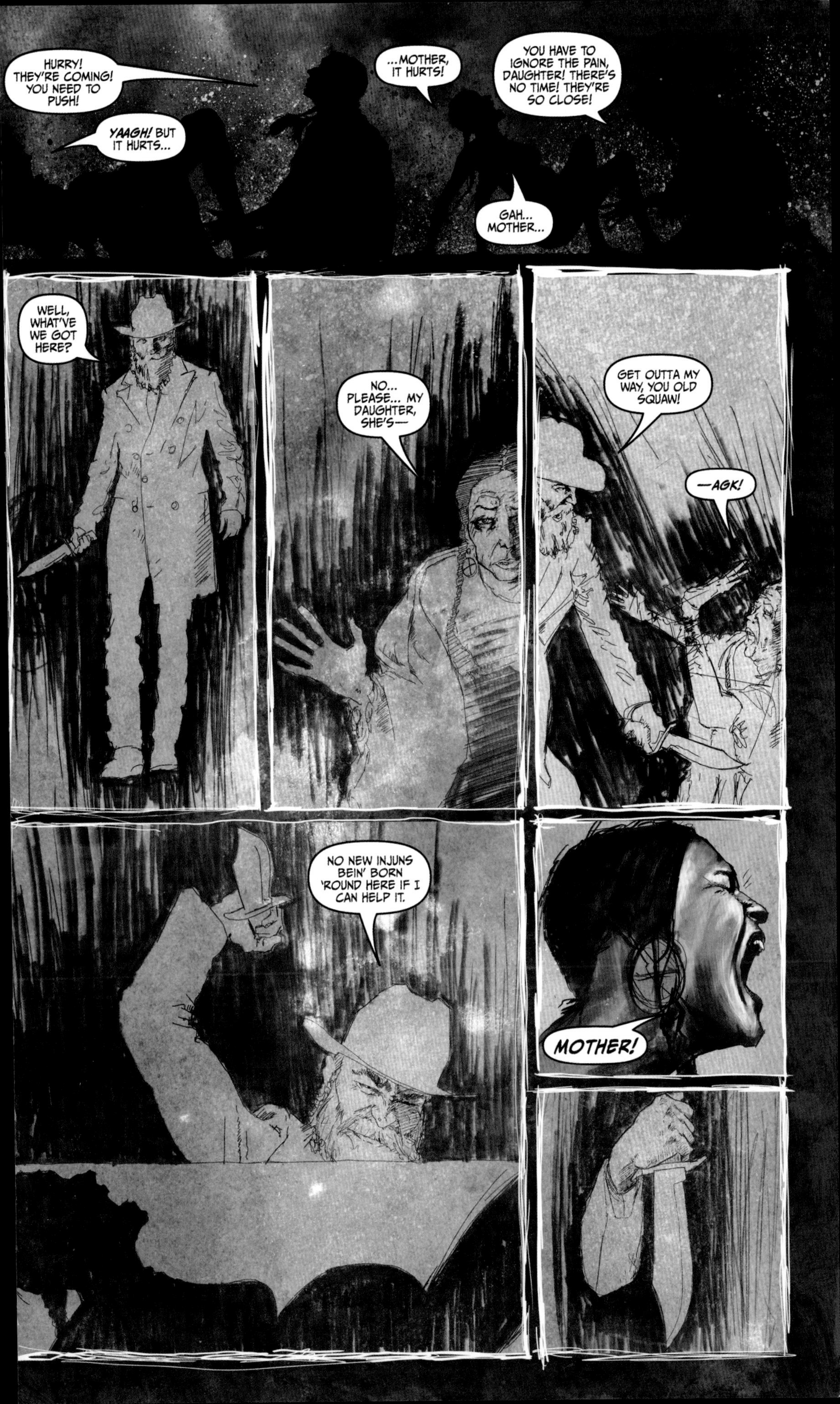
HURRY! THEY'RE COMING! YOU NEED TO PUSH!
YAAGH! BUT IT HURTS...
...MOTHER, IT HURTS!
YOU HAVE TO IGNORE THE PAIN, DAUGHTER! THERE'S NO TIME! THEY'RE SO CLOSE!
GAH... MOTHER...
WELL, WHAT'VE WE GOT HERE?
NO... PLEASE... MY DAUGHTER, SHE'S—
GET OUTTA MY WAY, YOU OLD SQUAW!
—AGK!
NO NEW INJUNS BEIN' BORN 'ROUND HERE IF I CAN HELP IT.
MOTHER!

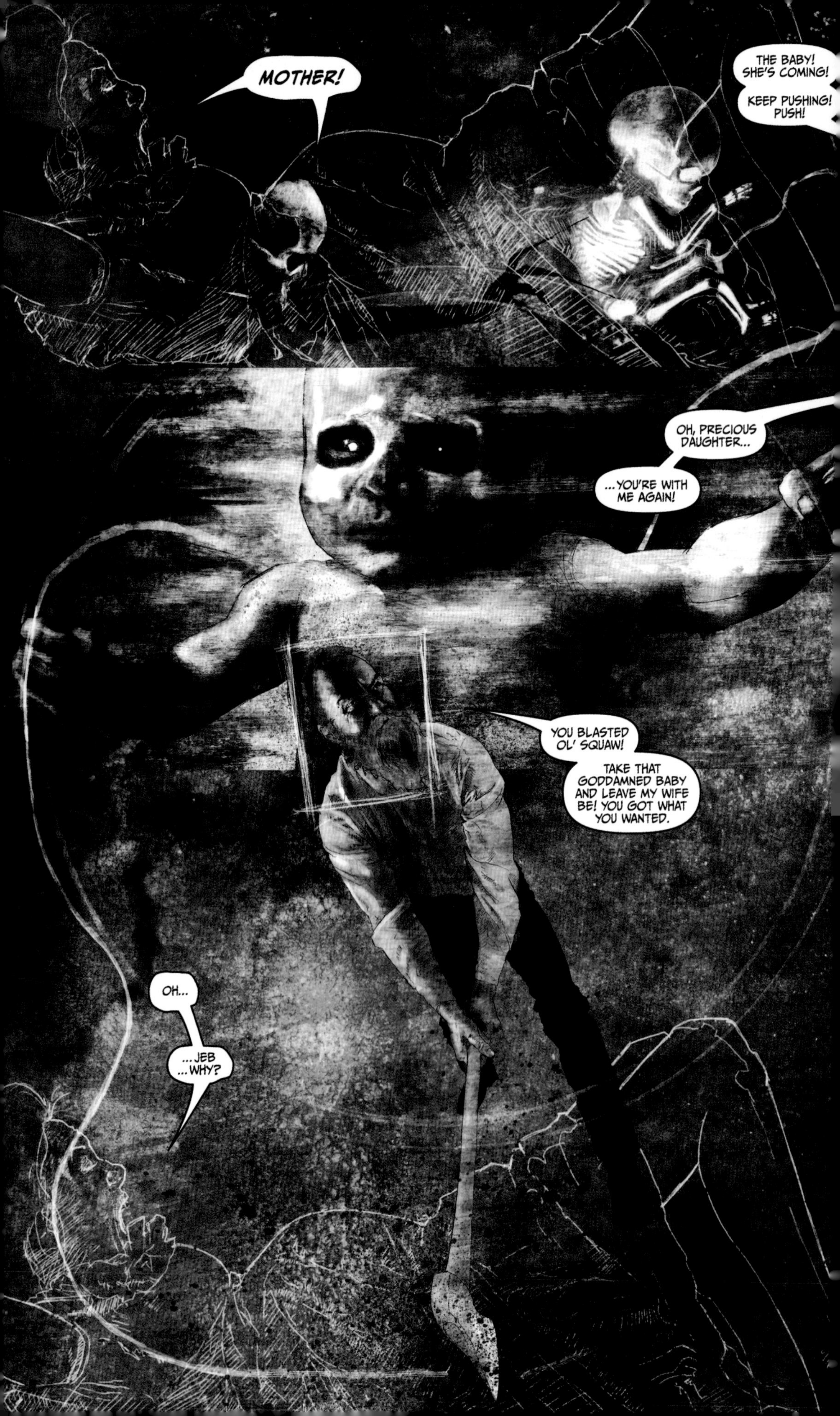
MOTHER!
THE BABY! SHE'S COMING!
KEEP PUSHING! PUSH!
OH, PRECIOUS DAUGHTER...
...YOU'RE WITH ME AGAIN!
YOU BLASTED OL' SQUAW!
TAKE THAT GODDAMNED BABY AND LEAVE MY WIFE BE! YOU GOT WHAT YOU WANTED.
OH...
...JEB ...WHY?

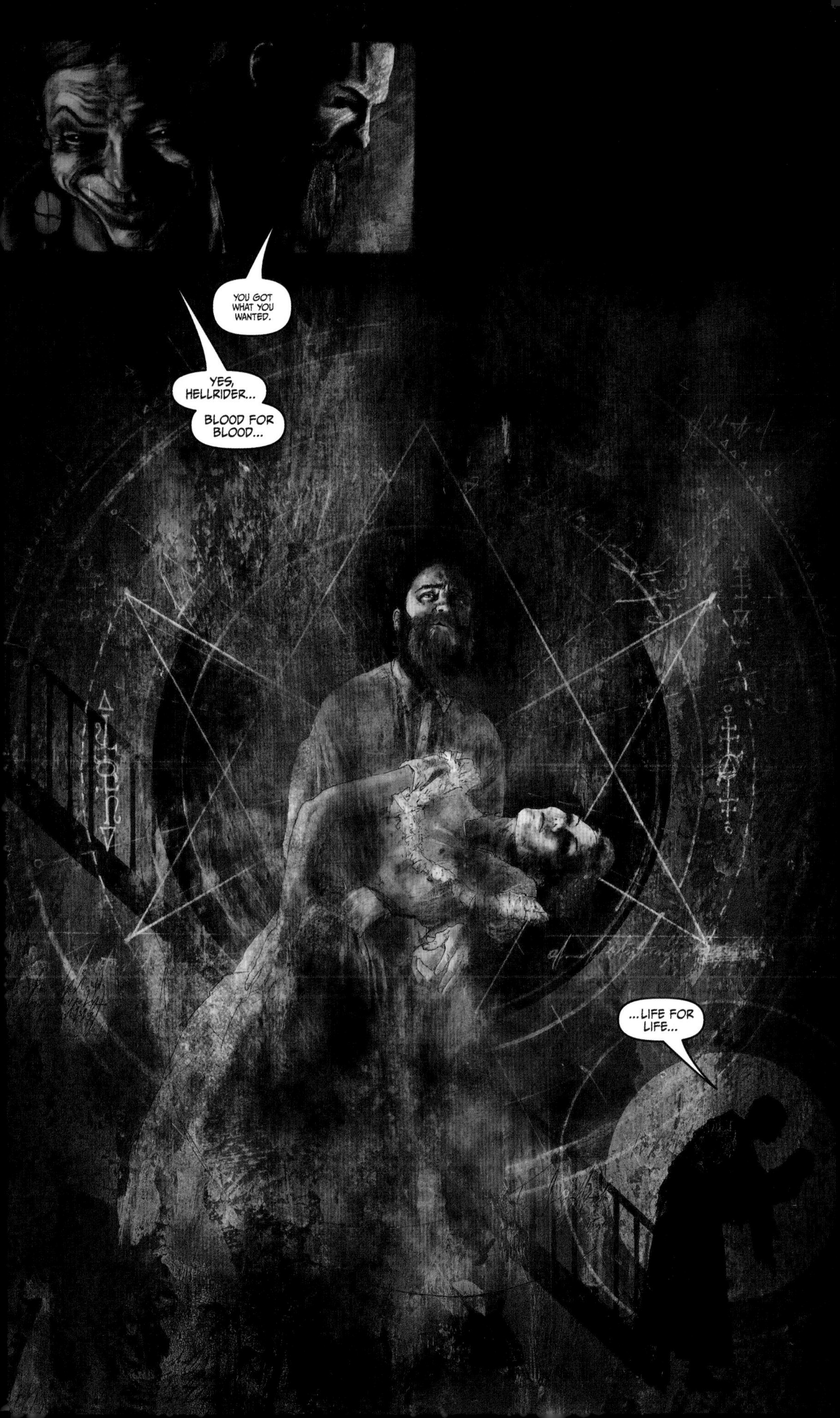
YOU GOT WHAT YOU WANTED.
YES, HELLRIDER...
BLOOD FOR BLOOD...
...LIFE FOR LIFE...

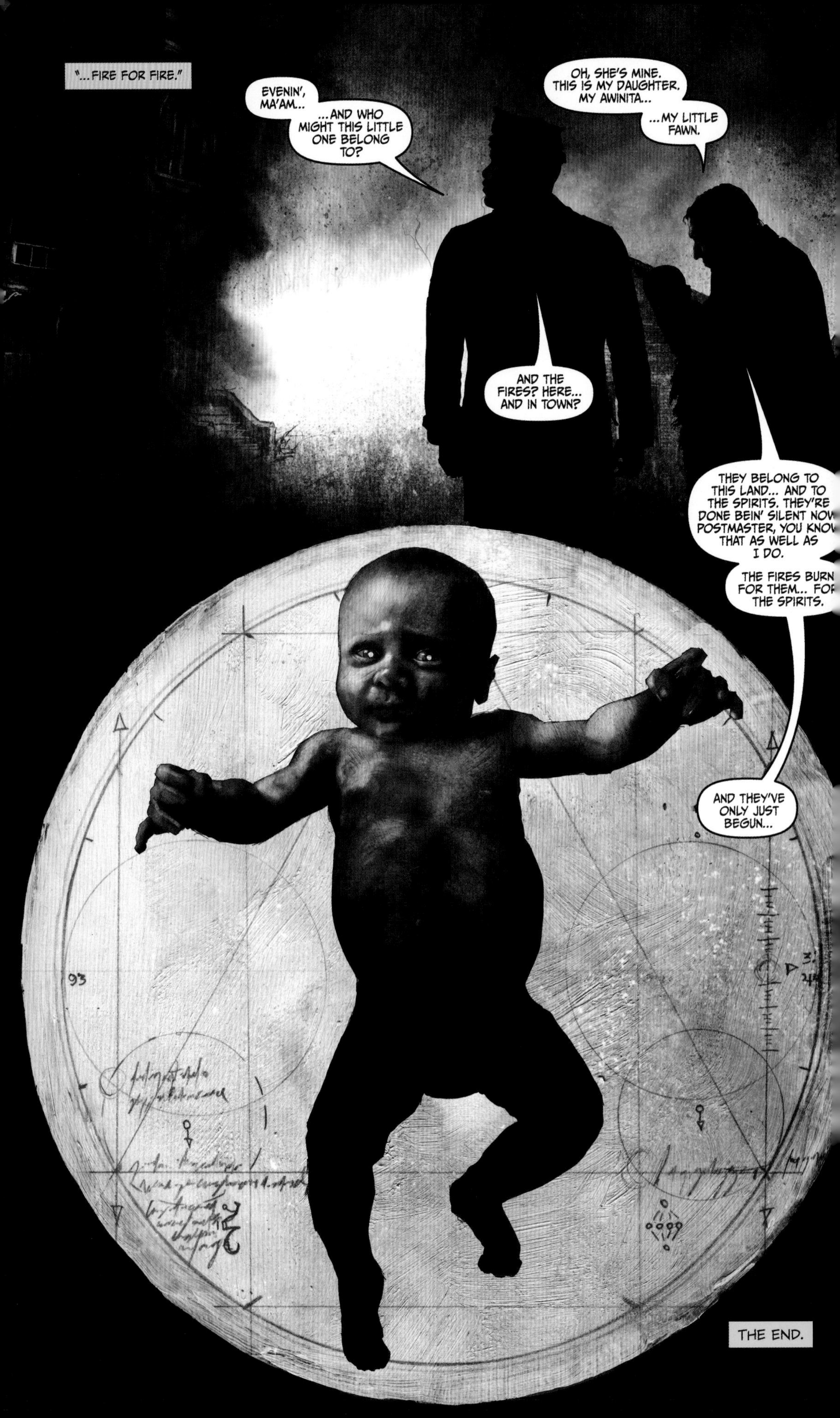
"...FIRE FOR FIRE."
EVENIN', MA'AM...
...AND WHO MIGHT THIS LITTLE ONE BELONG TO?
OH, SHE'S MINE. THIS IS MY DAUGHTER. MY AWINITA...
...MY LITTLE FAWN.
AND THE FIRES? HERE... AND IN TOWN?
THEY BELONG TO THIS LAND... AND TO THE SPIRITS. THEY'RE DONE BEIN' SILENT NOW POSTMASTER, YOU KNOW THAT AS WELL AS I DO.
THE FIRES BURN FOR THEM... FOR THE SPIRITS.
AND THEY'VE ONLY JUST BEGUN...
THE END.

Art Gallery

ART BY MENTON 3

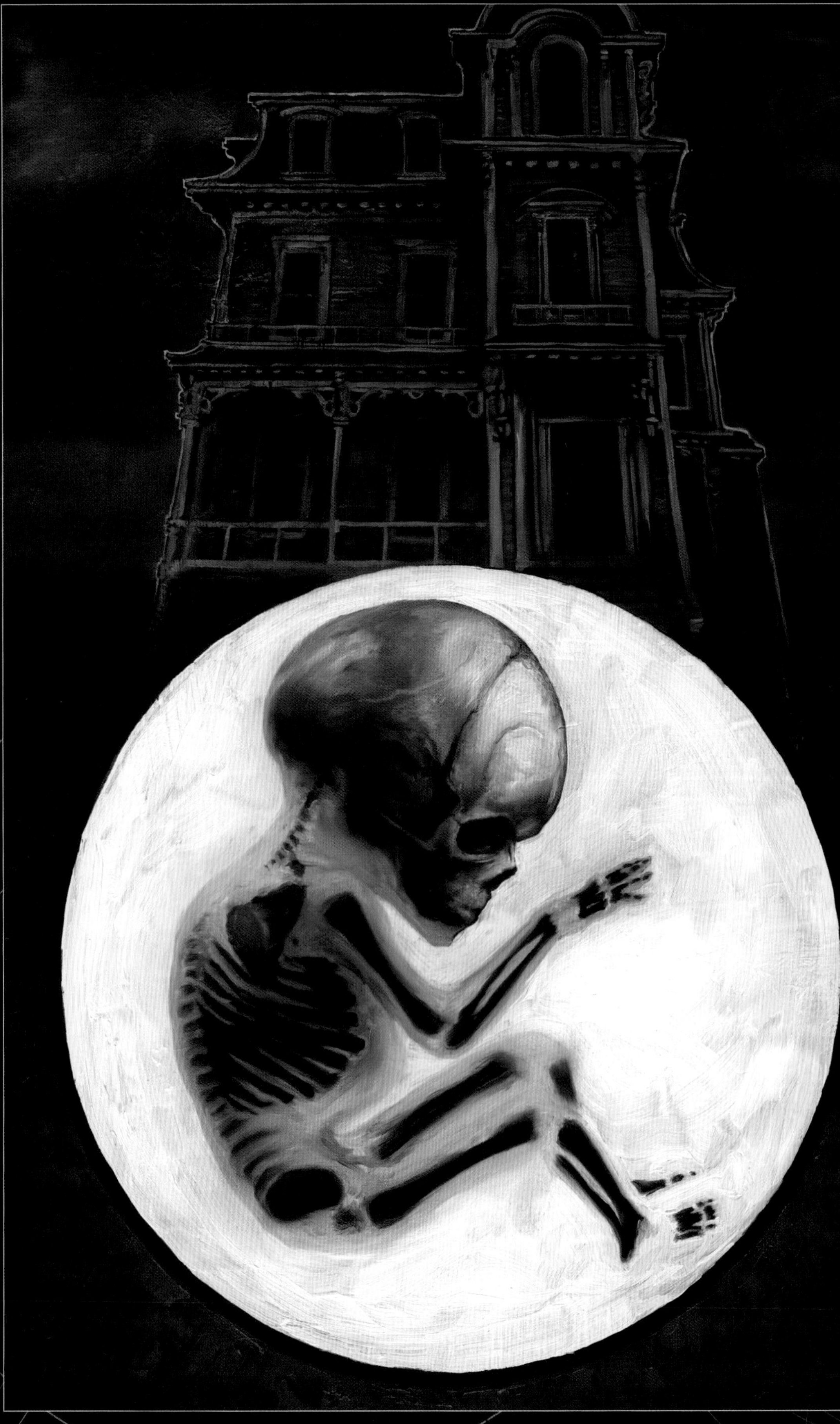

ART BY JUSTIN RANDALL

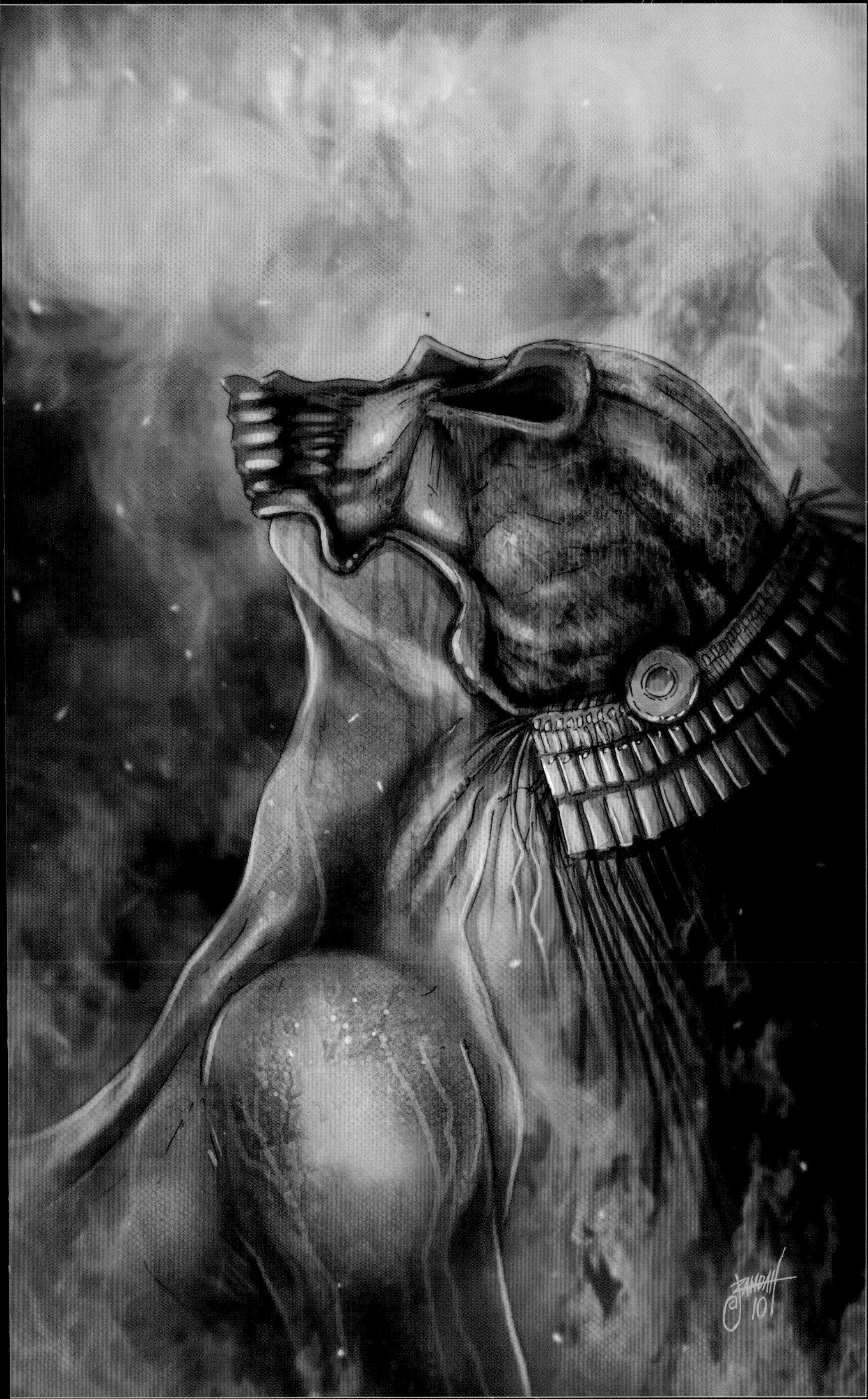

ART BY MENTON 3

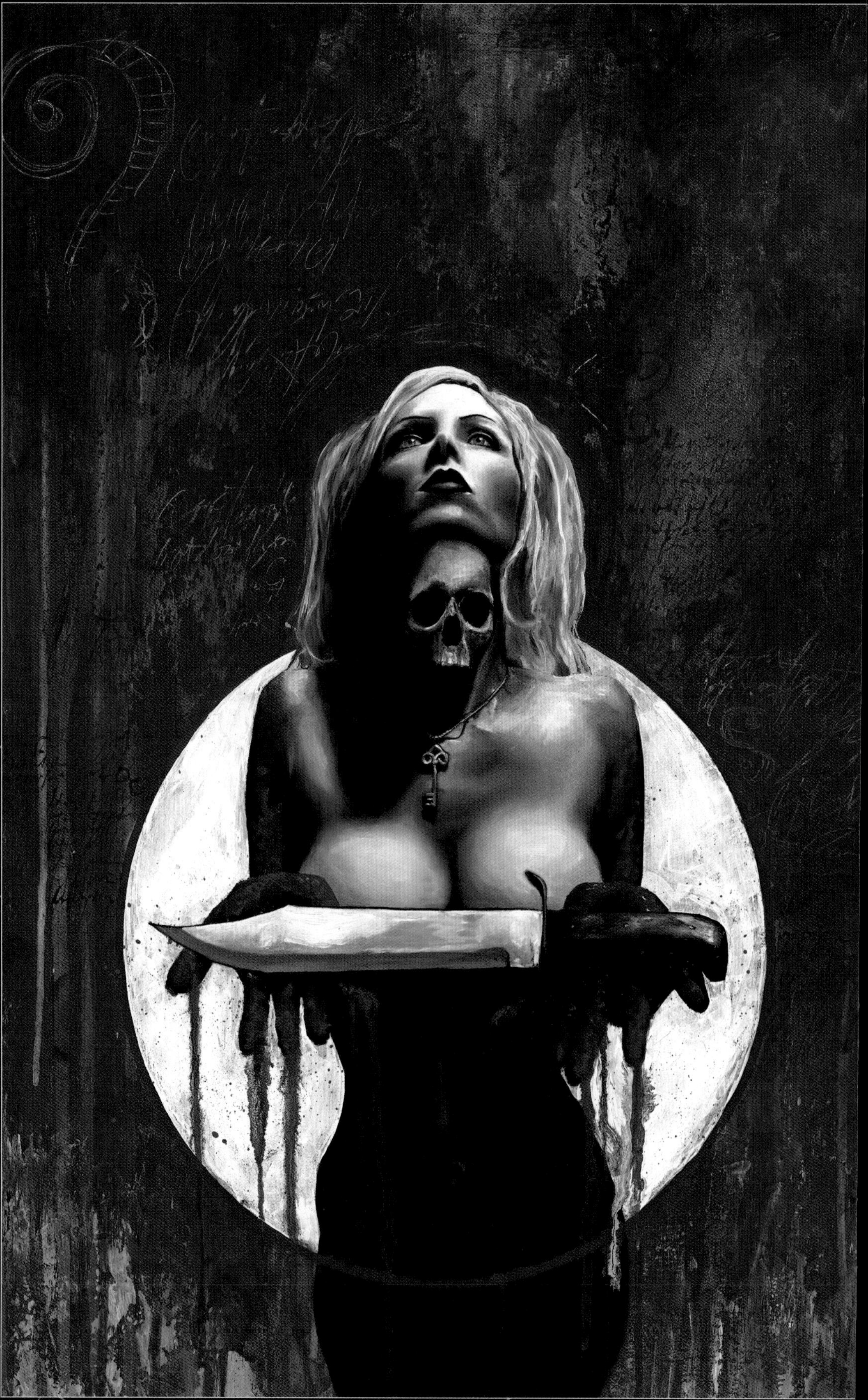

ART BY JUSTIN RANDALL

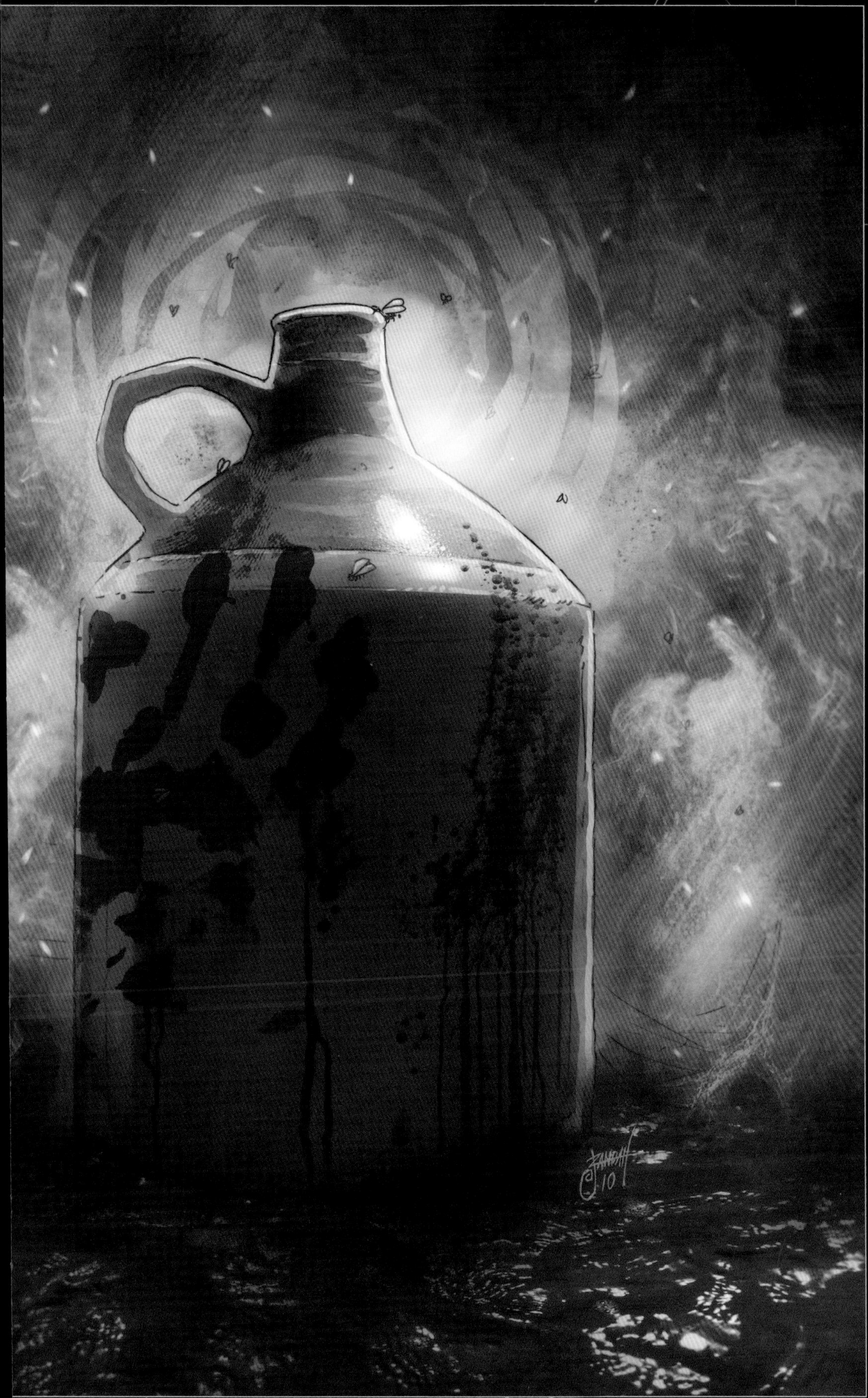
RANDALL
'10

ART BY MENT'ON 3

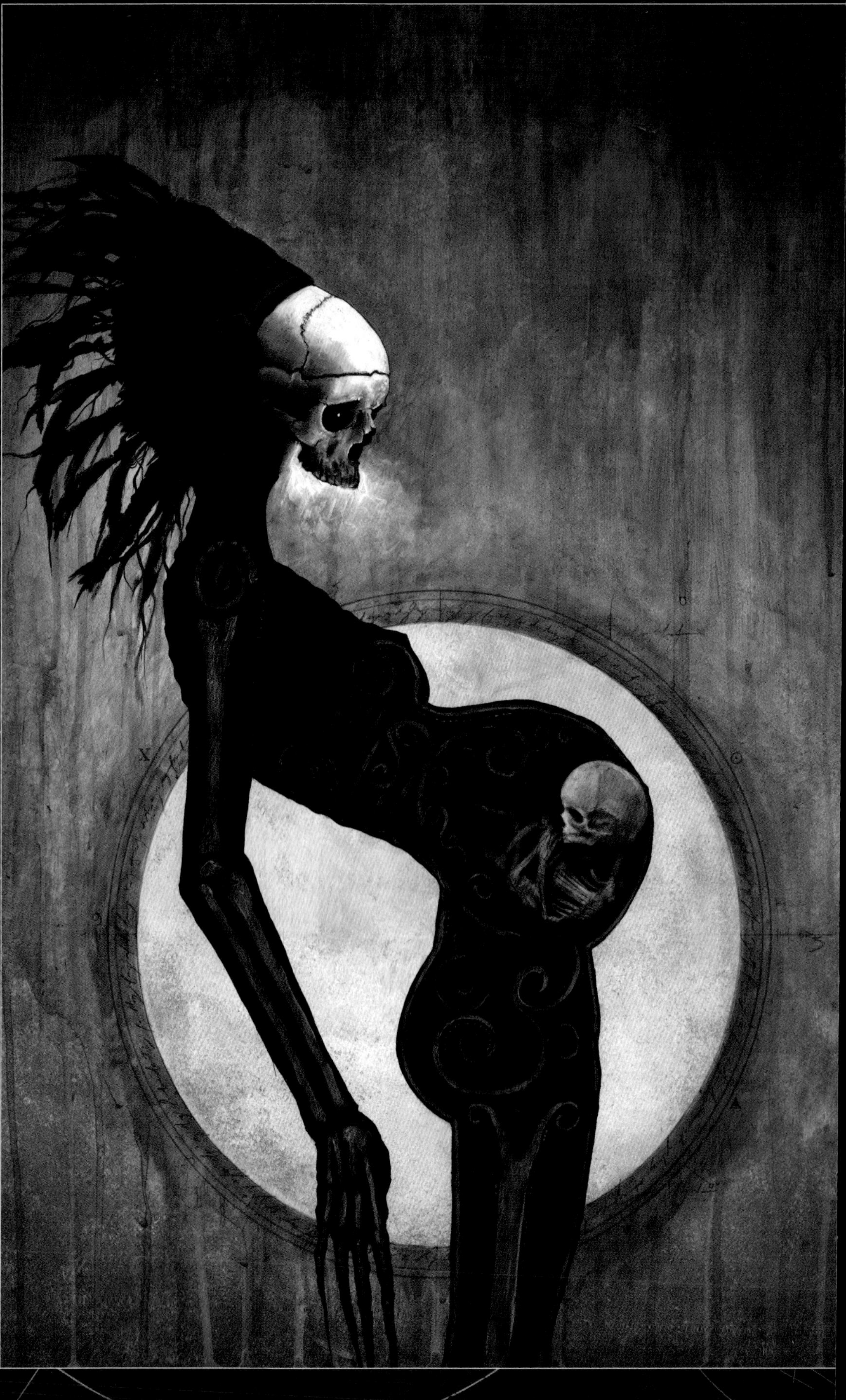

ART BY JUSTIN RANDALL

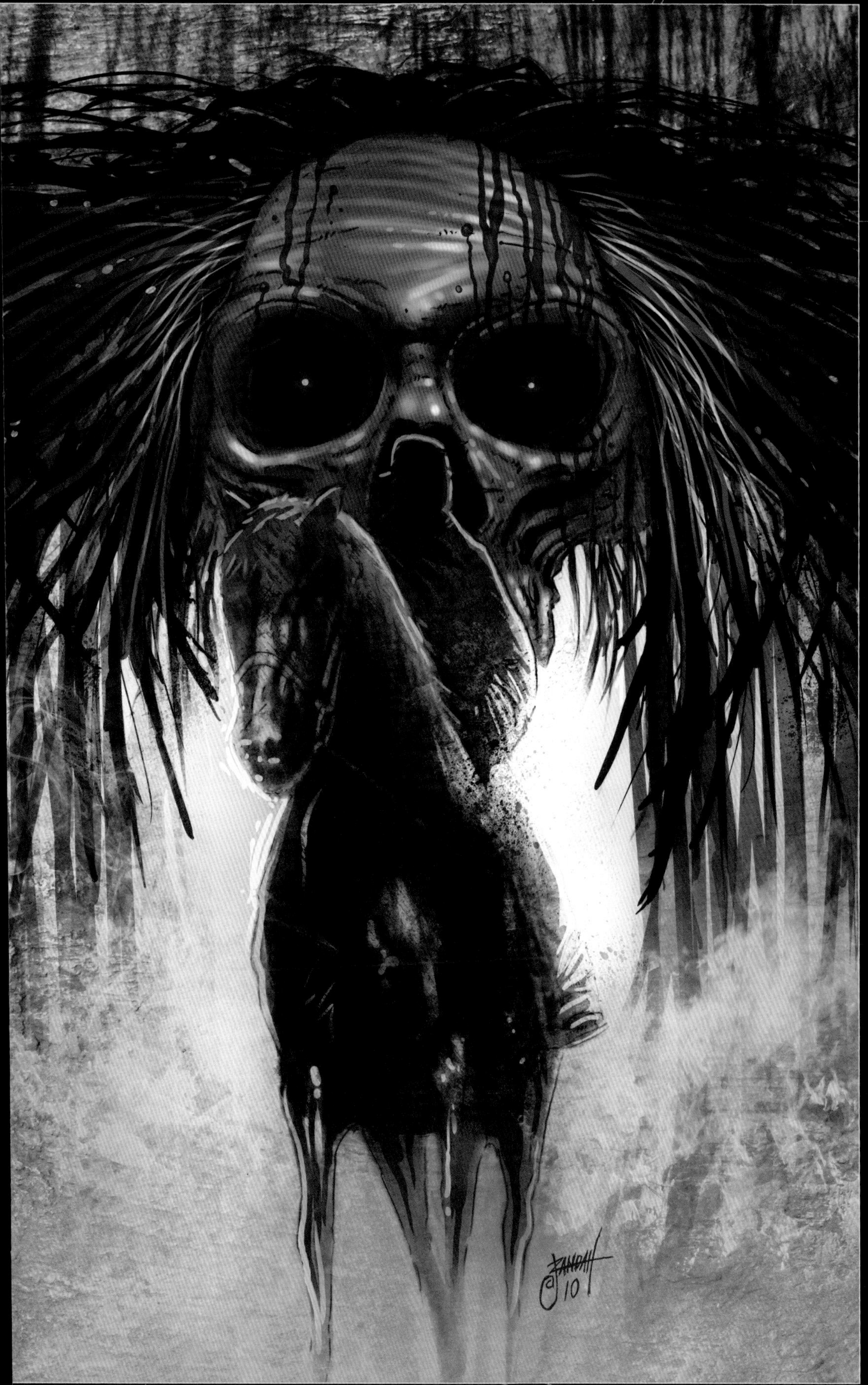
RANDALL
©10

ART BY MENTON 3

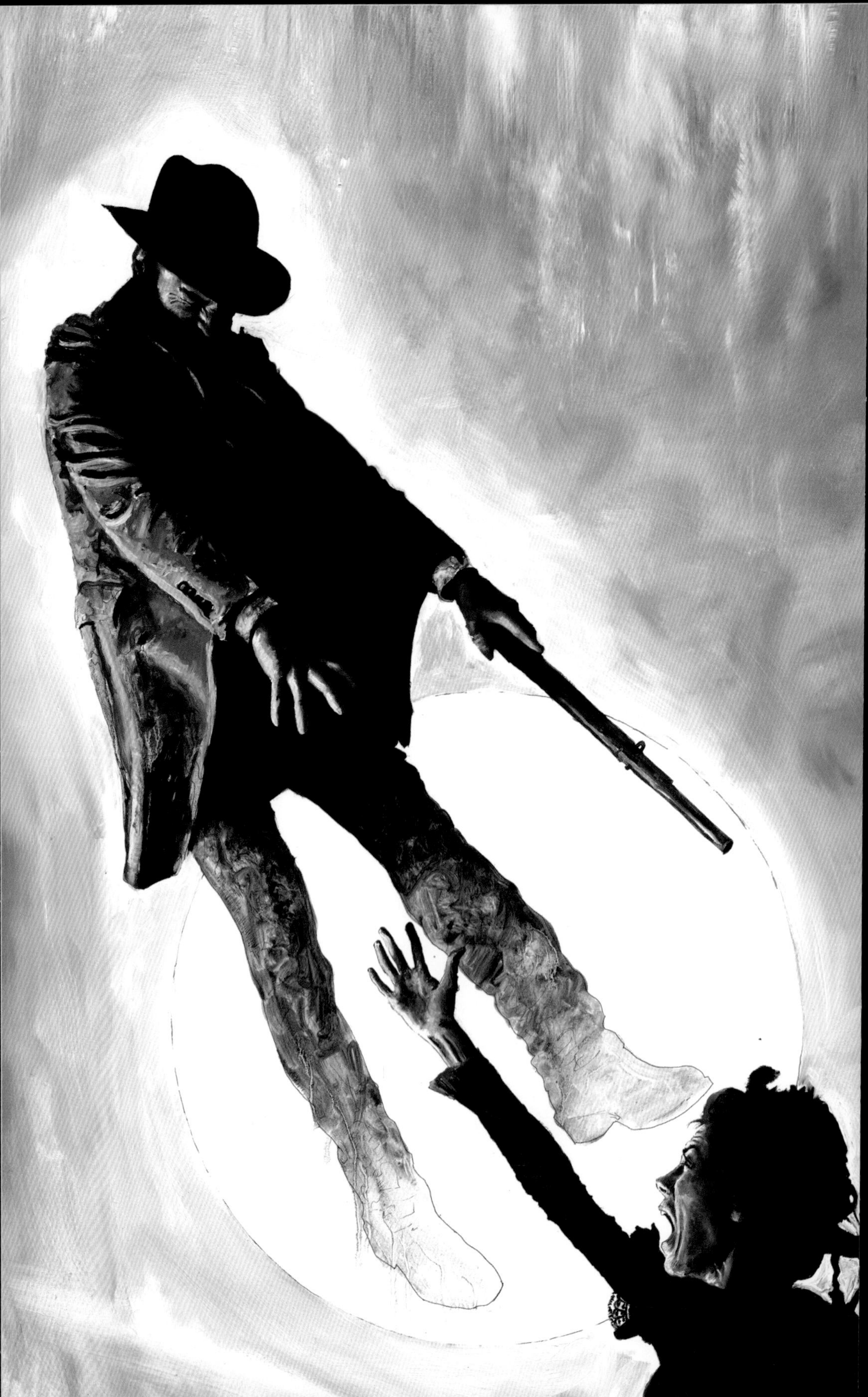

ART BY **JUSTIN RANDALL**

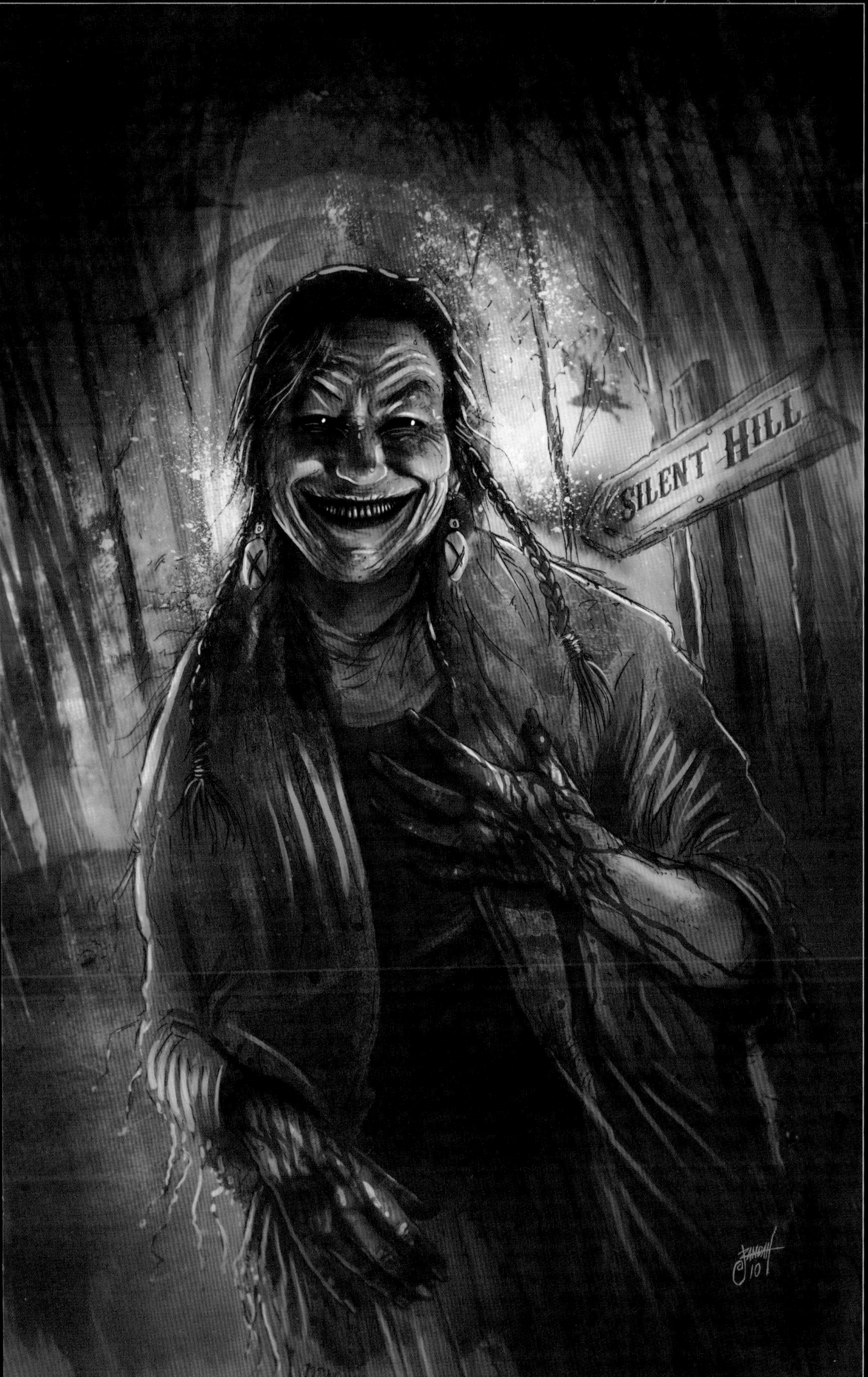
SILENT HILL

ART BY MENTON 3

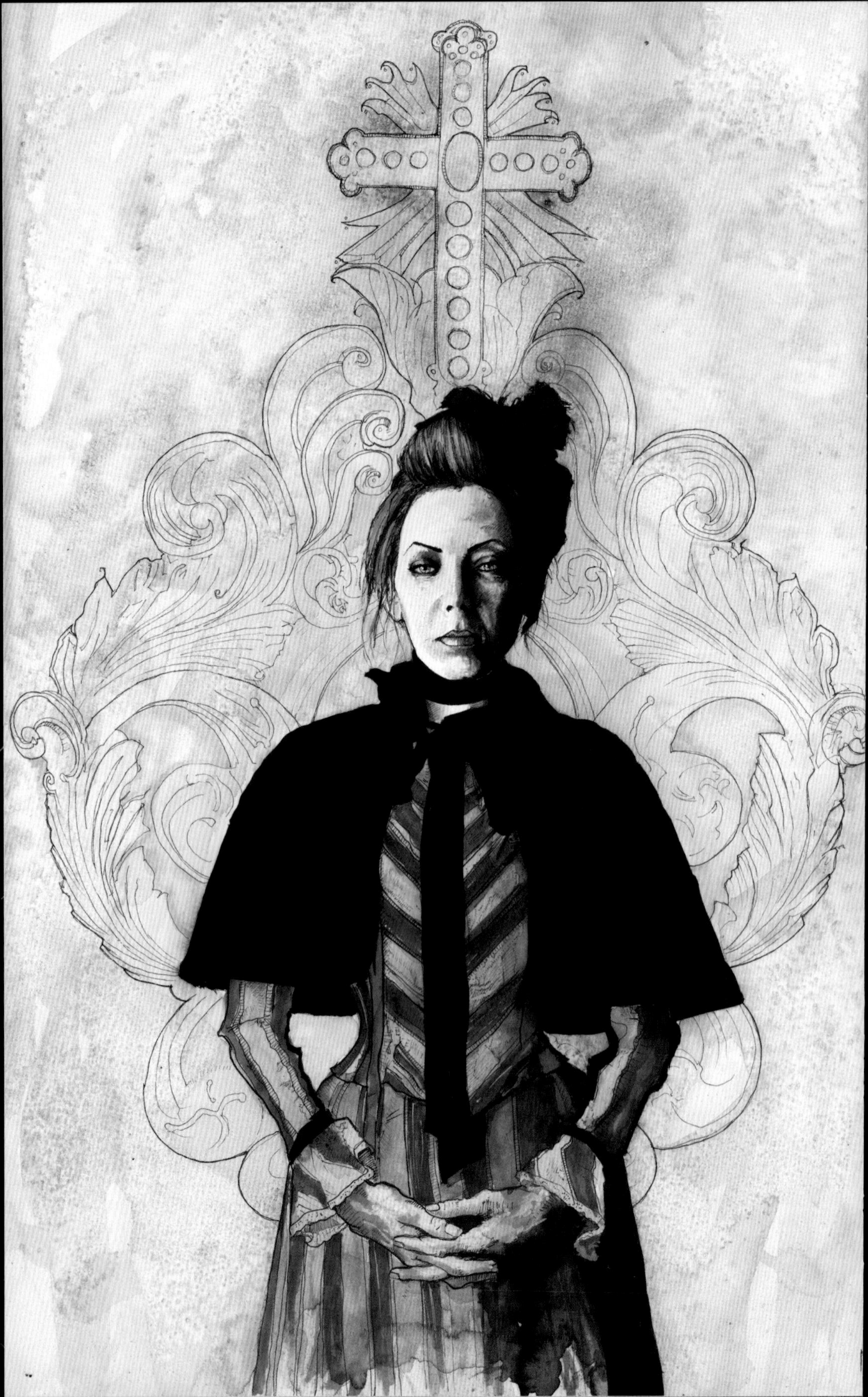

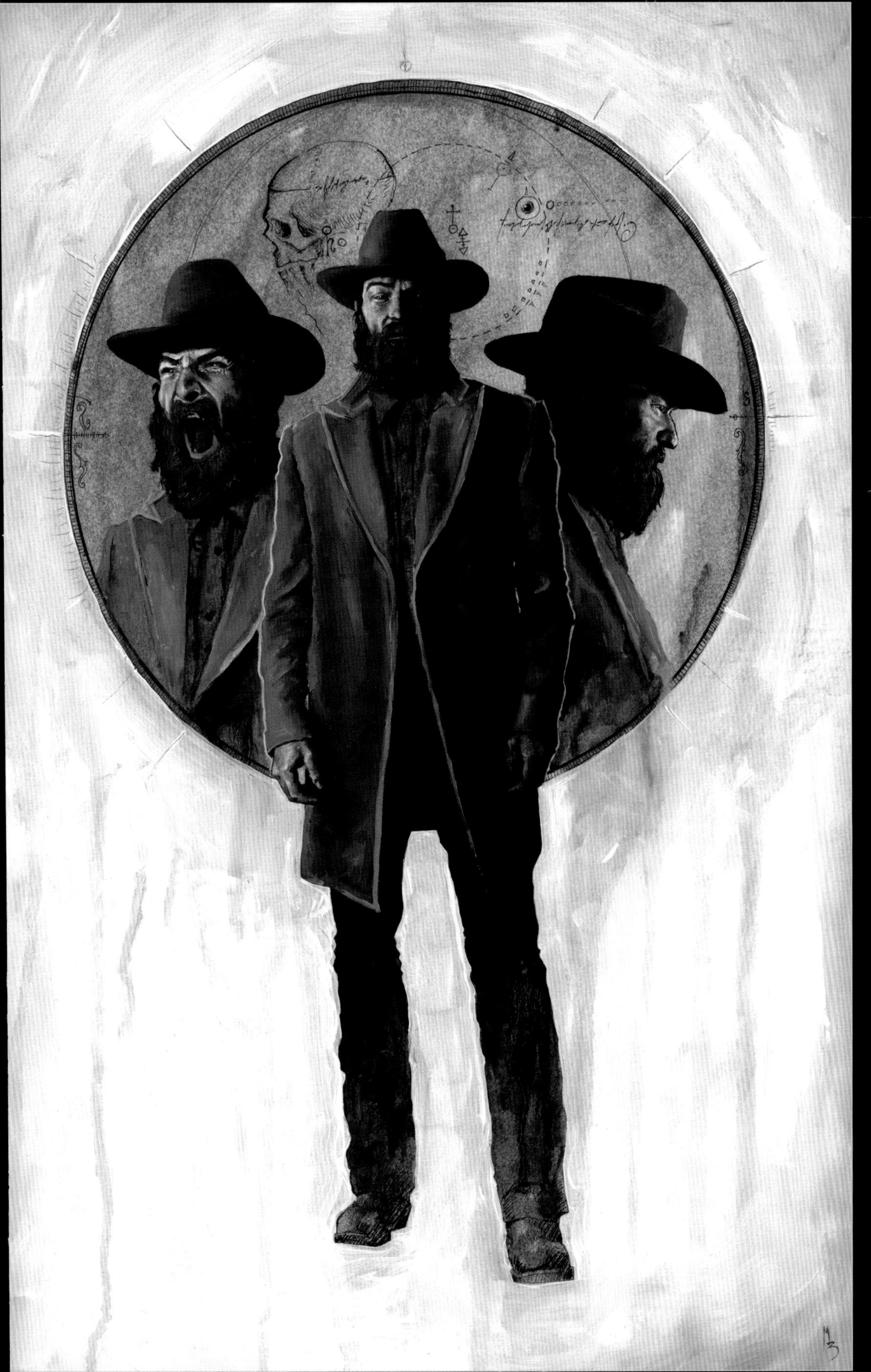

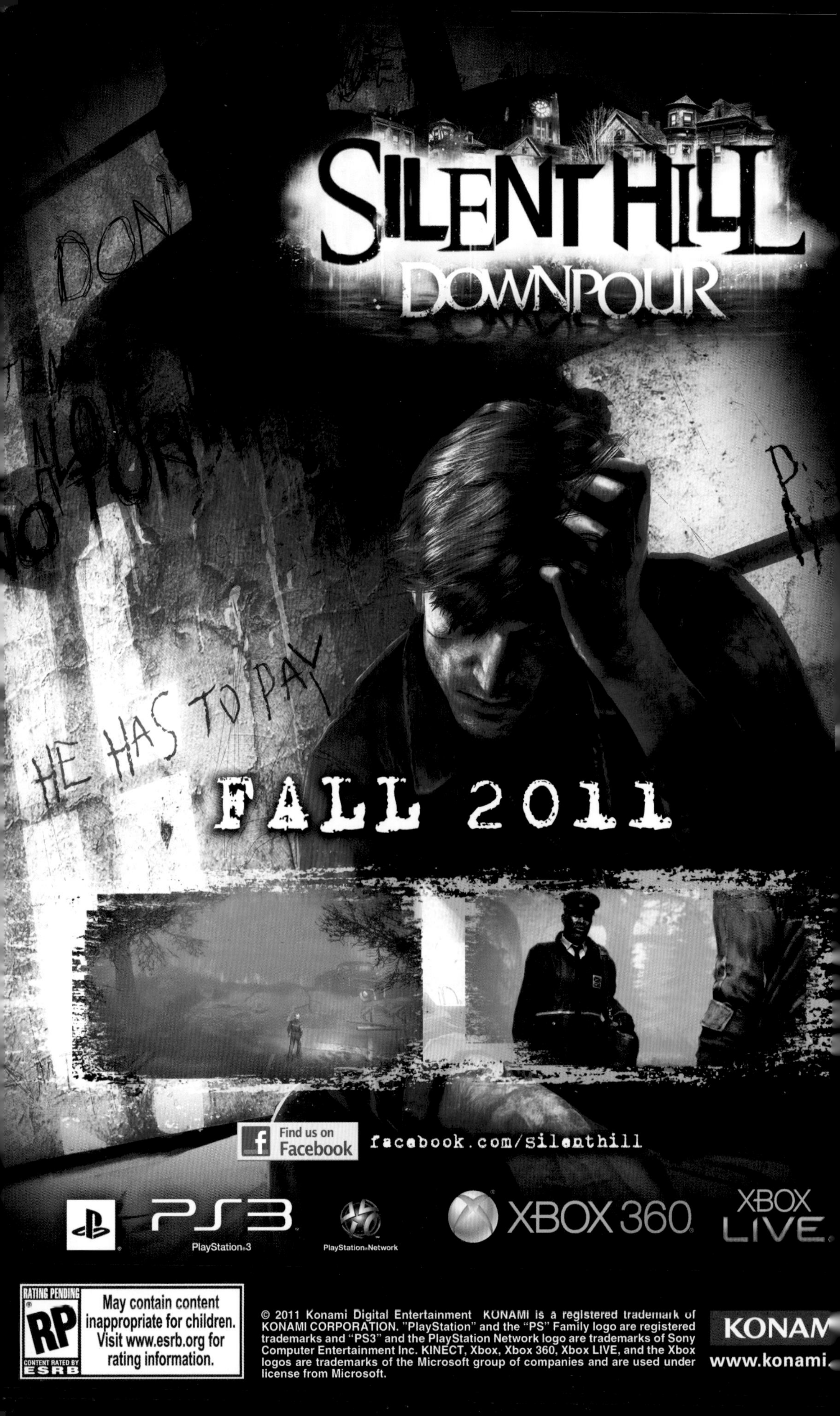
SILENT HILL
DOWNPOUR
HE HAS TO PAY
FALL 2011
Find us on Facebook
facebook.com/silenthill
PS3
PlayStation®3
PlayStation®Network
XBOX 360
XBOX LIVE
RATING PENDING
RP
CONTENT RATED BY ESRB
May contain content inappropriate for children. Visit www.esrb.org for rating information.
© 2011 Konami Digital Entertainment KONAMI is a registered trademark of KONAMI CORPORATION. "PlayStation" and the "PS" Family logo are registered trademarks and "PS3" and the PlayStation Network logo are trademarks of Sony Computer Entertainment Inc. KINECT, Xbox, Xbox 360, Xbox LIVE, and the Xbox logos are trademarks of the Microsoft group of companies and are used under license from Microsoft.
www.konami.